GLOBAL CONSTITUTIONALISM AND ITS CHALLENGES TO WESTPHALIAN CONSTITUTIONAL LAW

Westphalian constitutionalism has shaped our understanding of politics, socio-political institutions and personal and political freedom for centuries. It is historically based in the foundations of Western modernity, such as humanism and rationalism, and is organized around familiar principles of national sovereignty, the rule of law, the separation of powers and democracy. But since the end of the 20th century global constitutionalism has gradually emerged, challenging both the constitutional ideology and the constitutional design of Westphalian constitutional law. This book critically assesses the structural and functional transformations in the Westphalian constitutional tradition produced by the emergence of supranational and global constitutionalism. In so doing, it evaluates the theory of global constitutionalism, its legal and socio-political limits, and important issues concerning the supranational constitutionalism of the EU. This leads to an articulation of the constitutional theory of the emerging post-Westphalian constitutionalism, examining its development during a period of significantly increased access to and sharing of information, increased mobility and more open statehood, as well as the rise of human rights and its encounter with populism and nationalism. It will be of great interest to scholars of constitutional law and theory, particularly those with an interest in globalization and supranationalism.

European Academy of Legal Theory Monograph Series: Volume 14

EUROPEAN ACADEMY OF LEGAL THEORY MONOGRAPH SERIES

General Editors
Professor Mark Van Hoecke
Professor François Ost

Titles in this Series

Moral Conflict and Legal Reasoning
Scott Veitch

The Harmonisation of European Private Law
Edited by Mark Van Hoecke & Francois Ost

On Law and Legal Reasoning
Fernando Atria

Law as Communication
Mark Van Hoecke

Legisprudence
Edited by Luc Wintgens

Epistemology and Methodology of Comparative Law
Edited by Mark van Hoecke

Making the Law Explicit
The Normativity of Legal Argumentation
Matthias Klatt

The Policy of Law
A Legal Theoretical Framework
Mauro Zamboni

Methodologies of Legal Research
Which Kind of Method for What Kind of Discipline?
Edited by Mark van Hoecke

Objectivity in Law and Legal Reasoning
Edited by Jaakko Husa and Mark van Hoecke

An Introduction to Comparative Law Theory and Method
Geoffrey Samuel

The Tapestry of Reason
An Inquiry into the Nature of Coherence and its Role in Legal Argument
Amalia Amaya

Democracy and Ontology
Agonism between Political Liberalism, Foucault and Psychoanalysis
Irena Rosenthal

Global Constitutionalism and Its Challenges to Westphalian Constitutional Law

Edited by
Martin Belov

•HART•
OXFORD • LONDON • NEW YORK • NEW DELHI • SYDNEY

HART PUBLISHING
Bloomsbury Publishing Plc
Kemp House, Chawley Park, Cumnor Hill, Oxford, OX2 9PH, UK

HART PUBLISHING, the Hart/Stag logo, BLOOMSBURY and the Diana logo are trademarks of Bloomsbury Publishing Plc

First published in Great Britain 2018

A catalogue record for this book is available from the British Library.

Library of Congress Cataloging-in-Publication data

Names: Belov, Martin, editor.

Title: Global constitutionalism and its challenges to Westphalian constitutional law / Edited by Martin Belov.

Description: Portland, Oregon : Hart Publishing, 2018. | Series: European academy of legal theory monograph series | Includes bibliographical references and index.

Identifiers: LCCN 2017054354 (print) | LCCN 2017055293 (ebook) | ISBN 9781509914906 (Epub) | ISBN 9781509914883 (hardback : alk. paper)

Subjects: LCSH: Constitutional law. | Law and globalization. | Peace of Westphalia (1648) | Sovereignty.

Classification: LCC K3165 (ebook) | LCC K3165 .G58 2018 (print) | DDC 342—dc23

LC record available at https://lccn.loc.gov/2017054354

ISBN: HB: 978-1-50991-488-3
ePDF: 978-1-50991-489-0
ePub: 978-1-50991-490-6

Typeset by Compuscript Ltd, Shannon
Printed and bound in Great Britain by TJ International Ltd, Padstow, Cornwall

To find out more about our authors and books visit www.hartpublishing.co.uk. Here you will find extracts, author information, details of forthcoming events and the option to sign up for our newsletters.

Contents

Notes on Contributors

Jean-Bernard Auby is Professor of Public Law, Sciences Po Paris, Director of 'Centre on Changes in Governance and Public Law', Former Deputy Director of the Oxford Institute of European and Comparative Law. Professor Auby is a member of the advisory boards of *European Public Law*, *Review of European Administrative Law*, *International and Comparative Law Quarterly*, *European Review of Public Law*, *Italian Journal of Public Law*, *Rivista Italiana per le Scienze Giuridiche*, *Rivista Trimestrale di Diritto Pubblico*, *Rivista Italiana di Diritto Pubblico Comunitario*, *Revista Internacional di Direito Publico*, *Studi di Diritto Pubblico*, *Global Law Press*, *Revista Derecho, Empresa y Sociedad*, *Rivista Giuridica di Urbanistica*, *Revista Galega de Administracion Publica*, *Comparative Administrative Law* and *Catolica Law Review*.

Martin Belov is Chief Assistant Professor in Constitutional Law at the University of Sofia 'St Kliment Ohridski' Faculty of Law. Dr Belov has been project researcher at the Max-Planck Institute for European Legal History (Frankfurt am Main, Germany) and the Institute for Federalism (Fribourg, Switzerland). He has been guest lecturer in European and Comparative Constitutional Law in many European universities: University of Frankfurt/Oder (Germany), European Law and Governance School (Athens, Greece), University of Södertorn (Stockholm, Sweden), Scuolla Superiore Sant'Anna (Pisa, Italy), Staatlichen Studienakademie (Dresden/Bautzen, Germany), University of Warsaw (Poland), University of Lisbon (Portugal), State University of Milan (Italy), University of Cologne (Germany) etc. Martin Belov has published eight books and more than 70 scientific papers. In the field of global constitutionalism he has published *Global Governance and Its Effects on State and Law* (Peter Lang, 2016). His personal website is: www.martinbelov.eu.

Manuel Gutan is Professor at the Lucian Blaga University of Sibiu, Faculty of Law, where he teaches history of law and comparative law. His main areas of research are history of constitutional law, history of public administration, constitutional transplants, law and culture. Dr Gutan is currently the Editor-in-Chief of the *Romanian Journal of Comparative Law*. He recently published a book on 'Constitutional Transplants and Constitutionalism in Modern Romania 1802–1866' (2013, in Romanian). His recent publications include: 'The Infra-Constitutionality of European Law in Romania and the Challenges of the Romanian Constitutional Culture' in R Arnold (ed), *Limitations of National Sovereignty through European Integration* (Dordrecht, Springer Netherlands, 2016; 'Legal Transplant as Socio-Cultural Engineering in Modern Romania' in Jani Kirov, Gerd Bender and Michael Stolleis (eds), *Konflikt und Koexistenz. Die Rechtsordnungen Südosteuropas im 19. und 20. Jahrhundert Bd. I: Rumänien, Bulgarien, Griechenland* (Duncker & Humblot, 2015); 'Le droit comparé contemporain et l'actualité de la théorie des « formes sans fond » en Roumanie' (2013) 90 *Revue de droit international et de droit comparé*; 'The Challenges of the Romanian Constitutional Tradition. I. Between Ideological Transplant and Institutional Metamorphoses' (2013) 25 *Journal of Constitutional History*.

Balázs Fekete has an LLM degree (magna cum laude, 2007) from the Katholieke Universiteit Leuven and he completed his PhD studies at the Pázmány Péter Catholic University Faculty of Law and Political Sciences (summa cum laude, 2011) under the supervision of Prof Zoltán Péteri. He has been participating in the Ius Commune Casebooks project focusing on the relationship of national private laws and primary European Law (2013–2017) chaired by Professor Arthur Hartkamp. He is a member of the Coordinating Board of the CEE Forum of Young Legal, Political and Social Theorists, and he has been organising the Italian-Hungarian Comparative Law Workshop for five years together with Katalin Kelemen. His main articles were published in the *Review of Central and East European Law*, *Maastricht Journal of European and Comparative Law* and *Jahrbuch für Ostrecht*, and he has also contributed book chapters to volumes published by Hart, Springer and Peter Lang. He is senior lecturer in law at the ELTE University and fellow of the Hungarian Academy of Sciences Centre for Social Sciences, both in Budapest.

Konrad Lachmayer is Professor of Public Law, European law and foundations of law at Sigmund Freud University in Vienna (www.lachmayer.eu). He studied law at the University of Vienna and visited the University of Cambridge (United Kingdom), the Max-Planck-Institute for Comparative Public Law and International Law (Germany) and the Central European University (Hungary). From 2013/14 to 2016/17 he held a research chair at the Institute of Legal Studies, Centre for Social Sciences at the Hungarian Academy of Sciences and was a research fellow at Durham Law School. His research and teaching focuses on international constitutional law, especially the methodology of constitutional comparison, counter-terrorism measures and data protection as well as Austrian public law.

Giuseppe Martinico is currently Associate Professor of Comparative Public law at the Scuola Superiore Sant'Anna, Pisa. Prior to joining the Scuola Sant'Anna, he was García Pelayo Fellow at the Centro de Estudios Políticos y Constitucionales (CEPC), Madrid and Max Weber Fellow at the European University Institute, Florence. He is also Honorary Professor at the University of Henan (China) and Research Fellow at the Centre for Studies on Federalism, Turin.

Marta Simoncini is an FWO post-doctoral fellow at the University of Antwerp and King's College London. Currently, she is also a teaching fellow at University College London (UCL). Previously, she was a Max Weber Fellow at the European University Institute (EUI). Dr Simoncini obtained her PhD in Administrative Law from the University of Pisa. She is an expert in EU administrative law and governance, in particular in the checks and balances applicable to discretion, especially in the context of risk-based regulation. In these areas, she has published extensively in international and national law journals. She has also authored a monograph on risk regulation.

Introduction

Global Constitutionalism and Its Challenges to Westphalian Constitutional Law provides a critical analysis of the challenges of global constitutionalism to traditional theoretical paradigms and concepts as well as to the normative order and the institutional design of modern constitutional law in an early post-Westphalian situation. It is meant to present in a multi-discursive and critical manner the current clash between national and post-national, national and supranational, Westphalian and post-Westphalian constitutionalism. The book presents some of the developments in post-Westphalian global constitutionalism by exposing its achievements, shortcomings, legal and socio-legal limitations and determinants.

The book is grounded and framed on the constitutionalist paradigm. Despite the underlying constitutionalist approach, the analysis of the general theoretical and the specific issues of global constitutionalism is multi-discursive. This is due to the fact that the contributors come from different, but interrelated scientific fields such as public law (Auby); European and comparative constitutional law (Belov, Martinico, Fekete and Lachmayer); European administrative law (Simoncini); history of law and general theory of comparative law (Gutan). The book is a conference volume. It contains papers presented at the conference 'Global Constitutionalism and Its Challenges to Westphalian Constitutional Law' organised by the European Academy of Legal Theory and the University of Sofia 'St Kliment Ohridski', Faculty of Law on 7 April 2017 in Sofia, Bulgaria.*

Global constitutionalism and Westphalian constitutionalism are used as alternative and opposite normative paradigms that set the framework of the scientific analysis provided by the book. Both paradigms are abstract and extensive thus being open to multidimensional scientific exploration. The initial part of the book, which is devoted to the theory of global constitutionalism, uses that conceptual paradigm in its proper meaning. The papers of Auby, Martinico and Lachmayer, as well as my own, provide research of the fundamental issues of the emerging supranational constitutionalism on both regional and global levels. The papers of Gutan, Fekete and Simoncini are much more focused on a specific type and specific regional manifestation

* I would like to express my acknowledgement to Professor Mark van Hoecke, President of the European Academy of Legal Theory and Professor Sasho Penov, dean of the Faculty of Law of the University of Sofia 'St Kliment Ohridski' for their support in organising the conference 'Global Constitutionalism and Its Challenges to Westphalian Constitutional Law'.

of the global constitutionalism, namely the supranational constitutionalism of the EU, with its innovative solutions, sui generis concepts, and socio-legal and legal limits. Hence, the book has a double target. It provides for analysis of both global constitutionalism and EU supranational constitutionalism as its most advanced form.

The book is engaged with the issues of global, late Westphalian and post-Westphalian constitutionalism. Global governance issues are explored by only a few of the presentations included in it, such as Auby's and mine. Moreover, the book is characterised by a predominantly European perspective addressing contemporary issues of global constitutionalism.

Globalisation imposes several groups of challenges to the institutional design and the normative ideology of the constitutional systems of the early twenty-first century. The most important of these are the emergence of a global normative (dis)order, the crisis of classical ordering and explanatory paradigms able to structure the constitutional system in its different aspects (system of sources of law, institutional system, human rights system etc), the increased conflict potential between different regulative philosophies, constitutional designs, constitutional cultures and socio-legal practices, the structural shifts and alterations of the socio-legal preconditions of authority, legitimacy, public power, public coercion, democracy, representation and rule of law producing dysfunctionalities of Westphalian constitutional orders and national constitutions, the rise of the political power and constitutional importance of the supranational technocratic elites, the supranational bureaucracies and the judiciary (with regard to both the supranational and international courts and the constitutional and supreme courts of the states), the blurring of the 'public–private' divide as a structural precondition for modern public law etc.

The modern constitutional axiology of Westphalian constitutional law is also questioned and distorted by globalisation. This is especially true for the fundamental constitutional principles established in Western Modernity, namely sovereignty, (representative) democracy, the rule of law and the welfare state.

The current book tries to address most of these issues by providing a critical assessment of the theoretical heritage, legal background and socio-legal context of both Westphalian constitutional law and the challenges it experiences from the emerging global constitutional law in the early post-Westphalian epoch. The recent developments in world politics have demonstrated that the cleavage between the 'left and right' segments of the political spectrum has been partially dismantled and replaced by the 'globalism vs nationalism' cleavage. In the EU the latter divide is clearly defined in 'Euro-optimist' as against 'Euro-pessimist' tones. In fact, these oppositions are the result and manifestation of a deeper clash between Westphalian and post-Westphalian, between national, supranational and global constitutionalism. Thus the current volume tries to contribute to the scientific analysis and problematisation of these relatively novel tendencies, which are gaining momentum in the world in general and in the EU and the US in particular.

Westphalian constitutionalism is the denomination for the modern Western constitutionalism which emerged from the late eighteenth century onwards, but which has its intellectual and conceptual roots—and in some countries also legal and socio-legal traditions—in the late seventeenth century. The concept of Westphalian constitutionalism is used in the current volume instead of modern constitutionalism for several reasons. It better reflects the ideas of closed statehood, of territorial statehood and of national statehood which have been deeply intertwined concepts throughout the whole constitutional Modernity. Moreover, it exposes the fundamental role of the concept of sovereignty, which has been established as a key normative ideology and ordering scheme of the public power since the Treaty of Westphalia of 1648 and was later codified by the constitutions as a principle of the modern nation-state constitutionalism. Last but not least, Westphalian constitutionalism is related to the intergovernmental approach in public international law which puts strong emphasis on the central and even exclusive role of the state represented through its executive power institutions in international relations structured as intergovernmental relations.

Westphalian constitutionalism is based on several structural and conceptual preconditions enshrined in the national constitutions and reflected in international public law. Westphalian constitutionalism presupposes the exclusive territorial organisation of the public power, the hierarchical structure of its institutional and normative order safeguarded legally by the supremacy of the constitution and politically by the principle of sovereignty, the state's monopoly over coercion,[1] the clear delimitation between the spheres of the state and civic society and between the public and the private power, the monopoly of the state institutions over the 'classical' public functions consisting in production, implementation and control of the proper implementation of law[2] and the non-political role of the courts and the administration.

These Westphalian constitutional ideologies predetermined the outlook of the constitutional systems from the beginning of the 'long nineteenth century' until the end of the 'short twentieth century'.[3] Thus they were capable of serving as a more or less reliable background for structuring political relations and for imposing constitutional conditionality on politics

[1] M Weber, *Wirtschaft und Gesellschaft* (Tübingen, Mohr Siebeck, 2002).

[2] K Loewenstein, *Verfassungslehre* (Tübingen, Mohr Siebeck, 2000), 39–50.

[3] These concepts are launched by E Hobsbawm in his books *The Age of Revolution: 1789–1848* (New York, First Vintage Books, 1996), *The Age of Capital: 1848–1875* (New York, First Vintage Books, 1996) and *The Age of Extremes: the Short Twentieth Century, 1914–1991* (London, Abacus, 1995) 3.

for approximately two centuries in the countries which have adopted the Western type of constitutionalism.

The last phase of globalisation, which started at the end of the 1970s but has accelerated its dynamics since the 1990s, has changed the world in many senses and aspects. Combined with the technological—more precisely information and transport—revolutions, which have boomed since the beginning of the twenty-first century, it induced profound changes in the socio-legal context in which both constitutional and international law are allocated; shifted and blurred the boundaries between 'public' and 'private', global', 'regional', 'national' and 'local'; and brought 'time–space compression'[4] to life. The crisis of territoriality,[5] experienced by most states during the last few decades, has been paralleled by the promotion of 'open statehood'.[6] State-centred constitutionalism has been challenged by societal constitutionalism[7] and different forms of 'constitutionalism beyond the state'[8] (supranational constitutionalism, global constitutionalism etc).

Consequently, the state and its legal dimension—the constitution and constitutional law—have experienced deep structural challenges.[9] They are currently exposed to pressure for adjustment and change which produced two-track remodelling of the Westphalian concept of public power and thus of Westphalian constitutional law.

First, the domestic constitutions are being reformed as a response to globalisation and its regional manifestation—Europeanisation in its different variants such as EU integration, integration in the Council of Europe etc.[10] In other words, Westphalian constitutional law is partially and asymmetrically adjusted to the requirements of the post-Westphalian

[4] N Brenner, 'Beyond state-centrism? Space, Territoriality and Geographical Scale in Globalization Studies' (1999) 28 *Theory and Society* 39.

[5] P Cuttitta, 'Points and Lines: A Topography of Borders in the Global Space' (2006) 6 Ephemera 27–40 and M Belov, 'Globalisation, Crisis of Territoriality and Their Effects on the Constitutional Principles' in M Belov (ed), *Global Governance and Its Effects on State and Law* (Frankfurt am Main, Peter Lang, 2016).

[6] S Hobe, 'Statehood at the End of the 20th Century—The Model of the 'Open State': A German Perspective' (1996) 12 *Austrian Review of International and European Law* 127–54.

[7] G Teubner, *Constitutional Fragments. Societal Constitutionalism and Globalization* (Oxford, Oxford University Press, 2012).

[8] For the concept of constitutionalism beyond the state see, eg, JHH Weiler and M Wind, *European Constitutionalism beyond the State* (Cambridge, Cambridge University Press, 2003) and T Isiksel, *Europe's Functional Constitution. A Theory of Constitutionalism beyond the State* (Oxford, Oxford University Press, 2016).

[9] M Belov, 'Can We Still Drive the State Machine the "Old School Way"? Structural and Functional Deficits of the Modern State' in L Burasin, D Gardasevic and A Sardo (eds), *Law and State. Classical Paradigms and Novel Proposals* (Frankfurt am Main, Peter Lang, 2015), 153–71.

[10] A Albi and S Bardutsky (eds), *National Constitutions in European and Global Governance: Democracy, Rights and the Rule of Law* (The Hague, TMC Asser Press (forthcoming)).

constitutionalism produced by the global, transnational and partially post-national and post-territorial situation. Second, the rise of supranational and global constitutionalism, resulting in constitutionalisation of public international law,[11] is also the result of and response to globalisation and forms of post-Westphalian constitutionalism.

The emerging post-Westphalian constitutional law demonstrates both theoretical novelties and innovations related to the constitutional design. Relatively novel theoretical paradigms such as multilevel constitutionalism and constitutional pluralism represent the paradigmatic shift produced by the emerging post-Westphalian constitutionalism. The global governance paradigm is a response to the blurring of the divide between 'public' and 'private' based on the intermingling between public and private power and functions. The early post-Westphalian theoretical realm comprises the theories of fragmented sovereignties, pooling of sovereignties, open statehood, atteritorial public power, supranational sector-based constitutionalism, constitutional identity, supranational judicial dialogue, post-national citizenship, global but discursive and fragmented public sphere, and dispersed and networked global democracy.

The Westphalian constitutional design is reformulated—deconstructed, adjusted or transplanted in different socio-legal and institutional contexts—by the constitutionalisation of global or regional international organisations, the emergence of supranational constitutional regimes such as the EU and of sectoral humanitarian or financial quasi-constitutional regimes such as the Council of Europe or the World Trade Organisation. The innovative projections of early post-Westphalian global constitutionalism on the domestic level concern the devices for internationalisation and supranational opening of the national constitutions as well as for supranational engagement of the domestic institutions outside the realm of the executive power, such as courts and parliaments.

Some of the most important examples of such institutional novelties, gradually changing the Westphalian into a post-Westphalian constitutional law, are the integration clauses of the constitutions related to the opening of statehood towards participation in supranational and international constitutional organisations and towards supranational and international law and legal standards; the setting of counter-limits[12] to such supranational and international legal exposure of the domestic constitutional order;

[11] A Peters, The Merits of Global Constitutionalism (2009) 16 *Indiana Journal of Global Legal Studies* 397–400.

[12] For the concept of counter-limits see G Martinico, 'Complexity and Cultural Sources of Law in the EU Context: From the Multilevel Constitutionalism to the Constitutional Synallagma' (2007) 8 *German Law Journal* 205–30.

the definition and development of national constitutional identity; the inclusion of non-executive power institutions in the accomplishment of the external power of the state;[13] the increasing role of the courts and especially of the constitutional courts and the supreme courts in the multilevel judicial dialogue[14] with other state courts or with supranational and international courts; the development of existing or the provision of new devices for political and legal control on the activity of state institutions (especially the governments) while participating in supranational decision making; and the provision of enhanced mechanisms for political inclusion of foreign citizens (the most powerful of which is EU citizenship).

Post-Westphalian constitutional law is still a project in a rather early phase of its development. It is not a project per se or laboratory experiment, but is actually a conscious response to the challenges of globalisation to 'classical', 'modern' or 'Westphalian' constitutional law. In fact, post-Westphalian constitutional law and post-Westphalian constitutionalism are still to a great extent intuitive, fragmented, eclectic and, on many occasions, also dysfunctional. Some of the post-Westphalian constitutional theories still seem rather vague and incapable of giving feasible solutions to practical problems.[15] The post-Westphalian institutional design sometimes looks like an inappropriate alteration of classical Westphalian constitutional design paralleled by mechanical transplantation of institutions developed for the nation state on the international and supranational levels. The rough and unfinished adaptation of Westphalian nation state institutional design to the post-Westphalian and supranational socio-legal context is not able to substantially remedy or give appropriate answers to the pressing issues produced by globalisation, information revolution, global fluidity of the demos[16] and global risk society.[17]

However, the above-mentioned challenges to Westphalian constitutionalism, produced by globalisation, the information revolution and the global risk society, seem to be both objective and irreversible. Thus they need proper constitutional responses on both the conceptual and institutional

[13] For the external power of the state see M Belov, 'Separation of Powers Reconsidered: a Proposal for a New Theoretical Model at the Beginning of the 21st Century' in A Geisler, M Hein and S Hummel (eds), *Law, Politics and the Constitution. New Perspectives from Legal and Political Theory* (Frankfurt am Main, Peter Lang, 2014) 47–60.

[14] For the judicial dialogue see G Martinico and O Pollicino (eds), *The Interaction between Europe's Legal Systems. Judicial Dialogue and the Creation of Supranational Law* (Cheltenham, Edward Elgar, 2012).

[15] For important arguments against the critic of vagueness of the concept of international constitutionalism see A Peters, above n 11, 402.

[16] M Belov, 'Globalisation, Crisis of Territoriality and Their Effects on the Constitutional Principles' in M Belov (ed), above n 5, 53–81.

[17] For the global risk society see U Beck, *Risikogesellschaft. Auf dem Weg in eine andere Moderne* (Frankfurt am Main, Suhrkamp, 1986).

levels. It seems that Westphalian constitutional law and constitutional theory are (unfortunately) incapable of providing durable and viable answers.

The fundamental conceptual and methodological dilemma exposed and emphasised by the current volume is whether the key concepts and paradigms developed in Westphalian constitutionalism can be used in order to explain the phenomena and processes which are currently unfolding in the context of the early phase of post-Westphalian constitutionalism. If this is not the case, constitutional theory should develop genuinely new post-modern concepts and paradigms adequate to the challenges of post-Westphalian constitutionalism at the beginning of the twenty-first century.

The task of this book is to problematise both the challenges of global constitutionalism, perceived as a holistic concept and composite phenomenon, to the classical Westphalian outlook of the constitutional systems, and the responses of the constitutional systems to them in the form of gradually emerging post-Westphalian features of national and supranational constitutionalism. Thus it considers both the post-Westphalian challenges to Westphalian ideas, theories, concepts and institutions, and the Westphalian heritage and determinants of post-Westphalian constitutional theory and constitutional law. Naturally, the book does not provide for either exhaustive analysis of the issues of global constitutionalism or final and definitive answers and solutions. It contains just topical and multi-discursive analysis of some issues of concern related to the constitutional dimensions of the globalisation of law.

The book provides both conceptual and abstract theoretical analysis of global constitutionalism and an approach to global constitutionalism rooted in comparative constitutional and comparative historical analysis. The book is structured in three parts. The first part is devoted to the general theory of global constitutionalism. It is focused especially on the crisis of hierarchy as normative paradigm of the Westphalian constitutional geometry in the context of post-Westphalian and global constitutionalism while discussing also the idea of open statehood as a bridging normative concept between the constitutionalist and pluralist approaches to global constitutionalism. The second part analyses the limits to global constitutionalism. The third part contains contributions which explore key issues of the EU constitutionalism as the main manifestation of the emergent supranational constitutionalism.

There are several common topics in the papers published in the book. These are key issues which determine the overall contribution of the volume. In general, the book problematises the need for new constitutional paradigms sufficiently adequate to grasp the complexity of the current constitutional situation and to serve as a theoretical background to the emerging global and post-Westphalian constitutionalism.

The volume assesses the deficiencies of sovereignty in the post-Westphalian context especially with a view to EU constitutionalism. These deficiencies are predetermined by factors which frequently simultaneously produce a crisis of hierarchy as theoretical ordering paradigm that has been fundamental for Westphalian constitutional law. This issue is directly addressed and profoundly discussed in Jean-Bernard Auby's paper as well as in my own. However, the contradiction between holistic and hierarchical versions of classical Westphalian constitutionalism and polycentric constitutional pluralism is also analysed in Giuseppe Martinico's paper. Martinico uses constitutional openness as an analytical criterion bridging the 'constitutionalism–pluralism' and the 'hierarchy–polycentrism' divides.

Another topic relating to the crisis of hierarchy and sovereignty is the emergence of open statehood. The opening function of the constitution, the constitutional conditions for open statehood and the role of the domestic constitution as a linking factor between the national and supranational legal orders is a common topic for most of the papers in this volume. Constitutional openness is explored with regard to its prerequisites, instruments and limitations. These issues are widely analysed in the papers of Jean-Bernard Auby, Giuseppe Martinico and Balazs Fekete, and in my paper. Moreover, the stretching of global constitutionalism between constitutional openness and culturally predetermined identitarian self-restraint is the axis of intellectual juxtaposition and analytical encounter between the papers of Giuseppe Martinico and Manuel Gutan. Thus constitutional openness is a central topic of the book as a whole.

The preservation and safeguarding of the rule of law as a key constitutional principle of global constitutionalism in the early post-Westphalian situation is an object of scientific concern for many of the papers published in this volume. The need for a rule of law oriented approach to global constitutionalism and global governance and the necessity of safeguarding the achievements of the rule of law in the post-Westphalian context is one of the central appeals of Auby's paper. However, the issue of the rule of law as element of constitutional axiology and as ordering principle of constitutionalism is discussed by most of the papers, starting with my concern about the proper model for constitutional geometry as ordering paradigm of the contemporary constitutional system, going through Giuseppe Martinico's analysis of the theories of global constitutionalism and constitutional pluralism, offering different schemes for provision of the rule of law and Konrad Lachmayer's analysis of the adverse effects of anti-global constitutionalism and global anti-constitutionalism, and ending with the research into the effects of agencification in the EU on the rule of law presented by Marta Simoncini.

So far a clarification has been provided of the common issues and the common objects of research that are analysed to a different extent and from different viewpoints by all or most of the contributors to the book. Let us turn now to a brief summary of the main ideas launched by the different authors. This short outline of the key conceptual content presented by the authors should inform the reader and form the framework of their expectations. It must demonstrate which issues of global constitutionalism are analysed by the distinct presentations and what are the main arguments and conclusions of the contributors.

In his paper Auby derives the legitimation of the theories of global constitutionalism from the crisis of state-centred national constitutionalism produced by globalisation. According to him, this crisis has a twofold nature. The structural crisis, which concerns the organisation of the legal order, is paralleled by a functional crisis, being a crisis of the production of law, which is related to both form and content of the normative and institutional order.

Hence the Westphalian nation state legal order is increasingly dismantled and replaced by post-Westphalian global disorder. According to Auby this situation is a result of the multiplication and plurality of both legal producers and places of legal production. In fact, the very concept of 'place of legal production' proposed by Auby has the potential to be a revolutionising concept which is additional but also alternative to the traditional concept of territorial jurisdiction.

The structural and functional challenges to normative production posed by globalisation are key issues of Auby's paper. The plurality of norm producers and norm-producing realms and places which may be ordered in multilevel or pluralistic ways or may remain unorganised thus forming normative (dis)orders underline the whole logic of the paper and frame Auby's theoretical concerns. The multiplication of places of norm production, the interconnectedness of legal orders, the growing 'permeabilisation' and competition between legal systems and the partial dismantling of the 'public–private' divide are defined by Auby as key challenges to the normative hierarchies as ordering schemes of Westphalian constitutional systems. Thus Auby comes to the conclusion that 'the legal world no longer constitutes a fairly organised state-centred system'. All these phenomena produce the need for global constitutionalism as post-Westphalian ordering and explanatory paradigm.

Globalisation is conceived by Auby as a producer of normative disorder, but also as a chance for restructuring of the constitutional paradigm around a mixture of novel and traditional constitutional paradigms. Indeed hierarchy and state-centred solipsistic constitutionalism are in crisis, but rule of law in the context of internationalised 'open statehood' national constitutions and constitutionalised international law may serve as a partial remedy to the dysfunctionalities of the post-Westphalian constitutional order. Hence theories of global constitutionalism are welcomed by Auby as producers of order, reason and values in the post-Westphalian 'global legal entropy'.

Auby focuses on the function of the constitution and constitutionalism to produce a coherent normative system as implemented and reinstated on a global scale. Hence his paper provides an analysis of the chances and channels for emergence of a global legal taxonomy. Auby differentiates between four main aspects of global constitutionalisation. These are: first, the constitutionalisation of international law and international institutions; second, the opening of the national constitutions to the international and supranational legal order; third, the reconceptualisation of classical Westphalian constitutional concepts to the challenges of globalisation; and fourth, the constitutionalisation of both (public) international law and public actors and the private actors of global governance. Auby is problematising the scope, focus and object of global constitutionalism theories according to their conceptual allocation along the 'public–private' divide, their methodological preference on prescriptive or descriptive approach and their emphasis on the specific phenomena of legal globalisation and structural shifts, cracks or adjustments in the constitutional design.

Auby determines the conditionality of the success of global constitutionalism as a theoretical approach. He recommends a broader version of global constitutionalism which encompasses all norm-setting agents allocated on the various levels of the emerging infrastructure of the global legal order. He opts for a value-oriented theory of global constitutionalism focusing on the issue of safeguarding a value-oriented version of rule of law in a global and post-Westphalian context. Hence the central concern of Auby is how to establish and sustain a global, value-based and ordered system of norm production.

The most important instances of post-Westphalian constitutional impetus of Auby's paper can be outlined as follows. Auby takes into account the plurality of the emerging global order. He asserts the translayered and multilevel character of the current normative order. Moreover, he admits the lack of a single ordering scheme centred on the nation state, the relativisation of the 'public–private' divide and the crisis of the predominance of nation state constitutionalism produced by globalisation and the emergence of a postmodern constitutional attitude.

Auby detects two types of legal disorganisation produced by globalisation. These are normative disorganisation and institutional disorganisation. According to him there are two reasons for this phenomenon. The first is related to the insufficient legitimacy of the agents of globalisation and the international and supranational agenda setters and norm producers. This is also one of the main issues of Simoncini's paper, which may be considered as a specific concretisation of the general problem detected by Auby. The second reason concerns the normative arrangements, substantive hierarchies and dissemination of the essential principles of the rule of law. The issue of the crisis of normative hierarchies is also central to my paper. In that regard it is part of an intellectual dialogue with the Auby's contribution.

Furthermore Auby analyses the three main issues which, in his view, produce the dysfunctionalities of 'classical' or 'Westphalian' constitutionalism. These are the dysfunctionalities of the linking mechanisms between the legal producers and the legal orders in the global constitutional context, the mechanisms of hierarchical normative arrangements and the channels of dissemination of the essential principles of the rule of law. Consequently Auby outlines the main directions of the challenges of the post-Westphalian situation to the normative and institutional infrastructure of the constitutional order as well as to its capability to master the complexity of global constitutional pluralism.

Auby explores the opening function of the domestic constitutions to the international and supranational legal orders. He analyses the instruments and mechanisms for adjustment of the plurality of constitutional and quasi-constitutional orders in the current global constitutional pluralism. He stipulates the inadequacy of the traditional and simple hierarchical models of Westphalian constitutionalism to reconcile and explain the interrelation between the orders in the global world disorder (a topic central also to my paper).

Judicial dialogue as an instrument for adjustment of the increasing plurality of legal orders in the post-Westphalian situation is also explored by Auby. He describes the role of the courts in linking the 'international constitutions' of constitutional or quasi-constitutional regimes such as the EU and the WTO with domestic constitutional orders. Auby stresses the non-hierarchical, asymmetrical and frequently controversial jurisprudence of supranational and national courts sometimes producing 'double mirror effects' and situations.

Auby outlines the role which is played by non-traditional agenda setters and norm producers in the post-Westphalian context. It should be noted that Simoncini's paper, which is devoted to the role of agencies in European constitutionalism, is a kind of further specification and continuation of this general concern expressed by Auby.

Auby emphasises the multiple dimensions of the rule of law to the current post-Westphalian and global legal context—international, supranational and domestic. Again he points out the necessity of taking into account both the constitutionalisation of international law and the internationalisation of domestic constitutional law with a view to the principle of the rule of law. On the other hand, Auby notices that there are international regimes, such as the World Bank, the WTO and the IMF, which still do not match the rule of law requirements. Thus there is an inherent controversy between one of the most important principles of Westphalian constitutionalism, which also seems to have a strong chance to persist in the post-Westphalian situation, and the evolution of some international organisations into supranational quasi-constitutional regimes pretending to expose constitutional features without a sufficient bond to key constitutional principles such as the rule of law. Last but not least, Auby demonstrates the challenges of the quasi-constitutional activity of non-state actors to the rule of law as a key principle of both Westphalian and post-Westphalian constitutionalism.

Auby concludes with an analysis of the advantages and disadvantages, the capabilities and limits of global constitutionalism. He suggests that global constitutionalism is an instrument of 'disciplining normative pluralism in legal globalisation'. His thesis that the national constitutions became 'partial constitutions', incapable of resolving alone the constitutional issues of globalisation without the necessary support of the emerging global constitutionalism, is a clear manifestation of the transition from Westphalian to post-Westphalian constitutionalism.

My paper aims to clarify the analytical concept of constitutional geometry, explaining the constitutional geometry of Westphalian statehood and demonstrating the evolution of the Westphalian constitutional geometry of the constitutional nation state to the post-Westphalian constitutional geometry of the supranational and global constitutional law at the time of globalisation and information revolution. The paper reflects on the challenges to constitutional semiotics produced by the current early post-Westphalian situation.

The first part of the paper is devoted to defining and explaining the concept of constitutional geometry. Constitutional geometry is proposed by me as a semiotic constitutional law concept. I am launching it as both an analytical paradigm of constitutional theory and a constructive (ordering) paradigm of constitutional law.

Constitutional geometry is a semiotic phenomenon which aims to analyse the meaning of visual codes and visual representations of fully or partially institutionalised normative ideas. The function of constitutional geometry is to serve as an additional explanatory paradigm that exemplifies the main structural features of the constitutional order and the constitutional system. Constitutional geometry is a creative collection of supportive ideologies, concepts, paradigms and structural codes developed by different constitutional, legal and political theories throughout Western Modernity which try to explain the state, the constitution and the constitutional order by using geometric metaphors. The constitutional geometry of modern constitutional law is a device for rationalisation via formalisation and abstract and symbolic depiction of the constitutional order, the normative order, the institutional sub-systems of the constitutional system and the inter-institutional dynamics in it.

The second part of the paper presents the constitutional geometry of modernity, the reasons for its emergence in that concrete design and outlook and its most important structures, shapes and forms. Constitutional geometry was born out of the general pathos of Western modernity to rationalise, systematise and construct socio-political relations and the realm of the public power. It is closely related to some of the most important concepts and paradigms of Western modernity and modern constitutional law and constitutional theory, such as the concepts of state institution, institutional system, system of sources of law and territorial structure of public power.

Westphalian constitutional geometry is predominantly organised in hierarchies and pyramids. It rarely uses circles and networks as analytical matrixes for description and representation of institutional, normative or power relations. The network has failed to serve as either analytical or normative concept of Westphalian constitutional law with the victory of the territorial state. The network and the circle regained their explanatory and normative importance only with the development of the international legal order in the second half of the twentieth century and with the pluralisation and constitutionalisation of that order at the end of the twentieth and the beginning of the twenty-first century.

The hierarchy is used both normatively and analytically as the natural power matrix, explanatory and ordering scheme and intellectual and ideological code of modernity from the age of the absolute monarchy until the second half of the twentieth century. It is the most widespread, typical and frequently used form of constitutional geometry in Westphalian constitutional law. With the emancipation and differentiation of the public power from the broader category of social power and with the emergence of the state as governing system and mechanism for introduction and maintenance of social order, the hierarchy has become a universal code for structuring power relations. The victory of the territorial nation state over alternative models for organising the public power, the necessity for providing a conceptual model for accomplishment of the public authority, the need for maintenance of the interstate equilibrium, for sustainable and durable legitimation of public coercion and for rational explanation of constitutional ontology have produced universal recognition of the hierarchy as the main shape of modern constitutional geometry.

Westphalian constitutionalism has additionally reinforced the hierarchy as an instrument for national unification, centralised political domination and rational government. The establishment of efficient central government required the hierarchy as a universal ordering model. One important but not immediately obvious aspect of political, administrative, legal and constitutional modernisation resulted in 'hierarchisation'. The latter consisted in the introduction of the hierarchy as a universal ordering code and of the pyramid as a key matrix for the rational-emotional visualisation of the structure of the public order. The constitutional entrenchment of the hierarchy led to the establishment of the pyramid as the central form of modern constitutional geometry.

The third part of my paper concerns the post-Westphalian challenges of supranational constitutionalism, global governance and information revolution to the constitutional geometry of Westphalian constitutional law. It demonstrates that there is an increasing dysfunctionality of the analytical shapes of Westphalian constitutional geometry in the early post-Westphalian context which is caused by several complex, but to a large extent objective factors relating to supranational and global constitutionalism, global governance, globalisation and the information revolution. They produce structural changes in the ordering and organising schemes of the public power and in its constitutional design and start to change the constitutional geometry of modern statehood.

I am systematising the structural changes of Westphalian constitutional geometry in three main groups. The first group encompasses challenges to constitutional geometry imposed by the constitutionalisation of international and EU law that has led to the emergence of supranational constitutionalism. The second group includes changes of constitutional geometry produced by global governance as a broader governance paradigm that takes into account both the supranationalisation and globalisation and the privatisation of public power. The third group concerns the emergence of the Internet as a global virtual reality.

My key thesis is that the hierarchy and pyramid are challenged, partially dismantled and replaced by the network and the circle as explanatory and ordering schemes of constitutional epistemology and constitutional semiotics. Thus the objective processes of globalisation and the information revolution are producing structural changes in Westphalian constitutional geometry and are fostering the emergence of a new visual and normative world of post-Westphalian constitutional geometry. I provide a critical assessment of the leading constitutional paradigms relating to global constitutionalism, such as multilevel constitutionalism and constitutional pluralism, from the viewpoint of constitutional geometry. I also present concrete examples that should prove my hypothesis of the partial dismantling of Westphalian geometry by post-Westphalian constitutional geometry.

The issue of constitutional openness is central for Martinico's paper. Martinico tries to demonstrate that there is no 'Chinese wall' between the concepts of constitutionalism and pluralism.[18] He stresses the fact that currently both concepts aim to provide solutions for the opening of the domestic constitutional order and for linking the plurality of legal orders in the post-Westphalian situation.

One of Martinico's main assumptions is that the initial telos of specific types of constitution, which he denominates as 'constitutions born out of resistance', is generally directed towards the achievement of constitutional openness. In his view the 'resistance constitutions' are capable of serving as a basis for maintenance of open statehood, especially with a view to its human rights dimension, due to the internal logic and domestic reasons which have been developed in the context of late Westphalian Modernity during the second half of the twentieth century.

[18] For the opposition between constitutionalism and pluralism see A Peters, above n 11, 403–04.

The original contribution of Martinico is the demonstration of the endogenous causes for the development of constitutional openness. Martinico convincingly shows that multilevel constitutionalism and constitutional pluralism as post-Westphalian concepts have their foundations and origin in the domestic constitutionalism of the latest period of the development of the nation state. From such a perspective, these theories seem to have a stronger ontological bond than usually considered in the supranational constitutionalism doctrine. The inherent openness of constitutionalism to supranational, international and comparative migration, reception and transplantation of ideas is also exposed in Lachmayer's paper.

Martinico's contribution belongs to the post-national and supranational constitutional law paradigm, but is also rooted in the comparative constitutional law perspective. Martinico explicitly defines that the aim of his paper is 'to show how a comparative law based analysis can be helpful to overcome this false dichotomy (that between pluralism and constitutionalism)'.

Martinico enters the debate on internationalisation of domestic constitutions from a specific angle. On the basis of comparative and comparative historic examples he demonstrates the tendency of many European post-totalitarian constitutions to perform the opening function and to link the national with the international and supranational legal orders especially with a view to the rule of law and human rights. Thus Martinico exemplifies the general need for reconstruction and continuation of the rule of law in a post-Westphalian context which is already stipulated as a principal concern in Auby's paper.

Martinico critically analyses the opposition between constitutionalism and pluralism as launched in the constitutional discourse by prominent authors such as N Krisch. According to Martinico this is a false dichotomy based on outdated and not properly conceptualised perceptions of both of these normative paradigms of the global constitutionalism theory. Martinico believes that in fact both paradigms may be reconciled with a view to the implicit openness of the 'resistance constitutions' existing in many EU Member States. According to him, 'openness, described as one of the pillars of the pluralist paradigm, can also be seen as one of the building blocks of the post-World War II constitutionalism'.

Martinico's opposition of 'foundational constitutionalism' to 'resistance constitutionalism', 'thin constitutionalism', 'evolutionary constitutionalism' and, implicitly, to global constitutionalism is in line with the idea of transition from Westphalian to post-Westphalian constitutionalism. Such transition is based on the assumption that some core concepts of classical constitutionalism that emerged in the initial phase of Western constitutional civilisation have to be reconsidered and reassessed in the light of the current post-modern and post-national challenges without necessarily being radically replaced by genuinely new concepts.

In fact, the idea of 'evolutionary constitutionalism' as an ever-present dimension of constitutionalism transcending the historical context of Westphalian constitutional law and continuing its existence under post-Westphalian conditionality, as well as the idea of 'resistance constitutions' containing capabilities for constitutional openness which are adequate to the current socio-political situation, demonstrate the fact that post-Westphalian constitutionalism is not pure negation, but is actually a continuation of intellectual trends, conceptual lines and institutional design which also existed before the current phase of globalisation.[19]

Martinico detects the emergence of 'osmotic law' produced by 'axiological (desired) continuity that exists between the domestic and the international levels, and by the efforts made to construct a better society, even at the international level'. Hence what he describes as 'double orientation (internal and external) of the constitutional project' allows for the emergence of a post-Westphalian constitutional order grounded on pillars, principles and elements which have started to emerge during the late phase of the development of Westphalian constitutional law. It is characterised by both internationalisation of constitutional law and constitutionalisation of international law, as Auby's paper describes this fundamental interpenetration and mutual cross-fertilisation of the supranational and domestic constitutional orders.

Lachmayer's paper exposes the current dynamic of contradiction between globalisation optimism and globalisation scepticism, universal and contextual constitutional values and institutional design, open and closed statehood. It proposes a new typology of the anti-globalist and illiberal phenomena currently distorting the universalising trend in the spread of Western liberal-democratic civilisation which has been the mainstream during the decades since the fall of the Berlin Wall.

Lachmayer's contribution to this volume analyses the reasons for and the results of the migration of anti-constitutional ideas. The paper explores 'anti-globalisation developments and anti-constitutionalism developments' as well as 'the interrelations between the two'. It researches the emergence of global anti-constitutionalism and anti-global constitutionalism.

The recent developments of illiberal or even authoritarian constitutionalism demonstrate in the opinion of Lachmayer 'how strongly constitutional law depends on an intact constitutional culture based on constitutionalism. The question … remains: how to fight for constitutionalism if the ideals of constitutionalism can no longer be protected by constitutional documents, constitutional institutions and constitutional law'.

[19] For the idea that each political regime contains 'capabilities' for the emergence and unfolding of the new phases of socio-political developments see S Sassen, *Territory, Authority, Rights. From Medieval to Global Assemblages* (Princeton, NJ, Princeton University Press, 2006) 21, 148–204.

A common issue between the papers of Konrad Lachmayer and Manuel Gutan is the importance of illiberal and even anti-liberal political culture and constitutional self-identification as limits and impediments to the development of both classical liberal-democratic constitutionalism (based on democracy and rule of law) and of post-Westphalian global constitutionalism (predetermined by open statehood, jurisdictional proliferation and interpenetration and transnational constitutional dialogue).

The re-emergence of constitutional nationalism and identitarian or expressivist[20] constitutionalism is underlined by both authors. Lachmayer demonstrates the growing importance of these phenomena in an abstract theoretical and comparative perspective while Gutan provides a case study on the matter. Lachmayer differentiates between constitutional patriotism and constitutional nationalism, while Gutan demonstrates the impossibility of establishing constitutional patriotism based on civic values and civic virtues in the context of constitutional nationalism concealed as 'tendential constitutionalism'.

Lachmayer researches the preconditions and factors for the new tendency towards a rise in constitutional authoritarianism. He makes use of a socio-legal approach for examining the novel trends of suppression of global constitutionalism and liberal constitutionalism and for launching traditional and novel forms of illiberal constitutionalism. The research is allocated in a comparative and multi-discursive approach exploring phenomena and tendencies on both national and supranational levels.

Lachmayer warns that in 'times of re-emerging illiberalism, populism and authoritarianism, there is an increasing need for us to attempt to find new academic concepts to describe the phenomena that are arising'. Lachmayer critically assesses the concept of authoritarian constitutionalism, defining it as 'misleading, conceptually wrong and politically dangerous'. He points out that constitutionalism is an essentially liberal concept which cannot be deprived of its liberal philosophic background and normative content thus being installed with illiberal philosophical and normative content instead. On the contrary, authoritarian constitutionalism is 'factual ways of dealing with constitutional law in (semi-) authoritarian regimes'. Lachmayer believes that 'the term authoritarian constitutionalism' is 'politically dangerous' because it 'enables authoritarian governments to claim that their approach of authoritarian constitutionalism is at least an approach of constitutionalism'.

That is why Lachmayer suggests using the concept of constitutional authoritarianism instead of authoritarian constitutionalism. He defines

[20] M Tushnet, *Weak Courts, Strong Rights: Judicial Review and Social Welfare Rights in Comparative Constitutional Law* (Princeton, NJ, Princeton University Press, 2008) 5.

constitutional authoritarianism as a 'conceptual category of authoritarianism, which uses constitutional law (not the normative concept of constitutionalism) to stabilise governments politically and which misuses and distorts certain constitutional institutions (without giving them full powers)'.

Lachmayer delimits two threats to global constitutionalism. These are anti-global constitutionalism and global anti-constitutionalism. According to him, examples of anti-global constitutionalism are Brexit and recent developments in US policy. Lachmayer believes that the threats to constitutionalism 'beyond the state' simultaneously endanger and produce adverse effects on constitutionalism 'within the state'.

Having in mind this consideration of Konrad Lachmayer one can conclude that in the current context constitutionalism is, in one way or another, necessarily a composite concept consisting of both national and global dimensions. Thus the emergence of supranational and global constitutionalism and the migration, reception and transplantation of constitutionalist ideas create a transnational constitutional space which predetermines the existence of national and subnational constitutionalism. In other words, the emergent post-Westphalian constitutionalism also seems a crucial safeguard for the persisting elements of Westphalian constitutionalism.

The finding of Konrad Lachmayer that the 'politics of nationalism are re-emerging from their decades-long dormancies' is in compliance with and corresponds to the concern of Manuel Gutan that illiberal constitutionalism in Central and Eastern Europe was never meant to disappear but has only been hidden for a while for tactical political purposes.

Lachmayer's thesis that 'globalisation in the context of constitutional law can not only serve to support ideas of constitutionalism, but can also spread ideas opposing the values of constitutionalism' is a rather pressing, immediate and topical finding in the context of the current period of challenges to globalisation in general and to global constitutionalism in particular. It demonstrates that both constitutional democracy and competing power models, such as authoritarianism, have inevitably become global in the current post-Westphalian context. Consequently Lachmayer's assumption of the existence and unfolding of global anti-constitutionalism as a second challenge to global constitutionalism together with anti-global constitutionalism should again demonstrate the intrinsic link between constitutionalism and globalisation in the contemporary expansion of the scale of socio-political relations and their constitutional shapes and forms beyond the 'territorial container' of the state.[21]

To some extent paradoxically, the 'global legal order led to the fast migration of anti-constitutional ideas' as ascertained by Lachmayer. Hence the

[21] N Brenner, 'Beyond state-centrism? Space, Territoriality and Geographical Scale. Globalization Studies' 28 (1999) *Theory and Society* 55.

geographical 'world' has irreversibly become also a socio-political and constitutional 'world'. Thus the objectively emerged global scale of law, politics, economy and social relations, predetermined by the information revolution, defines the inevitably global dimension of either constitutionalism and democracy or authoritarianism, oligarchy and technocracy. Consequently Lachmayer's intermediate conclusion is that 'the new forms of authoritarianism ... are much more a transnational than a national phenomenon'.

The early post-Westphalian conditionality, established by globalisation and the information revolution, imposes restrictions, but also creates new opportunities for the spreading of global anti-constitutionalism. On the one hand, the new production, trade, mobility and information opportunities give rise to the need for adoption and maintenance of at least formal and façade constitutionalism which produces some loose limitations to public power. On the other hand, the emergence of transnational and global public space also facilitates the spread of anti-constitutional and anti-democratic ideas. Lachmayer concludes that 'an authoritarian turn, however, cannot ignore (especially) economic globalisation'. Thus he asserts the chances of further development of constitutional globalisation due to the interest also of authoritarian regimes in the continuation of some of the trends in neo-liberal globalisation and because of the objective existence and increase in global interdependencies.

Lachmayer's conclusion is that a new radical constitutionalism has to be shaped and adopted. The process of its elaboration should consist both in a return to the roots of constitutionalism (thus containing elements of the classical Westphalian constitutional design) and in a search for new paradigms, concepts and institutions adequate to the contemporary post-Westphalian developments. According to him, this is the only way to prevent the domination of global authoritarian tendencies. Following the theories of G Teubner and P Blokker, Lachmayer proposes to use the paradigms of societal constitutionalism and decentralised direct democracy in order to achieve some viable form of global constitutionalism in the post-Westphalian situation.

Manuel Gutan's paper is devoted to the limits imposed by the Romanian ethnocentric and illiberal constitutional identity to modernisation, Europeanisation and integration in forms of supranational and global constitutionalism. This case study demonstrates how important the deep socio-legal determinants are for the proper understanding of the resilience of the national constitutional systems to the development of global constitutionalism. The need for wider and deeper research of the determinants of post-totalitarian Central and Eastern European constitutionalism outside of the mainstream 'one-way transition to democracy' discourse is emphasised also in Balazs Fekete's paper. Gutan demonstrates that while being formally actively engaged with forms of post-Westphalian global constitutionalism,

Romania still remains deeply bounded by the classical Westphalian content of its constitutional culture and normative ideology.

The author defines the crisis of European civic constitutionalism as a crisis of both liberalism and multiculturalism producing a considerable rise of 'illiberal democracies' and of 'constitutional illiberalism'. These tendencies endanger both democracy in the EU Member States and the development of European and global constitutionalism—a view shared with Lachmayer's paper.

The reaction of national societies to the challenges of the emerging post-Westphalian global constitutional order triggered by globalisation and Europeanisation is demonstrated by Gutan on the basis of historical and comparative historical research. His analysis is focused predominantly on the Romanian case, but the author also provides comparative examples from other Central and Eastern European states, such as Hungary. On the basis of the Romanian experience, Gutan demonstrates how national identities and national constitutional identities can serve as strong and unsurmountable limits to European and global constitutionalism.

Gutan's core assumption is the existence of a phenomenon which he calls 'tendential constitutionalism'. He defines tendential constitutionalism as 'endeavour of constitutional change grounded on the interest of the Romanian elites in the values and principles of liberal-democratic constitutionalism as reified aims of Europeanisation and a never-ending process'. Tendential constitutionalism is predetermined by the inner limits of societies to promote and sustain constitutional transplantation and exposure to globalisation and Europeanisation via superimposed modernisation.

In Gutan's view tendential constitutionalism is a result of the interplay between the modernisation strategies of the domestic political elites based on their desire to engage in forms of modernisation via participation in European constitutionalism while at the same time retaining the domestic ethno-cultural identity by allowing just formal transplantation of institutional design. Put in Gutan's words, it is a 'pattern of constitutional development that perpetually mediates between the need to become "European" and the need to remain "Romanian"'.

Hence tendential constitutionalism is a phenomenon related to both Westphalian and post-Westphalian constitutionalism. It has its roots both in ethnocentric nation state constitutionalism and in supranational EU constitutionalism as part of global constitutionalism. Paradoxically it serves as a device for reinforcement of the implicit but predominant and fundamental illiberal group identity through simulation of desire for modernisation currently accomplished as Europeanisation and constitutional globalisation.

Gutan criticises the insensitivity of the mainstream liberal-democratic constitutional theory of globalisation and Europeanisation to capture and explain the contextual peculiarities shaped and formed by deep historical and cultural determinants. According to him the EU constitutionalism debate is reductionist in the sense that it is

> focused on particular mechanisms of constitutional change, eg the transfer of particular European constitutional values and principles in the Central East European countries, and particular outcomes, eg Europeanisation. But it underrated the inherent (cultural) limits to constitutional change deeply rooted in the Central East European constitutional cultures.

Thus Gutan disagrees with the 'European constitutional convergence' theory with regard to its superimposed and universalist optimism which underestimates the (dis)functionality of legal transplants and the normative role of regional, national and local constitutional culture.

The general impetus behind Gutan's argumentation is that the single dimensionality of the 'liberal end of history' *à la* Fukuyama impedes the proper detection of residual nationalism and illiberal constitutionalism implicitly, but since recently also overtly functioning as limitations to Europeanisation and to development of supranational and global constitutionalism. Gutan warns:

> [W]e should take illiberal constitutionalism more seriously. From this point of view, enthusiastically discussing post-Westphalian global (European) constitutionalism while neglecting particular local constitutional developments would be like navigating at full sail on a sea of sand.

Gutan studies the limits of global constitutionalism and its particular form—the 'European constitutional convergence'—established in the course of instrumental transplantation of liberal-democratic values and institutions as a legitimising façade of the post-communist regimes in the Central East European states since 1989. Gutan believes that illiberal elements in the constitutional cultures of the Central East European countries have continued their existence since 1989. What is more—according to him, they were never meant to disappear.

Thus the transplantation of Western liberal-democratic constitutional values and constitutional design in the Central and East European countries in general and in the Central and East European EU Member States in particular concealed deeper illiberal and nationalistic socio-political structures, attitudes and mental predispositions due to the pragmatic need to subdue to contextual but superficial modernisation via Europeanisation. Hence in Gutan's view Romania, but also the Central and Eastern European region in general, is a territory of uneasy encounter between ethnocentric illiberal constitutionalism and (neo)liberal versions of globalisation, Europeanisation and global constitutionalism. Consequently a proper socio-legal analysis of the currently existing constitutional mentality and status quo in that part of the world requires problematisation of nationality, cultural relativism and group identity in the context of globalisation, global governance and global constitutionalism.

The resilience of the national identity serving as ultimate limitation to Europeanisation is well defined by Gutan. According to him 'Romania has not only an inherently conditioned appetite to fully join the European constitutionalism but also sufficient potential to fight back any attempt to equate the Romanian constitutional identity with the European one or to build a multi-layered European identity based on common anti-ethnos (civic) values'.

Gutan demonstrates the ability of the Romanian political elite to avoid value-based Europeanisation by instrumentally misusing the plurality of values, orders and identities existing in the European constitutional pluralism. This is exemplified by the frictions and tensions between the concepts of protection of human rights and group identities used by the EU, the Council of Europe and the Romanian state. This mismatch between the constitutional concepts in the human rights domain does not lead to mutual toleration and varied recognition, as presumed by the theory of constitutional pluralism. In Gutan's view, it serves as a tool for the Romanian political elite to adopt formal while avoiding substantial Europeanisation.

Thus global constitutionalism in its regional European manifestations paradoxically reinforces the ethnocentric domestic constitutional culture. Moreover, according to Gutan, 'the threat to core national and constitutional ethnocentric values is capable of fostering Euroscepticism more than any abstract issues such as "limitation of national sovereignty" or "the democratic deficit", which are in fact of completely secondary importance in Romania'. This is an indirect critical stipulation on the development of supranational self-referential modernisation discourses which do not have a substantial impact on the still fragmented national constitutional discourses. From this viewpoint, the advancing post-Westphalian supranational constitutionalism is paralleled by persisting and even reinforced and revived Westphalian constitutionalism on the nation state level.

Gutan draws rather pessimistic conclusions from a global constitutionalism perspective. He believes that the rebirth of illiberal constitutionalism is not coincidental. It is historically predetermined and was just temporarily covered for tactical reasons of the domestic elites. The illiberal ethnocentric constitutionalism will persist as an unavoidable impediment to the development of substantial Europeanisation, democratisation and as an impenetrable limit to the development of post-Westphalian global constitutionalism.

The topic of the limits of European integration is common for the papers of Gutan and Fekete. However, the limits they discuss are of a different nature. Gutan defines the ethnocentric national identity as a limitation to Europeanisation via constitutional transplantation, while Fekete analyses the limits of the concept of pooling of sovereignties in the current phase of recession of globalisation and Europeanisation optimism. Both papers share the admission that the constitutional concepts in general and the emergence of post-Westphalian concepts belonging to the ideal realm of global constitutionalism in particular are embedded in the constitutional culture and the socio-political context. Thus culture, identity and community serve as inevitable determinants and—in many instances—also limitations, for the emergence of supranational and global constitutionalism in general and for EU constitutionalism in particular.

Fekete defines sovereignty pooling as 'strategy for coordinating state behaviour'. He believes that it is a concept which is very much dependent on the socio-legal context and thus is exposed to its inherent limitations. According to the author, 'the more political are the goals to be achieved via sovereignty pooling, the less chance there is to realise them'. Fekete implies that although challenged by globalisation and Europeanisation sovereignty will persist, and with it, one of the main pillars, principles and supportive ideologies of Westphalian constitutionalism. Thus any transition to post-Westphalian constitutionalism is postponed or even rendered impossible so far as the socio-legal predispositions for overcoming sovereignty are missing. Fekete remains sceptical about 'sovereignty pooling' as an early post-Westphalian concept since 'European political culture is still heavily reliant on sovereignty at both the level of political rhetoric and that of constitutionalism'.

Fekete uses Michael Oakeshott's analytical paradigm of sovereignty as a starting point for construction of his critical assessment of Robert Keohane's theory of pooling of sovereignties. In fact, the theory of Oakeshott implicitly presumes the shift from late medieval particularism amounting to non-democratic structural pluralism to modern monism constructed around the concept of sovereignty. At the same time, Keohane's theory is an attempt at reconciliation of the modern sovereignty-based monism with the re-emerging plurality, this time of multiple, multilayered and perplexed constitutional orders. Hence the initial theoretical framework set by Fekete on the basis of Oakeshott's and Keohane's theories touches upon the problematics of normative (dis)order and the partial dismantling of hierarchy tackled by Auby in his contribution to this volume and to the challenges of the early post-Westphalian situation to the constitutional geometry of the Westphalian constitutional law analysed in my paper.

An interesting issue which may arise out of the reading of Fekete's interpretation of Keohane's and Jean Boden's theories concerns the ordering function of the concept of sovereignty 'in the turbulent era of pre-Westphalian Europe'. Now, it is questionable whether sovereignty still accomplishes this function sufficiently well in the age of globalisation. If not, one should look for additional or even alternative paradigms for 'ordering of the constitutional orders'.[22] Fekete denies the capability of the 'pooled sovereignties' concept to serve as a trustful and efficient post-Westphalian paradigm performing such an ordering task.

Another implication of the Keohane's theory as analysed by Fekete, which is related to the topic of global constitutionalism, concerns the socio-legal determinants of the split in the Western civilisation since World War II consisting in the adherence of the US constitutionalism to the classical versions of sovereignty paralleled by the emergence of post-sovereignty trends in the EU constitutionalism. Fekete stresses the re-emergence of sovereignty in the post-crisis political discourse in Europe during the last decade. Thus he challenges the inevitability and irreversibility of supranational constitutionalism as based on the 'pooling of sovereignty' concept. Fekete questions the idea and practice of pooling of sovereignty by analysing whether we are not witnessing a new phase of the development of sovereignty in Europe—'the nightfall of sovereignty pooling'.

Fekete critically analyses Keohane's thesis that sovereignty is being transformed from status into a toolkit and bargaining chip in the context of EU integration. In broader terms the fragmentation of sovereignty and its transformation from static into dynamic concept serving as procedural hurdle in multilevel games, sometimes structured as 'nested games',[23] is one of the most important issues to have emerged in the context of early post-Westphalian constitutionalism.

Fekete introduces some of the discussions related to the search of post-Westphalian explanatory paradigms of the emerging supranational constitutionalism of the EU by contrasting Samantha Besson's theory of cooperative sovereignty to Keohane's theory of pooling of sovereignties. He focuses on what he calls 'constitutional framework for sovereignty pooling'. In that regard he delimits static and dynamic aspects of the EU decision-making model and puts special emphasis on qualified majority voting (QMV) as a device for putting into practice the pooling of sovereignty concept.

The main idea launched by Fekete is that:

> sovereignty pooling has always been an underlying principle of the community toolkit of establishing its constitutional architecture. Although it has been almost unnoticeable in the early period of integration [the] post-Lisbon configuration of competence-sharing and broad range of QMV decision-making are logical consequences of the earliest intents of sovereignty pooling.

[22] For the concept of 'ordering of constitutional orders' see E Tanchev, 'The Contemporary Supranational Constitutional Pluralism or the Ordering of Constitutional Orders' in P Kirov (ed), *Constitutional Studies 2012–2013* (Sofia, 'St Kliment Ohridski' University Press, 2014), 171–98 (in Bulgarian).

[23] For the concept of nested games see G Tsebelis, *Nested Games. Rational Choice in Comparative Politics.* (Berkeley, University of California Press, 1990).

Fekete defines three phases of the historical development of sovereignty pooling in the EU: the first phase, from the establishment of the European Communities to the Single European Act; the second phase, from the Single European Act to the Lisbon Treaty; and the third phase, from the adoption of the Lisbon Treaty onwards.

Fekete argues that in the period since the Lisbon Treaty 'sovereignty pooling was a clear success in policy areas relating to the internal market in the broadest sense while it had only modest or even little impact on other important policy areas mostly associated with the traditional core of sovereignty'. He also believes that the current crisis of constitutional Euro-optimism sets new and revives old limits to sovereignty pooling. Consequently Fekete provides an analysis of this recent trend which according to him leads to the eventual 'nightfall of sovereignty pooling in Europe'.

Fekete concludes that the events during the last decade, marked by the financial and the migrant crises, have triggered new dynamics in the development of the European concept of sovereignty. He outlines two main phenomena which challenge the concept of pooled sovereignty and produce dynamics revitalising more traditional or Westphalian approaches to sovereignty. These are the 'external judicial resentment to the deepening of sovereignty pooling' and the 'internal scepticism towards the deepening of sovereignty pooling'.

Fekete finally reminds us of his two main theses exposed in the paper by presenting the current dissatisfaction of the 'Visegrad' countries with the decision on the redistribution of migrants in the EU and by pointing out the 'judicial revolts' of some EU Member States' constitutional courts against further 'sovereignty pooling'. The first thesis is that the sovereignty concept and sovereign perceptions in general and 'sovereignty pooling' in particular are a matter of constitutional identity and constitutional culture deeply rooted in socio-legal determinants which have been underestimated during the optimistic periods of EU integration. The second thesis is that sovereignty, as the most obvious Westphalian constitutional concept, is still a core principle of European constitutionalism, although tamed or tempered by post-Westphalian concepts such as 'constitutional identity' and 'pooling of sovereignties'.

The issues of political trust and accountability are common problems for the papers of Fekete and Simoncini. However, both papers analyse these problems from different perspectives, with different scientific aims and with regard to different analytical objects. Fekete explores whether the horizontal and vertical axes of trust in the EU constitutional construction, which are culturally and socio-politically predetermined, are sufficient to sustain a post-Westphalian concept of political authority which is not necessarily monolithic, supreme and hierarchical and thus inevitably bound to sovereignty. Simoncini is interested in a particular issue, which is again related to the emergence of supranational constitutionalism and to problems which did not exist in the context of Westphalian statehood. Her concerns relate to the constitutional dimension of the EU agencies as a framework that allows rendering them more accountable and thus making them more trustworthy from a democratic point of view and from a constitutionalist perspective. Thus she opposes the (global) administrative law perspective defining the EU as a 'form of deliberative supranationalism, distinct from a constitutional experience'.

Simoncini's paper explores the 'complexity of the EU identity as a legal order beyond the state'. The general theoretical framework of Simoncini's work is set by the tension between the delegation of constitutional competences to the EU by the Member States and the autopoietic[24] development of its constitutional order which determines the dynamics of EU supranational constitutionalism. The main aim of Simoncini's paper is to determine whether the 'agencification' at EU level has a constitutional and not just an administrative dimension and what is its impact on the rule of law and democracy in the context of 'constitutionalism beyond statehood'.[25]

Simoncini's paper tackles several important issues related to the supranational constitutionalism of the EU: the harmonisation of regulatory philosophies; the adjustment of constitutional and administrative orders; the rendering of supranational autonomous administrations democratically legitimate and accountable; and the reconciliation of the requirements of expertise and management of global risk society issues[26] by regional (EU) regulatory regimes providing for the rule of law with the need for preservation of trust, accountability, representative democracy and state self-determination.

The problem of agencification is a specific manifestation of the broader principle issue of the increasing role of technocracies in the context of globalisation, global constitutionalism and global governance. The question whether the increased technological knowledge and sector-specific expertise can be constitutionally framed is among the most important issues of the current global technological society, produced by the technical, information and mobility revolution experienced by the late modern societies at the end of the twentieth and the beginning of the twenty-first century.

Simoncini explores the shift of the EU agencies from executive institutions belonging to the realm of the administration to regulatory institutions with (still limited) rule making and policy determination functions thus also acquiring a constitutional role and dimension. Relying on the case law of the CJEU, Simoncini stipulates that 'the evolution of administrative

[24] G Teubner, *Law as an Autopoietic System* (Oxford, Blackwell Publishers, 1993).

[25] See also N Walker, 'Taking Constitutionalism Beyond the State' (2008) 56 *Political Studies* 519–43.

[26] U Beck, above n 17.

powers at the EU level ... presupposes the development of an autonomous supranational order that constitutionally frames EU agencies' powers'. She demonstrates that the constitutional dimension of the agencification is presupposed and triggered by the constitutional autopoiesis of the EU. Simoncini stipulates that 'the judicial evolution of the Meroni doctrine shows that from a supranational perspective, the EU is a legal order autonomous from its constituent Member States'.

The issues of accountability and legitimacy are central to Simoncini's paper. She considers 'the accountability and legitimacy issues on broader grounds. Both the supranational framework of EU powers and the multilevel structure of the EU shall contribute to understanding the legitimacy of the exercise of administrative powers by EU agencies.' Simoncini explores the different legitimation approaches proposed by the theory. She suggests that:

> the development of EU agencies' powers can be interpreted as further fragmentation of national normative powers which involves a relaxation of Member States' oversight aimed at the development of the (supranational) internal market. The autonomy of EU law legally justifies this development on the grounds of the constitutional status of the EU.

Simoncini distinguishes between supranational delegation of powers from the Member States to the EU and subsequent autonomous allocation of powers on an EU level. The latter is defined by her as 'a phenomenon of pluralisation and specialisation of EU powers'. Simoncini suggests that when analysing the case of the EU agencies 'the idea of a supranational administrative governance shall be complemented by and adjusted to the existence of an autonomous dimension of the EU legal order which cannot be explained only as a delegation of regulatory powers from the Member States, but needs to be understood within the specific categories of EU law'.

Simoncini explicitly defines two types of constitutional challenge to EU agencies: first, the political accountability issues; and second, legal accountability issues. Implicitly she also presumes the existence of legitimacy issues. With a view to political accountability, Simoncini suggests that 'the search for complementary accountability instruments that beyond their specific goals can set up a wider political accountability framework is key to reconnect EU agencies to the composite nature of the EU and to consolidate their legitimacy'.

Simoncini also delimits important issues relating to the legal accountability of the EU agencies which are preconditions for the establishment of an effective system of control for their activity as agents of the supranational constitutionalism of the EU. The most important of them are 'the existence of effective judicial protection' as 'a necessary precondition for the allocation of powers to EU agencies', the 'level of deference the judiciary takes towards EU agencies' acts when complex technical assessments are submitted to judicial review', the 'dichotomy between technical assessments by EU agencies and political discretion by EU institutions', 'the recognition of the existence of a specific administrative decision-making space in the EU' in order to 'avoid blending discretionary choices of EU agencies' and the confrontation of the activity of the EU agencies with the 'conception of legality that goes beyond the dichotomy between political and technical tasks'. Simoncini concludes that 'the introduction of an EU administrative procedure law would make the exercise of (regulatory) powers more visible to the Member States, as well as to European citizens and sector-operators'.

Part I

General Constitutional Theory of Global Constitutionalism

1

Global Constitutionalism and Normative Hierarchies

JEAN-BERNARD AUBY

I. THE BASIC PROBLEM: THE DISORDER CREATED BY THE MULTIPLICATION AND DISPERSION OF LEGAL PRODUCERS AND OF PLACES OF PRODUCTION OF LAW IN THE GLOBAL SPACE

IF THEORIES OF global constitutionalism arose, it is because, after some development of legal globalisation, it became obvious that the latter was in the process of transforming the legal functioning of the world so profoundly that the usual organisation of law, rooted in national constitutions and well structured around them, could soon be lost.

It is now clear that globalisation is changing dramatically global governance and the normative production mechanisms in the world.[1] The growing interconnectedness of legal systems has paved the way to a multiplication of law makers. In particular, one can observe an emergence of new law makers: some of them are new forms of public law makers (such as many global administrative entities), but others are outright non-state regulators.[2]

One can also argue that, in complement to these basic phenomena, others contribute to make normative hierarchies less clear. Among them, there is what can be described as a transformation in systemic relations between legal systems: growing 'permeabilisation' between legal systems, growing competition between legal systems, a trend towards a certain harmonisation.[3]

No need to insist on the fact that these transformations are a challenge to the traditional ordinance of law in the world, and that, because of them, the legal world no longer constitutes a fairly organised state-centred system like in the past. It is this new disorder in the system of production and the organisation of law at the international level which is inciting some people to advocate for a constitutionalisation of the global area, for a global constitutionalism.

[1] JB Auby, *Globalisation, Law and the State* (Oxford, Hart Publishing, 2016) 14 et seq.
[2] S Sassen, *A Sociology of Globalization* (WW Norton & Co, 2007) 214 et seq.
[3] JB Auby, above n 1, 80 et seq.

II. THEORIES OF GLOBAL CONSTITUTIONALISM AS EFFORTS TO INSTIL SOME ORDER AND VALUES INTO THE NORMATIVE DISORDER OF LEGAL GLOBALISATION

Ahead of what can easily be seen as global legal entropy, theories of global constitutionalism are efforts to restore some order and to impose the respect for certain values by using the proven recipes of constitutionalism.[4] Constitutionalism and constitutionalisation have two basic functions. One is to devise the relations between public authorities, to distribute roles and powers among them, to adjust the supervision by citizens. The other one is to marshal the production and implementation of norms in a legal system, by designating the bodies in charge of making law and the relations between norms produced in the system. In other words, it is to endow it with a viable normative architecture. It is on this second function that this chapter's discussion is centred.

One must make clear, though, that there is more than one theory of global constitutionalism.[5] There are in fact several, among which the main differences are as follows. They first differ according to their targets. Indeed, any global constitutionalism has to determine which entities involved in legal globalisation it considers as needing to be constitutionalised. Some will consider that the priority is to constitutionalise (by attaching to them a basic charter addressing the above-mentioned issues, or addressing them more completely than their current statutes) the main international organisations, such as the UN and the WTO, at a minimum. They then convey the conviction that global constitutionalism implies the constitutionalisation of international law,[6] while others will consider that no efficient constitutionalisation is doable without impacting on the national constitutions in order for them to organise better the relations between their systems and the global legal world. Some will go so far as to lay on the table the issue of how to constitutionalise non-state regulators.[7]

[4] See in particular B Ackerman, 'The Rise of World Constitutionalism' (1997) 83 *Virginia Law Review* 771; C Joerges and EU Petersmann (eds), *Constitutionalism, Multilevel Trade Governance and Social Regulation* (Oxford, Hart Publishing, 2010); J Klabbers, A Peters and G Ulfstein, *The Constitutionalization of International Law* (Oxford, Oxford University Press, 2009); D Schneiderman, 'A new global constitutional order?' in T Ginsburg and R Dixon (eds), *Comparative Constitutional Law* (Cheltenham, Edward Elgar, 2011) 189 et seq; C Tomuschat, 'International Law: Ensuring the Survival of Mankind on the Eve of a New Century', General Course on Public International Law, in (1999) 281 *Recueil des Cours* 10, 25.

[5] M Loughlin, 'What is constitutionalisation?' in P Dobner and M Loughlin (eds), *The Twilight of Constitutionalism* (Oxford, Oxford University Press, 2010) 47 et seq.

[6] J Habermas, *Plea for a constitutionalisation of international law*, 23rd World Congress of Philosophy, 4–10 August 2013; JM Sorel, 'La constitutionnalisation du droit international', in H Ruiz-Fabri and M Rosenfeld (eds), *Repenser le constitutionnalisme à l'âge de la mondialisation et de la privatisation*, Société de législation comparée, 2011, 28 et seq.

[7] G Anderson, *Constitutional Rights after Globalization* (Oxford, Hart Publishing, 2005).

Second, global constitutionalism theories adopt an approach which is either typically analytical, in the sense of observing the reality in order to detect the existence of a constitutional architecture underneath the global legal functioning, or prescriptive in the sense of pushing forward global constitutionalisation as a voluntary policy. The so-called 'societal constitutionalism' theory would tend to be on the first side, while theories aimed at constitutionalising the big international organisations would be more on the second one.

Third—and this divide is largely connected with the previous one—there are theories which mainly base constitutionalisation on mechanisms of private law, such as the chains of contractual and arbitral mechanisms in international business relations as constituting an underlying constitutional framework,[8] while others will insist on the contrary on public law realities and mechanisms, be they situated at the level of international organisations or also impacting on national constitutions.

The synthesis I make personally of these theories leads me to admit that the efforts of global constitutionalism only make sense[9] under three conditions. For a global constitutionalism approach to fully understand the issue it is trying to grasp, it must cover all possible targets, for example all global law makers. Second, it must adopt a 'multilevel' approach, in which the different levels of constitutionalisation more or less meet and complement each other. By the way, from the two preceding remarks it follows that the approach of global constitutionalism integrates a dimension of internationalisation of national constitutions: the latter must take their part in the overall constitutional organisation. Third, I believe that no global constitutionalism theory can stand upright if it does not convey the essential values of the rule of law, without the respect for which there is no just and stable legal order.

III. THE PROBLEM OF NORMATIVE HIERARCHIES IN LEGAL GLOBALISATION

We must then come back to the effects globalisation has on normative hierarchies. The institutional and normative disorganisation caused by

[8] G Teubner, 'Fragmented Foundations. Societal Constitutionalism beyond the Nation-State' in P Dobner and M Loughlin (eds), *The Twilight of Constitutionalism* (Oxford, Oxford University Press, 2010) 327; André-Jean Arnaud, 'Entre modernité et mondialisation. Leçon d'histoire de la philosophie du droit et de l'Etat', Librairie Générale de Droit et de Jurisprudence, 2004, p 254: 'Le droit privé trouve dans la globalisation un contexte favorable pour se transformer en droit constitutionnel pour les régimes globaux de gouvernance privée' ('Private law finds in globalisation a favourable context for transforming itself into constitutional law for the global regimes of private governance').

[9] A O'Donoghue, *Constitutionalism in Global Constitutionalisation* (Cambridge, Cambridge University Press, 2014).

globalisation raises two types of issue. One is related to the legitimacy of global bodies. It questions their accountability, in terms of supervision by their various stakeholders and in terms of legal imputation and liability mechanisms. The main corresponding approach, centred on the bodies and procedures, is typically the one adopted by the 'global administrative law' theory.[10] The other one is related to normative arrangements, substantive hierarchies and dissemination of the essential principles of the rule of law: the focus, there, is more on the substance and normative relations. Of course, there is a share of overlapping between the two sets of problems: for example, the implementation of norms is an issue that straddles the two. Nevertheless, they are two different sides of the coin.

It is on the second group of problems that we will concentrate in this chapter, aiming to determine what contribution global constitutionalism can make to its resolution. It can be said to contain three key questions. From the point of view of substance and normative relations, the level of disorder/order in a particular legal system can be considered dependent on three factors.

The first is about the existence and readability of linking mechanisms between legal producers and legal orders. A set of institutions and law-creating entities and mechanisms cannot perform like a viable legal system if it is not possible to determine if there are links between them and of what nature they are.

The second is the level of existence and clarity of mechanisms of arrangement between norms and in particular of hierarchical arrangements allowing us to solve situations of conflict when rules arising from various parts of the system are in competition for regulating the same situation.

The third is the level of existence of adequate channels of dissemination of the essential principles of the rule of law. One legal system cannot claim to be sustainable if it does not contain this key, which ensures that its legal subjects are encouraged by way of fundamental principles to respect the rules it produces.

The problem that must therefore be addressed is to what extent constitutionalism makes it possible to satisfactorily promote these three orders of reality in the global sphere.

[10] See, eg, S Cassese (ed), *Research Handbook on Global Administrative Law* (Edward Elgar, 2016), N Krisch, 'Global Administrative Law and the Constitutional Ambition' in P Dobner and M Loughlin (eds), *The Twilight of Constitutionalism* (Oxford, Oxford University Press, 2010) 245 et seq.

IV. GLOBAL CONSTITUTIONALISM AND LINKS BETWEEN LEGAL ORDERS[11]

One of the main functions traditionally assumed by constitutions is to lay down ground rules on the relationship between the legal order they organise and other legal orders, also between the partial legal orders they accommodate when they accept to any extent some internal pluralism.[12] Let us consider the instruments which can today be regarded as contributing to the constitutionalisation of the global order: that is to say, in the present state of things, national constitutions in proportion to their concern for international relations and founding treaties of certain major international and European organisations, which are close to constitutions. Are they concerned about the relations between the legal order which they form and other legal orders?

National constitutions, in general, contain rules concerning relations with the international legal order (at least as regards the authority of treaties in the domestic order): it is less common for them to regulate relations with other national legal systems (conflicts of laws).

What about international 'constitutions' such as the UN Charter and the European treaties? They sometimes deal efficiently with the issue of relations with other legal orders, but not always. European treaties are placed under the authority of the United Nations Charter, but conversely the WTO Treaty does not address the relationship between the legal order it creates and the national ones (particularly with regard to the issue of direct effect).

It is true that, as Santi Romano has shown,[13] the links between legal orders are variable and cannot be reduced to the most ordinary figure of recognition and domination: legal order B is instituted by A, and hence its existence depends on A. In fact, and the observation of legal globalisation clearly shows it, the links between legal orders are more varied: for example, they may relate to the distribution of roles, in the sense that order B assumes a different function (this may be the judicial sanction of the norms laid down in system A) or both orders apply only partially in the same material domains. Thus, the instruments through which the constitutionalisation of the global order is carried out can be imaginative as to the figures of relation between legal orders.

[11] JB Auby, 'Repenser le droit à l'aune de la globalisation juridique?' in B Bonnet (ed), *Traité des rapports entre ordres juridiques* (Librairie Générale de Droit et de Jurisprudence, 2016) 261–77.

[12] It is possible to plead that any kind of territorial decentralisation—and all states contain some degree of it—induces some legal pluralism (JB Auby, *La décentralisation et le droit* (Librairie Générale de Droit et de Jurisprudence, 2006)), but not all constitutions and constitution drafters share this view.

[13] S Romano, *L'ordinamento giuridico*, 1918.

However, things are made more complicated by the fact that legal producers, and hence the institutions that house partial legal orders which must be combined, have become increasingly numerous and varied: to states and interstate institutions have been added non-state regulators (ICANN, ISO, etc), global administrative agencies, infra-state communities (the increasingly frequent occurrence of sub-state communities that have significant normative power in federal or regional systems).

It is not easy for global constitutionalism to master this complexity and to organise the very diverse multilateral relations it entails and, as things stand at present, their organisation remains very incomplete. For example, standards made within the ISO system have varying effects according to the national legal systems with which they come into contact: in some, they retain a contractual and soft law nature while in others they acquire a formal regulatory value.

Are 'international constitutions' and national ones addressing the problem of the emergence of non-state law makers and the development of the constantly thriving participation of regional and local governments in international legal life?[14] Not often, since both still reflect a vision of the law in which states and interstate organisations remain at the centre of all normative production.

Could they do otherwise? It will never be easy: even in federal and regional states, where sub-state entities have legislative powers—because they are more or less considered as having the same nature as the central state—in general, the relations between the law they produce and the international ambit is filtered by the central state. Concerning the non-state law makers, it is very difficult to admit them to the dignity of law makers recognised by constitutions because they will usually lack the required legitimacy ingredients.

V. GLOBAL CONSTITUTIONALISM AND NORMATIVE ARRANGEMENTS

The next question extends the previous one. It concerns the case where two norms coming from different legal orders and put in relation by the routes that have just been mentioned are in competition to regulate a given legal situation. It raises the problem of normative hierarchy conceived in the broad sense. This problem is obviously of particular frequency in legal globalisation, which multiplies both the sources of law and the concrete

[14] Y Blank, 'The City and the World' (2005–2006) *Columbia Journal of Transnational Law* 875; Y Blank, Localism in the New Global Legal Order (2006) 47 *Harvard International Law Journal* 263.

opportunities to see norms coming from different legal orders collide: in particular because of the multiplication of situations of transnationality and of extraterritoriality in an increasingly interconnected legal world.[15]

Constitutionalisation can obviously provide solutions: constitutions are commonly concerned both with their internal hierarchy and with the relations of precedence between the norms arising from their legal order and those that come from other legal orders. In particular, when, relying more or less on a monist or a dualist view, they pronounce on the relations between treaties and the national legislation.

In the globalised world, however, things are presented in a particularly complicated light. The enormous production of norms in various ways makes it more difficult than ever to establish primacy relations. This is shown, for example, by the increasingly frequent issue of conflicts between international conventions. In the rather frequent silence of the conventions, judges are led to question their respective fields of application and then, if this test does not solve the problem, to identify their common objectives in such a way as to give priority to the one which appears the most effective to pursue them or, if this criterion does not give the solution, to make the one which carries the most essential values prevail.

More broadly, it can be said that in the globalised legal world, the strictly hierarchical relationships between norms coming from different systems are less frequent. One of the reasons for this is that, in the globalised world, legal systems are frequently confronted with one another at levels where it becomes impossible for them to bow hierarchically before another one. This is perfectly demonstrated by the relations between the treaties of the European Union and the constitutions of the Member States: whereas the Court of Justice considers that the European treaties prevail over all national norms, even at constitutional level, some national supreme courts have indicated that they do not accept this primacy, or at least accept it only relatively. This position, first expressed in the *Solange* jurisprudence by the German Federal Constitutional Court, can be labelled as admitting a situation of 'double mirror effect'.[16]

Another reason why global constitutionalism cannot be too ambitious in the establishment of clear-cut normative hierarchies is that it must adapt to frequent realities of multilevel governance, in which two or more tiers of public action and correlative normative creation combine and complement each other. If the Court of Justice of the European Union has ruled out the direct effect of the WTO standards, and has thus severed their authority,

[15] JB Auby, above n 1, 16.

[16] JB Auby, above n 1, 77; I Pernice and FC Mayer, 'De la Constitution composée de l'Europe' (2000) *Revue trimestrielle de droit européen* 631.

it is to give the Union authorities greater freedom to negotiate with the organs of WTO.[17]

Here again, another difficulty derives from the emergence of non-state global law makers, whether private global law makers or sub-state entities. Especially for the former, since, in general, constitutions—whether 'international constitutions' or national ones—simply ignore their existence as law producers. One may suppose that the regulations they produce are in essence inferior to state and interstate law, but this is not expressly ascertained by many constitutions.

VI. GLOBAL CONSTITUTIONALISM AND DISSEMINATION OF THE RULE OF LAW'S FUNDAMENTAL PRINCIPLES

Constitutions are a privileged place for the proclamation of the principles of the rule of law (and fundamental rights, which are neighbouring values). In fact, the global legal world is already largely covered by international standards that highlight the principles of the rule of law:[18] whether international texts of a quasi-constitutional nature (such as the European Convention on Human Rights or the Charter of Fundamental Rights of the EU) or provisions of national constitutions relevant to international relations (for example, relating to asylum). It has not been too difficult to attach quasi-constitutional texts conveying the principles of the rule of law (and the protection of fundamental rights) to the charters of various major international and European organisations (the UN, the Council of Europe and the European Union).

In other cases, however, this has proved less easy. This is the case with some international economic organisations, such as the World Bank, the WTO and the IMF, whose basic values did not integrate the heritage of rule of law and fundamental rights. In order to ensure that the due process and fair trial rules would be sufficiently respected within the WTO, a Dispute Settlement Body was created and developed that did not exist at the beginning.[19]

Even more difficult is the case of non-state regulators, which, being generally private legal entities, are not inherently governed by the principles of the rule of law and of respect for fundamental rights. The best solutions for

[17] F Berrod, 'La Cour de Justice refuse l'invocabilité des accords OMC: essai de regulation de la mondialisation', (2000) July–September, *Revue trimestrielle de droit européen*, 419.

[18] A Peters, 'The Globalization of State Constitutions' in J Nijman and A Nollkaemper (eds), *New Perspectives on the Divide Between National and International Law* (Oxford, Oxford University Press, 2007) 251.

[19] JE Alvarez, 'The New Dispute-Settlers: (Half) Truths and Consequences' (2003) 38 *Texas International Law Journal*, 405.

submitting them to these principles are either, in the event of litigation, to treat these entities as public bodies, therefore subject to the same rules as these, or to impose on them by legislation to integrate, through mechanisms of corporate governance, respect for the rule of law and fundamental rights in their internal functioning.[20]

This can be done in national constitutions (the legal personality of non-state regulators is immersed in national law) or in the fundamental texts of the international organisations with which these regulators wish to collaborate. But it is seldom done simply because national constitutions as well as 'international constitutions', in general, ignore non-state regulators.[21]

VII. CONCLUSION: NECESSITY AND LIMITS OF GLOBAL CONSTITUTIONALISM

The idea of global constitutionalism as a means of disciplining normative pluralism in legal globalisation is not only a good idea: it is a necessity. In the globalised world, national constitutions become, as it were, partial constitutions. They control only part of the legal relations in which the legal order concerned is inscribed. This is compounded by the fact that global constitutional or quasi-constitutional instruments are essential for the international promotion of certain fundamental principles: it is clear that a certain amount of submission to these principles is a necessary counterweight to globalisation.

However, the exercise has its constraints and limitations. Global constitutionalism is necessarily organised in a 'multi-level' way, which differentiates it strongly from classical constitutionalism, which rather is self-centred.[22] It will never allow the setting up of pure pyramidal organisations, as national systems may sometimes appear. It will always require hybrid compositions, echoing multiple arrangements, vertical as well as horizontal.

Finally, one must not exaggerate the scope of problems it can address. If we focus on the subject discussed in this chapter, it is at least worth pointing out that the relations between norms within national systems are generally not entirely regulated by the constitution. The law, the jurisprudence, often come to add their solutions.

The 'global' constitutions cannot aim to solve the problems of normative hierarchy in globalisation entirely. This is without prejudice to the political

[20] JB Auby, 'Contracting Out and Public Values' in S Rose-Ackerman and P Lindseth (eds), *Comparative Administrative Law*, 2nd edn (Aldershot, Ashgate, 2017).

[21] G Anderson, above n 7, 22 et seq.

[22] N Bamforth and P Leyland, *Public Law in a Multi-layered Constitution* (Oxford, Hart Publishing, 2003), P Popelier and W Vandenbruwaene, 'The Constitutional Adulthood of Multi-Level Governance' (2014) 21 *Maastricht Journal of European and Comparative Law*.

limitations of the constitutionalisation project, which it was not in the scope of this chapter to deal with. Surely, it would be unwise to think that global constitutionalism could solve all the problems of the world.[23] No doubt, too, that, in itself, constitutionalism does not provide an answer to another problem, as important as that of the normative disorder, which is that of the democratic deficit of the world in globalisation.[24]

[23] Z Laidi, *La norme sans la force. L'énigme de la puissance européenne* (Paris, Presses de Sciences Po, 2005) 247 et seq: 'Constitutionnaliser l'ordre mondial, c'est succomber à une vision salvatrice qui pense qu'en allant jusqu'au bout d'un processus, on règlera les problèmes du monde' ('To constitutionalise the world order is to succumb to a saving vision which thinks that by going through a process, we will solve the problems of the world').

[24] M La Torre, 'El Brexit y la miseria del constitutionalismo global' (2016) 64 *El Cronista* 4.

2

The Challenges to Westphalian Constitutional Geometry in the Age of Supranational Constitutionalism, Global Governance and Information Revolution

MARTIN BELOV

I. TAKING CONSTITUTIONAL GEOMETRY SERIOUSLY[1]

THIS CHAPTER AIMS to clarify the analytical concept of constitutional geometry, explaining the constitutional geometry of Westphalian statehood and demonstrating the evolution of the Westphalian constitutional geometry of the constitutional nation state into the post-Westphalian constitutional geometry of supranational and global constitutional law in the time of globalisation and information revolution. The chapter reflects on the challenges to constitutional semiotics[2] produced by the current early post-Westphalian situation.

Constitutional geometry is an important constitutional paradigm that has so far been underestimated by constitutional theory and overshadowed by more powerful and widespread analytical and constructive paradigms. In fact these paradigms are closely linked to the constitutional geometry serving as its background or supplement or exposing some of its aspects. Hence constitutional geometry is not a profoundly new concept. It has always been implicitly enshrined in the normative and institutional order—both

[1] Here I borrow that polemic construction from the title of Ronald Dworkin's book 'Taking Rights Seriously'. See R Dworkin, *Taking Rights Seriously* (Cambridge, Mass, Harvard University Press, 2001).

[2] Examples of semiotic studies of constitutional law are the works of D Brion, 'The Semiotics of Constitutional Meaning' (1995) *Semiotics* 137–45 and P Ahonen, 'The Semionics of Finnish Constitutional Law on Government Finance' in R Kevelson (ed), *Law and Semiotics* (New York, Plenum Press, 1988) 13 et seq.

constitutional and political—of the Westphalian statehood and has been indirectly used by modern constitutional theory. However, it has not been sufficiently emancipated as an independent analytical paradigm and as a key semiotic concept of constitutional law theory.

The concept of constitutional geometry has to be defined and discussed with a view to its general analytical role as a holistic phenomenon and its particular instantiations and manifestations in constitutional law. It has to be examined with regard to its features as both an analytical paradigm of constitutional theory and a constructive (ordering) paradigm of constitutional law.

Under 'analytical paradigm' I understand a system of interrelated analytical tools used by the theory to explain the constitutional law in its ideal dimension as a system of normative ideologies and ideas,[3] in its positive dimension as a constitutional order composed of norms, principles and institutions, and in its empirical dimension as 'constitutional law in action', which actually shapes human and institutional behaviour in its socio-legal context. Actually constitutional geometry is a phenomenon which is at the same time constructed by the theory, enshrined in the normative order and objectively produced by the social life or objectively moulded by the historical process of advance and adaptation of the constitutional system to the socio-legal context.

On the other hand, constitutional geometry is also a constructive (ordering) paradigm of constitutional law because it allows for the arrangement of the constitutional institutions into typical broader shapes and forms unified on the basis of specific logic and criteria. This is the logic of rational visualisation and symbolic structuring of constitutional relations which is based on the cumulative criteria of durability, persistence, capability of formal representation and strategic importance for the constitutional order, the constitutional system or their sub-systems.

Indeed, constitutional geometry is built upon the precondition of rationality while at the same time rests and depends on its own visual-emotional persuasiveness derived from the broader socio-legal, ideal and factual context. Thus constitutional geometry as a constructive (ordering) paradigm allows for macro structuring of constitutional relations and of the constitutional order in a way that also appeals to the set of preconceptions developed in the broader societal context. Constitutional geometry allows an interdisciplinary study of the macro structures of the constitutional order taken in their broader historical, cultural and socio-legal context. That is

[3] For the concept of normative ideology and normative idea see M Belov, 'The Ideological Heritage of Magna Carta and Its Reception in the Bulgarian Constitutionalism' in P Panayotov (ed), *Scientific Readings in Honour of Venelin Ganev and Nikola Dolapchiev* (Sofia, 'St Kliment Ohridski' University Press, 2017) 450–53 (in Bulgarian).

why it can be constructed and analysed also from the viewpoint and by using the achievements of other branches of human knowledge.

Just one example which might seem unusual and stunning at a first glance: the theory of Wassily Kandinsky on the methods for ascribing, objectivising and suggesting of meaning through artistic depiction of geometric forms[4] may serve as an incentive for using geometrical shapes and forms as symbolic representations of constitutional macro structures and phenomena. Naturally the use of knowledge from the art sciences has its objective limits in the nature of the law and the legal science and in the objective characteristics of the constitutional phenomena that should be depicted. Moreover, that knowledge has to be used in combination with the knowledge from other sciences that may shed contextual light on the analysed constitutional phenomenon. For example, political science, philosophy, sociology and history may inform us regarding the 'normativity of the facts and ideas'[5] allowing for the establishment and continuity of certain durable constitutional geometric forms. Consequently these forms are to a great extent objectively predetermined by the socio-legal context in which they are produced. Moreover, the constitutional geometric forms are both product and result of the socio-legal context and at the same time shape and frame it after they have been established. Thus they are both preconditioned on meta-legal factors and aim to serve as their regulatory and explanatory paradigms.

Modern social and political philosophy, constitutional theory and theory of state and law have created several explanatory paradigms that are supposed to define the way we think about the macro structures of the constitutional system. They should predetermine not only the legal and political culture but also the imagination of both the citizens and the political elite and have to structure their durable beliefs about the state, the constitution and the constitutional order. The system of these durable ideas aimed at the establishment of the ideal constitution[6] of the state can be defined as normative constitutional ideology.

Constitutional geometry is not only part of the normative ideology of constitutional law but it is also enshrined and objectivised in the institutional and normative dimensions of positive constitutional law. Constitutional geometry subsumes the institutions and the different sub-systems of the constitutional order under wider shapes on the macro and medium levels. Thus it builds upon and partially overcomes the traditional institutionalist systematisation of positive constitutional law.

[4] W Kandinsky, *Point and Line to Plane* (Dover Fine Art, 1979) 1–179.

[5] J Stalev, *The Normative Force of the Factual* (Sofia, Feneya, 2007) 1–280 (in Bulgarian).

[6] For the concept of ideal constitution see, eg, J Blondel, *Comparative Government. An Introduction* (Hemel Hempstead, Prentice Hall/Harvester Wheatsheaf, 1995) and E Tanchev, *Introduction in Constitutional Law* (Sofia, Sibi, 2003) 112 (in Bulgarian).

Hence constitutional geometry is closely related but not limited to legal institutionalism. Constitutional geometry can neither be reduced to nor does it equal institutionalism. Institutional theory in its different variants is focused on the origin, shape, constitutional model and functioning of the institutions whereas constitutional geometry uses the outcomes of the institutional approach, but its attempt to frame constitutional knowledge is not limited to institutional design. Constitutional geometry builds upon the institutional approach since it presupposes the institutional order of the constitutional system. However, it targets all possible modes for typical depiction of constitutional phenomena predominantly with regard to the macro and medium levels of institutional design. Hence constitutional geometry is a semiotic phenomenon which aims to analyse the meaning of visual codes and visual representations of fully or partially institutionalised normative ideas which in some cases builds upon the achievements of other legal theoretical approaches.

Moreover, constitutional geometry derives some of its shapes and normative ideas, for example the normative pyramid, from legal normativism. However, this is rather exceptional because the normative construction of the legal order is neither symbolically and visually appealing nor capable of being sculpted into macro shapes and forms. That is why the use of Kelsen's normative hierarchical pyramid[7] is one of the rare instances of borrowing of geometric metaphors from the theory of normativism. This is also due to the fact that the theory of legal normativism itself is not oriented towards production of such geometric shapes and forms which can consequently be used by constitutional geometry. One can speculate whether Kelsen's theory of international law is not open to the analytical extraction of some constitutional geometric forms, for example with regard to his approach to the centralisation and decentralisation of legal orders and to the problems of monism, dualism and pluralism.[8] However, I will refrain from entering that discussion due to space constraints.

Last but not least, some of the most important ideas developed in the modern theory of state have served as key pillars of the constitutional geometry of the Westphalian statehood. These are the idea of the hierarchical structure of public authority defined by Jean Bodin, Thomas Hobbes, John Austin and Max Weber, Max Weber's concept of the hierarchical structure of executive power and its pyramid-like construction with government at the

[7] For a critical analysis of Kelsen's theory of the hierarchical and pyramid-like structure of the legal order see F Ost and M van der Kerchove, *De la pyramide au réseau? Vers un nouveau mode de production du droit?* <www.dhdi.free.fr/recherches/theoriedroit/articles/ostvdkpyram.pdf> 1 et seq.

[8] A Kalisz and M Zalewska, 'Hans Kelsen in a Multicentric (Legal) World' in M Belov (ed), *Global Governance and Its Effects on State and Law* (Frankfurt am Main, Peter Lang, 2016), 115–29.

top and administration at the bottom, the linear structure of state formation and constitution building based on social contract, dividing the time-space continuum into natural and civic phases, provided by John Locke, Thomas Hobbes, Jean-Jacques Rousseau, John Rawls etc.

The fact that constitutional geometry makes use of the achievements of different schools of thought in constitutional, legal and political theory, which have taken the form of visual representation of power constellations and systemic relations, demonstrates that it is based on a creative mixture of different approaches. However, this mixture does not lead to an eclectic result. This is due to the fact that the function of constitutional geometry is to serve as an additional explanatory paradigm that exemplifies the main structural features of the constitutional order and the constitutional system. Constitutional geometry does not pretend to be a fully consistent and all-encompassing approach for explaining the organisation of normativity, the structure and system of the constitutional order which is the aim, for example of legal institutionalism, legal positivism and legal normativism.

Actually constitutional geometry is not a separate and distinct legal theory. It is an additional analytical paradigm which visually depicts and explains via a semiotic approach selected fragments or basic aspects of the constitutional order. Moreover, it uses the results of different theories. Constitutional geometry structures the scientific understanding of the constitutional order through exemplification and visualisation. It organises the constitutional order predominantly on the most abstract and highest level of the normative ideologies and normative ideas and to a lesser extent on the level of the constitutional institutions.

That is why constitutional geometry possesses the very broad framework and indirect normativity typical also of constitutional ideologies and ideas. Its organising power consists in the imposition of ideas or cornerstone concepts and codes for structuring the constitutional order on the constitutional system with its sub-systems which have to be further developed on the institutional and normative levels.

Consequently constitutional geometry is a creative collection of supportive ideologies, concepts, paradigms and structural codes developed by different constitutional, legal and political theories throughout the Western Modernity which try to explain the state, the constitution and the constitutional order by using geometric metaphors. However, it cannot be reduced to the theories and approaches from which it borrows and on which it builds not in a systematic manner but in the form of 'cherry-picking'. Constitutional geometry is a framework concept and broad depot for formal and visually structured depiction and clarification of constitutional typologies. It is a form of constitutional semiotics.

All theoretically defined shapes and forms, such as hierarchies, pyramids, triangles, rectangles, polygons, circles and networks, which are borrowed from mathematics by social, political and constitutional theory, can be defined as elements of 'constitutional geometry' if they possess an ordering and explanatory force with a view to the constitutional order. Thus constitutional geometry represents an intellectual enterprise and product addressing the need of the people to exemplify abstract constitutional concepts and to master the complexity of social and political life and of the constitutional discourse by reducing it to clearer and more easily comprehensible concepts, for example those of the illustrative and visual world of (constitutional) geometry. Hence constitutional geometry is a broad paradigm which has to conceptualise and render systematic the visual discourse of constitutional law and constitutional theory.

Constitutional geometry comprises normative models—both ideal and legal—for shaping, framing and describing the constitutional order and its particular sectoral, institutional and power aspects. It is a form of constructive imagination aimed at rational cognition, inventive and creative description of the constitutional system and rational prescription of the best way for systematising, ordering and typifying constitutional relations. The attempt to represent constitutional relations through the use of geometrical shapes and by depicting the constitutional order as a quasi-volumetric phenomenon which resembles the geometric relations of the physical world is a common denominator for all forms of constitutional geometry. Thus constitutional geometry tries to conceptualise the constitutional system, the constitutional order and constitutional relations by the use of analogy with geometry as a branch of mathematics.

Actually constitutional law and political science make use of non-legal concepts derived from the scientific apparatus of the natural sciences in general and of mathematics in particular due to their desire to rationalise and capture the diversity and changeability of socio-political reality and to reduce the complexity of the constitutional and political order. Modern constitutionalism was born during the 'long nineteenth century'[9] and developed throughout the 'short twentieth century'[10] as a phenomenon that strives to rationalise the structure and functioning of public power through formalisation, institutionalisation and proceduralisation of socio-political relations.

Hence the constitutional geometry of modern constitutional law is a device for rationalisation via formalisation and abstract and symbolic depiction of the constitutional order, the normative order, the institutional sub-systems of the constitutional system and the inter-institutional dynamics in it. Moreover constitutional geometry aims at rationalisation via simplification and reduction of the complexity of the public power and its constitutional

[9] E Hobsbawm, *The Age of Revolution: 1789–1848* (New York, First Vintage Books, 1996) and E Hobsbawm, *The Age of Capital: 1848–1875* (New York, First Vintage Books, 1996).

[10] E Hobsbawm, *Age of Extremes: the Short Twentieth Century, 1914–1991* (London, Abacus, 1995) 3.

foundations and the representation of the different power constellations through the use of visual depiction. Sometimes constitutional geometry appears as system of normative ideas which are imposed on and interpolated in the constitutional system or are extracted from the constitutional order. However, constitutional geometry is frequently not an all-encompassing and fully systematic phenomenon. Thus constitutional geometry cannot pretend to be an either all-organising scheme of the constitutional order or a coordinated and coherent scheme of normative beliefs resulting in a fully integrated system for visual representation of constitutional institutions and their inter-institutional dynamics.

Constitutional geometry has to be differentiated from constitutional symbolism. Constitutional symbolism targets the collective emotions of society through representative and symbolic metaphors of statehood provided by the constitution or constitutional law such as the flag, the anthem, the state motto etc. It aims to establish a constitutional pantheon that can serve functions of symbolic representation and integration of the political community. That is why constitutional symbolism is part of emotional constitutionalism—the constitutionalism based on the collective beliefs and emotions of the political community and on the constructed or inherited collective constitutional imaginary.

Constitutional geometry, in contrast to constitutional symbolism, is part of rational constitutionalism. It is a key strategy for rational comprehension of the most important schemes enshrined in the constitutional order. Constitutional geometry is part of the scientific collective imaginary of constitutional and political scholars. It is based on rationally proven or rationally constructed (geometric) metaphors and strives to delimit rationally convincing but also symbolically appealing matrixes of the structure of the constitutional order and its particular parts. Hence constitutional geometry, as with many elements of the constitutional discourse, comprises a mixture of rational and emotional elements. However, in the case of constitutional geometry the rational elements clearly dominate the emotional ones.

It should also be mentioned that constitutional geometry allows for an abstract analysis of the systemic adaptation of the constitutional system and the constitutional order to the structural and functional changes in the socio-legal context. It is a concept that detects the shifts and mutations of the structural matrixes and codes which both frame the constitutional dynamics and reflect the systemic alterations in the macro structures and schemes of the institutional design and the constitutional order. Thus the transition of the constitutional systems from Early Modernity (seventeenth to eighteenth centuries) through Modernity (nineteenth to twentieth centuries) up to Post-Modernity (the current age) produces fundamental structural changes in the socio-legal context. They result not only in different constitutional axiology and constitutional design but also in different matrixes for ordering and explaining the structural shapes and features of the constitutional order, or, in other words, in different constitutional geometries.

The definition of the concept of constitutional geometry sheds some light on this novel approach for framing classical constitutional issues relating to the question of how to master and comprehend the durable and fundamental structures of the constitutional order. However, the theory of constitutional geometry needs further elaboration by presentation of the constitutional geometry of Modernity, the reasons for its emergence in that concrete design and outlook and its most important structures, shapes and forms.

II. GEOMETRICAL EXPLANATORY PARADIGMS IN WESTPHALIAN CONSTITUTIONAL LAW

Constitutional geometry has been ever-present although in latent, implicit and semi-exposed ways since the emergence of constitutionalism in the eighteenth and nineteenth centuries and even since the emergence of some of its predecessors in the late pre-constitutional era of the early Westphalian epoch from the second half of the seventeenth century onwards. Hence the intellectual traditions of constitutional geometry can be traced down to the absolute monarchy and the early phase of the emergence of the territorial nation state with their corresponding and supporting political philosophy. In other words the roots of some of the main schemes, shapes and forms for visual geometric representation of power relations spread as far as early Modernity. With regard to the 'invented tradition'[11] of the ideal heritage of the Antiquity on which the modern Western civilisation, the constitutional civilisation included, has been built one can speculatively even go further back in political history.

However, until the emergence of the first constitutions the use of the term 'constitutional geometry' is incorrect. One can define the ways the constellation of public power has been visually exposed as either political geometry or constitutional geometry of the factual constitution, which are related to the theoretical or the empirical but not to the legal dimension of public power. This is due to the fact that the shapes and forms in which public power has been demonstrated, structured, moulded and described have been the product of either the collective imagination of the political community negotiated by the people or imposed on them by state officials and the intellectual elite or the theoretical depiction of the power constellation by the political and social philosophy.

The modern constitutions are the first systematic, rational and written attempts at establishing durable power schemes and long-lasting patterns of

[11] E Hobsbawm and T Ranger (eds), *The Invention of Tradition* (Cambridge, Cambridge University Press, 1983).

inter-institutional relations that can be structured around the achievements of political and social theory. Hence constitutional geometry is a modern concept that has implicitly emerged in the context of Westphalian constitutional theory and positive constitutional law. An important part of the normative ideology of modern constitutionalism concerns the shapes and forms in which the people are supposed to conceive the constitutional reality and some of the central phenomena of the constitutional discourse. The system of sources of law, the system of power and authority, the territorial structure of the state and the system of state institutions and inter-institutional relations are typically defined by the constitutional theory and imagined by the political community in the shapes of constitutional geometry.

Thus constitutional geometry is closely related to some of the most important concepts of Western Modernity and modern constitutional law and constitutional theory. These are the concepts of state institution as a normative model and legal framework for public officials' behaviour, sources of law as formal and usually written repositories of legal normativity and public power and state authority as phenomena which are emancipated from other forms of social power and authority and thus from their pre-modern syncretism. Even the concepts of state understood as either a system of territory-based socio-political relations of the nation structured by public power and state authority[12] or as an impersonal normative order[13] are essentially modern. That is why constitutional geometry has been born out of the general pathos of Western Modernity to rationalise, systematise and construct socio-political relations and the realm of public power.

Westphalian constitutional geometry is predominantly organised in hierarchies and pyramids.[14] Triangles and rectangles are also used but not as framing categories on a macro level that aim to explain the general characteristics of the constitutional order. Triangles and rectangles are typically put in practice as schemes for analytical-symbolical depiction of inter-institutional relations between the central state bodies—the monarch or the president, government and parliament, eventually the constitutional courts and the supreme courts and in some cases also the second chambers conceived as individual institutional actors. Other forms of constitutional geometry such as lines, trees and spirals are also present and have some epistemic and symbolic importance in the context of modern constitutional law.

The constitutional geometry of Westphalian constitutional law and statehood rarely uses circles and networks as analytical matrixes for the description and representation of institutional, normative or power relations. The network has failed to serve as either analytical or normative concept of

[12] G Jellinek, *Allgemeine Staatslehre* (Nabu Press, 2010) 1–835.

[13] H Kelsen, *Allgemeine Staatslehre* (Gehlen Verlag, 1966).

[14] For these 'traditional models' for organisation of the legal system see F Ost and M van der Kerchove, above n 7, 1 et seq.

Westphalian constitutional law with the victory of the territorial state over the city-state confederations such as the Hanseatic League or the global network-based trade empires as the predominant model for structuring the state and public power in Western Modernity.[15] The clear advantages of the territorial state in political, military and economic terms structured on the basis of hierarchy and pyramid-like power relations doomed the circle and the network to disuse for several centuries. The network and the circle regained their explanatory and normative importance only with the development of the international legal order in the second half of the twentieth century and with the pluralisation and constitutionalisation of that order at the end of the twentieth and the beginning of the twenty-first centuries.[16]

Hence Westphalian constitutional theory has created its own visual world of constitutional geometry. It is primarily structured around the hierarchy as universal explanatory scheme of the world in general and socio-political relations in particular. The hierarchy is used both normatively and analytically as the natural power matrix, explanatory and ordering scheme and intellectual and ideological code of Modernity from the age of the absolute monarchy until the second half of the twentieth century.

Here I will focus predominantly on the hierarchy and the pyramid as the most important normative shapes and analytical tools of modern constitutional law and constitutional theory. That analysis, however, should be preceded by a presentation of the line as a deeper and not immediately visible but fundamental concept of modern constitutional geometry.

The line is a powerful analytical tool around which the evolution of the constitutional and political order has been organised by many political theories. Moreover, the line is presupposed by constitutional theory and constitutional law as an initial ordering scheme serving for allocation of the institutions on the same level of the territorial structure of the state and public power. Here the line denominates one of the segments of the hierarchical pyramid, namely the institutional level which symbolises formal institutional equality.

Last but not least the line serves as a temporal axis depicting the temporal dimension for the unfolding of political power relations and for construction, deconstruction and reconstruction of institutional design through which the constitutional system adjusts itself and adapts to the changing socio-political, economic and most importantly technological and

[15] For a critical analysis of the mainstream view of the definitive advantages of the territorial state over such network-based political regimes see JG Ruggie, 'Territoriality and Beyond: Problematizing Modernity in International Relations' 47 (1993) *International Organization* 155–56.

[16] For the challenges of the network to the pyramid, the effects of the dynamic interplay and competition between these constitutional semiotic concepts and the chances of the network to replace the pyramid see F Ost and M van der Kerchove, above n 7.

information context. Apart from this macro temporal aspect the line may symbolise coequal and synchronic or asynchronous institutional timelines determining symphony or polyphony of temporal institutional horizons.

Consequently the line has two main functions and typical meanings in modern constitutional geometry. First, it is a way of depicting institutional relations. Second, it is a device for representation of the historical development of the socio-political process and of the emergence and evolution of its constitutional dimension. Thus it is a temporal axis for exposure of the institutional development of the constitutional order. This second meaning of the line is the more important one, both from the viewpoint of theory and of praxis. It is much more frequently used and persistent in constitutional theory and bears much richer symbolic meaning.

In addition a third and lesser known function and meaning of the line can be interpretatively extracted from Saskia Sassen's theory of the 'transversally bordered spaces'.[17] In the context of her theory the line implicitly functions as a symbolic representation of the cross-cutting claims for authority raised by the actors of global governance such as global religions, transnational corporations, supranational courts, sovereign funds etc, which penetrate the 'bordered space'[18] of the Westphalian statehood and constitutional order. This issue will be examined again in the context of the analysis of the current challenges to the Westphalian constitutional order and its constitutional geometry.

The line is not very productive as a device for representation of relations between institutions on the same level of the territorial structure of the state, for example on a national or local level. Such relations are visually sufficiently clear and easy to comprehend also without the use of constitutional geometrical forms. The inter-institutional lines, in contrast to the inter-institutional triangles or rectangles, usually neither bring more clarity nor produce additional meaning. That is why they are rarely used in constitutional theory as a device for visual representation of institutional behaviour, institutional relations or institutional dynamics.

The line symbolising institutional equality has been useful for emphasising the lack of superiority and institutional domination of the monarch in constitutional-parliamentary and parliamentary monarchies and of the parliament in post-communist systems which have rejected the Soviet type of government. Here the line is a sign for the reflexivity and reactivity[19] of the new democratic constitutions towards the previous constitutional order which was based on the supremacy of the monarch, the supreme council

[17] See S Sassen, When Territory Deborders Territoriality (2013) 1 *Territory, Politics, Governance* 23.

[18] ibid.

[19] For the concept of reactivity of constitutions see, eg E Tanchev, above n 6, 198.

or the parliament. Thus the line has served some role for reforming the constitutional and political culture in systems undergoing transition from a concentrated authority enshrined in a dominant institution such as the monarch or the parliament (serving as supreme council in the context of Soviet systems) to separation of powers based simultaneously on institutional dispersion and sharing of the public authority.

In such cases, however, the line equals the level which is a concept with different semantics. The use of the line as a synonymous concept for the level is grounded on the only common aspect of their semantics—the semantics of equalisation, and on the pursuit of the aim to align institutions allocated on the same axis of the constitutional design. It has to be taken into account that both the line and the level are rarely enshrined in positive constitutional law as legal terms. The line and the level are concepts of constitutional theory. They are either extracted through systematic and teleological interpretation of the constitution and constitutional law or imposed on them as explanatory paradigms or even as tools for constitutional modernisation via conceptual reform.

The line is used as an instrument for geometrical visual depiction of institutional relations also with regard to other aspects of horizontal power polycentrism and of relations concerning representative democracy. The line may represent the genetic and functional relations[20] between parliament and government in parliamentary systems. Here the line denominates the complex linkage between these key institutions of parliamentary republics and monarchies. The line may be used as a device for visualisation of the inter-institutional relations between the organs of the legislative and the executive power also in systems with rigid separation of powers such as some versions of the constitutional monarchy and presidential republics. Here the line serves as a tool for geometrical representation of institutional independence and to a lesser extent of institutional interdependence.

However, such use of the line is not of great epistemic benefit. Indeed it emphasises the legal relation or the system of legal relations between state institutions which are central for the constitutional system. However, their visual representation via geometrical metaphors does not bring much additional meaning and knowledge regarding their functioning.

In the context of parliamentarism the line may be used also for visual depiction of the system of representative relations between the people,

[20] For the genetic and functional relationship between the Parliament and the government see, eg, P Kiiver, European scrutiny in national parliaments. Individual efforts in the collective interest? in O'Brennan and Raunio (eds), *National Parliaments Within the Enlarged European Union. From 'Victims' of Integration to Competitive Actors?* (London and New York, Routledge, 2007) 73 et seq; A King, 'Modes of executive-legislative relations: Great Britain, France and Germany' in (1975) 1 *Legislative Studies Quarterly* 11–34; and G Sartori, *Comparative Constitutional Engineering. An Inquiry into Structures, Incentives and Outcomes* (Houndmills, Macmillan Press, 1994) 101.

the electorate, parliament and other state institutions elected fully or partially by parliament. An excellent example of the function of the line as a form of constitutional geometry capable of visually representing chains of political representation of political will and interests rooted in the people as sovereign, mediated through the parliament and spreading through the institutional system with parliamentary endorsement, is one decision of the German Constitutional Court.[21] According to it there is an 'uninterrupted democratic chain of legitimation' that stems from the people, concentrates the 'input' democratic legitimacy[22] in the Bundestag, which then distributes it to other state institutions. This symbolic presentation of the constitutional geometry of the representative parliamentary systems is not limited to the German constitutional model, but has universal significance.

The constitutional geometrical metaphor used by the German Constitutional Court is the chain and not the line. However, the chain can be reduced to a line for analytical simplification. And again, the chain may be used as an independent form of constitutional geometry, if its specific semantics can contribute to the better visual exposure of the characteristics of the constitutional design. Actually the constitutional geometrical form which has been drawn by the German Constitutional Court is not only a chain reduced to a line but also resembles a tree depicted by the use of a system of lines.

The line might seem a more appropriate device for description of the system of inter-institutional relations in the representative parliamentary republic. This is due to the fact that the tree seems to be insufficiently universal, durable and clearly shaped. Moreover, it can be reduced to a system of lines. On the other hand, the tree as a form of constitutional geometry has the advantage of visualising systemic relations which stem from one ideal, normative or empirical power source and spread in different branches of the institutional system. The tree is especially adapted to represent the relationships of the pure parliamentary republics where the source of law is the people and the main distributor of 'input' democratic legitimacy is the parliament as national representative institution. Hence the tree exemplifies the fact that the forms of constitutional geometry may stand in complementary but also in competitive and alternative relation to one another.

The line may also be employed as a representation of the time-space continuum, the emergence and development of the constitutional statehood and authority and for depiction of the temporal dimension of the evolution of the constitutional order. The line as a device for depiction and representation of the historical process of the development of the constitutional system

[21] BVerfGE 83, 60, 73.

[22] For the input democratic legitimacy see, eg P Craig and G de Búrca, *EU Law. Text, Cases and Materials*, 4th edn (Oxford, Oxford University Press, 2008) 65; and P Kiiver, *The National Parliaments in the European Union: A Critical View on EU Constitution-Building* (The Hague, Kluwer Law International, 2006) 95.

has two main forms and displays. First, the line can serve as an arrow pointing at some definite political end or indefinite constitutional future. Second, the line may turn itself into a spiral denominating the uneven development of the constitutional system and combining the evolutions with the revolutions and showing the gradual process of gaining of shape and substantial meaning of the constitutional order.

The shift of the line into a spiral similar to the turning of the line into a tree which has been analysed above demonstrates again the transformation and mutation of the forms of constitutional geometry which are dependent on the best way of visual representation of constitutional systemic relations and of the broader framework of the constitutional order. Hence the spiral may be used as either a specific manifestation of the line or can be defined as separate form of constitutional geometry.

One of the most popular temporary-historical dimensions of the line is based on the presumption for the continuous and evolutionary character of constitutional history which has its beginning, intermediate stops, aim and eventually an end. The end might be constructed differently, such as the Hegelian state as final destination in the journey of the 'world spirit' throughout history,[23] as class-free Marxist society, or as Fukujama's liberal end of history.[24]

The line may also be infinite. This is the case of the social contract theories in which the line visualises the development of mankind from a gathering of people into society and from non-constitutional pre-modern society into constitutionally organised modern society. Here the line is important not as an arrow reaching a definite end but as an arrow demonstrating the direction which is accentuated somewhere in the course of its development in the moment of conclusion of the constitutional social contract.

Most of the above-mentioned theories do not explicitly use constitutional geometry in general or the line as a form of constitutional geometry in particular. However, the systematic reading of their core ideas can be visually described well through the use of the line. Hence the line is implied by the meaning provided by the above-mentioned theories and can serve as a tool for visual representation of their temporal constitutional dimension.

The hierarchy is the most widespread, typical and frequently used form of constitutional geometry in Westphalian constitutional law. It has been the natural model for ordering political power relations during the whole history of mankind with some negligible exceptions. With the emancipation and differentiation of public power from the broader category of social power and with the emergence of the state as governing system and

[23] GWF Hegel, *Outlines of the Philosophy of Right* (Oxford, Oxford University Press, 2008).

[24] F Fukuyama, *The End of History and the Last Man* (New York, Free Press, 2006).

mechanism for introduction and maintenance of social order, the hierarchy has become the universal code for structuring power relations.

Consequently the hierarchy is a durable, persistent, logical and efficient structure for organising the state's institutional system throughout history. However, with the increase in the role of the state during the age of Modernity as an ordering and governing mechanism of human society resulting in the attribution of new functions to it, such as management of large parts of the social fields defined as social policies, governing of public finance and economy, application of a nationwide unified model for conflict resolution etc, the importance of the hierarchy and later the pyramid as institutional framing and representation schemes considerably increased.

Several factors have contributed to the universal recognition of the hierarchy as the main shape of modern constitutional geometry. The victory of the territorial nation state over alternative models for organising the public power, for example the empire, the networked confederation of city-states or the aterritorial religious-based realms and communities, and its establishment as the dominant form of statehood in Western Modernity has been paralleled by the necessity of providing a conceptual model for accomplishment of public authority. The need for maintenance of the interstate equilibrium, for sustainable and durable legitimation of public coercion and for rational explanation of the constitutional ontology has led to the emergence and constitutional entrenchment of the principle of state sovereignty especially in its form as monarchical sovereignty that marked the beginning of Westphalian statehood.

Thus the need for constructing the territorial structure of the state power provoked by the emergence of the sovereign territorial nation state objectively triggered the use of the hierarchy and the pyramid as dominant forms of modern constitutional geometry. The territoriality of public power itself was an objective determinant of the increasing importance of the hierarchy and the pyramid as ordering schemes of Westphalian statehood and as explanatory and analytical paradigms of Westphalian constitutional and political theory.

Indeed the modern territorial nation state has inherited the hierarchy from the multicultural empires—both pre-modern and early modern. However, in this imperial context the hierarchy has been complemented and has been partially competing with the asymmetric and mosaic structure of the estate-based medieval society. Moreover, the medieval and early modern hierarchies were not based upon constitutionally entrenched rationality and they did not make systematic use of the hierarchy as a holistic ordering scheme of the constitutional geometry.

With that background in mind, it seems proper to conclude that Westphalian constitutionalism has additionally reinforced the hierarchy as an instrument for national unification, centralised political domination and rational government in different aspects. The establishment of efficient central government including, but not limited to, general administration, tax administration and military and police administration, the development of unified national written law applied and safeguarded by well-ordered, rationally constructed and efficient courts' and state prosecutors' systems required the hierarchy as a universal ordering model. The medieval heritage of networked clientelistic power relations, autonomous cities, estates, guilds and local communities has been partially deconstructed and replaced by formalised, rationalised, proceduralised, legally institutionalised and then constitutionalised universal power schemes applicable for the whole territory and for a wide range of spheres of socio-political relations.

These processes of deconstruction, construction and reconstruction were accomplished under the banner of modernisation. One important but not immediately obvious aspect of this political, administrative, legal and constitutional modernisation resulted in 'hierarchisation'. The latter consisted in the introduction of the hierarchy as universal ordering code and of the pyramid as key matrix for the rational-emotional visualisation of the structure of the public order. The constitutional entrenchment of the hierarchy led to the establishment of the pyramid as the central form of the modern constitutional geometry.

That is why the hierarchy, which also existed in pre-modern times, has been used to its furthest extent as a rationalising and modernising matrix during Westphalian pre-constitutional and then constitutional Modernity. Thus the hierarchy and the pyramid as its more evident and visually convincing form have served as both bearers of order and tradition and as key modernising strategies and tools in the hands of the central state government and the emerging national political elite. Hence the hierarchy has become a point of interception and intertwining of both tradition and modernisation with regard to the models for structuring the public power and the shapes of political geometry which was later transformed into constitutional geometry. The hierarchy has proved to be the most useful and natural matrix for restructuring power relations in the early modern period (sixteenth to seventeenth centuries) and then for their constitutionalisation in the form of written constitutions and modern constitutional law from the eighteenth to nineteenth centuries onwards.

Here are some examples of the universal creative application of the hierarchy and the pyramid as central organising and ordering schemes of modern constitutional law, key concepts of modern constitutional theory and the most important figures of modern constitutional geometry. They demonstrate not only the rationalising results of modern constitutional law and constitutional theory, but also the continuity and inheritance of some of the key normative ideologies of medieval public law and the political philosophy which have been reconstructed in order to serve as ordering schemes and normative ideologies of Modernity and as forms of its constitutional geometry.

The hierarchy was also the central organising scheme for medieval political orders. The God as supreme source of the political order and the monarch as divinely appointed supreme leader of the community inaugurated by recourse to sacred tradition were key normative ideologies of medieval statehood. The Pope was an institution which merged both medieval concepts for legitimate hierarchical domination—the religious and the secular. Westphalian constitutional law as well as constitutional and political theory have partially reconstructed and laicised these traditional ways for legitimising the power hierarchy.[25] They have also additionally reinforced the hierarchy as an explanatory scheme of modern constitutional geometry.

The supremacy of the monarch was initially overemphasised and strengthened in the early Westphalian age. Absolute monarchy drove the concept of the supremacy of the monarch to excess by merging the figure of the monarch with the concept of the state. This strategy led to legitimation of the monopoly of the monarch and the state over the accomplishment of hierarchical public coercion and superimposed policy making. In that way the political power resting upon hierarchy and subordination has been emancipated from the other forms of socio-political governance, some of which have been achieved in non-hierarchical but in horizontal or networking ways.

Examples of such more horizontal and network-based forms of governance were the relationships in the Protestant political communities which were grounded on the idea of equality of all people in front of God, for example the Protestant colonists' town meetings in North America, the confederal unions of free cities such as the Hanseatic League, the world trade empires such as Netherlands and the confederations. However, even in systems which were governed basically in accordance with the principle of hierarchy there were social power centres, such as the estates and the free cities, which achieved horizontal and network-based forms of governance.

Thus, to some extent paradoxically, the absolute monarchy has paved the way for the partial emancipation of the state from society, for the delimitation of state power from other types of social power and for the establishment of its formal neutrality and hierarchical supremacy. The second kind of emancipation—the emancipation of the state as an impersonal and increasingly formalised institutional system from the figure of the monarch—became possible with the adoption of the first constitutions. They transformed the monarch from unlimited demiurge into state institution with constitutionally provided competences. The modern constitutional territorial state required a hierarchical and pyramid-like structure of its constitutional geometry as an all-encompassing ordering scheme

[25] For the traditional legitimacy see M Weber, *Soziologie. Weltgeschichtliche Analysen. Politik* (Stuttgart, Kröner Verlag, 1968) 151.

especially due to its de-personalisation and increasing constitutional institutionalisation. However, the need for hierarchical structuring of modern statehood concerned all its dimensions—the state as factual power relations, the state as institutional system and the state as normative order.

Sovereignty as one of the central and key concepts of Westphalian constitutional law has been typically defined in hierarchical terms. It is a concept that both requires and reinforces the hierarchy as ordering scheme of the political and constitutional order. Sovereignty is both the hierarchical top and the hierarchical source of the authority of the Westphalian state, which system has been structured as a power pyramid.

Westphalian constitutional modernity has been stretched between several extremities. Its rationalist pretention and pathos had to be balanced with the need for assuring the emotional persuasiveness of its institutions, principles, values and ideologies. The enhancement of the socio-political pluralism which has been required by the increasing complexity of modern society triggered by the emergence of the mass society as a result of the industrial revolution and urbanisation should not have been provided to the detriment of the efficiency and authority of the state. In that context the sovereignty, hierarchy and pyramid-like structure of the institutional, normative and power order have been necessary preconditions for safeguarding the authority and efficiency of the public power, for its emancipation from the private sources of socio-political governance and for generating both rational legitimacy[26] and emotional comprehensiveness of the constitutional model. Moreover, they proved to be mutually interdependent phenomena.

That is why an important part of modern constitutional theory is based on the idea of hierarchy as an explanatory scheme of modern constitutional geometry. Sovereignty as key principle of modern constitutional law and as fundamental organising tool for the constitutional order is grounded on and preconditioned upon the hierarchy. Even many of the social contract theories which are capable of explaining the constitutional system and political order in non-hierarchical and more horizontal ways actually presuppose the hierarchy. This is especially evident in the Hobbesian *pactum subjectionis*, but is also clearly recognisable in John Locke's theory of the legitimate king which served a pivotal role in the establishment of the constitutional monarchy as the predominant constitutional model of the 'long nineteenth century'.[27] Jellinek's 'three element theory',[28] which is maybe the most important socio-legal theory of the state elaborated in the age of late Modernity, also suggests the hierarchical scheme of the political order structured by the public power. Moreover, in his theory the hierarchy is preconditioned upon the territoriality of the nation state.

[26] ibid.
[27] E Hobsbawm, above n 10.
[28] G Jellinek, above n 12.

The mutual interdependence of sovereignty, hierarchy and pyramid-like structure of the constitutional order can be well exemplified by the comparison of two seemingly antagonistic theories—Carl Schmitt's political decisionism and Hans Kelsen's legal normativism. Schmitt defines sovereignty as an empirical existentialist category which predetermines the legal order and (re)creates the constitutional and other legal rules in a situation of anomy. Thus the sovereign will is actually a secular version of the will of God and the sovereign as a secular God can structure and restructure the constitutional order and the socio-political world to his liking. The sovereign will has total hierarchical supremacy in the constitutional, political and social system. On the other hand, Kelsen uses the Grundnorm as functional equivalent of God. Similarly to the function of God in medieval scholastic theory, the Grundnorm is an axiomatic suggestion which is used for hierarchical deduction of the legal order.[29] In Kelsen's theory the world is limited to the legal system in its reductionist version as normative system. Both Schmitt and Kelsen use the hierarchy as a universal ordering scheme for their conceptual models of the statehood and its constitutional and legal order.

Both theories compared lead to several conclusions. Both sovereignty and the Grundnorm presuppose and are grounded on hierarchy. The normative hierarchy and more precisely the supremacy of the constitution safeguard sovereignty. Sovereignty is the source and safeguard for constitutional supremacy and for the hierarchical order of the constitutional system. Thus sovereignty and the pyramid-like structure of the constitutional order based on the axiomatic suggestion of the existence of the Grundnorm are interdependent concepts which perform a mutual safeguarding function. Sovereignty and the supremacy of the constitution are the two sides of the coin named 'hierarchy' and are both cornerstones of Westphalian constitutional law.

Naturally these conclusions oversimplify the theories of Kelsen and Schmitt and neglect some of their postulates. However, they prove the fact that sovereignty and constitutional supremacy are interdependent central phenomena of Westphalian constitutionalism with strategic importance for modern constitutional law and theory. And they are both based on the concept of hierarchy as a key figure of Westphalian constitutional geometry. Last but not least, it should be noticed that Kelsen further develops the idea of hierarchy as a form for organising the legal and constitutional order by virtue of providing the pyramid as a powerful and convincing form of modern constitutional geometry.

Consequently a very important intellectual heritage which has contributed to the establishment of the hierarchy as a predominant ordering and

[29] According to R Tashev, 'the basic norm is methodological suggestion with operational character' which allows for the establishment of self-referential system based on deduction. See R Tashev, *General Theory of Law* (Sofia, Sibi, 2004) 19–20 (in Bulgarian).

explanatory paradigm of Westphalian constitutional law consists in the conceptual organisation of the constitutional system around the axiomatic presumption of the existence of a supreme ordering power. This power is supposed to be the source of the constitutional system's ontology and to some extent also to its teleology thus being the driving force for the maintenance of constitutional equilibrium and a key source for legitimation. During the Middle Ages this function has been performed by the God. In the context of Western Modernity and Westphalian constitutionalism the God has been replaced in its function as source of the validity of the legal order and of the legitimacy of the political order by the sovereign in its different manifestations and later also by the Kelsenian Grundnorm. Hence both the Grundnorm and sovereignty are concepts based on hierarchy. Thus they have massively contributed to the centrality of the hierarchy in modern constitutional geometry.

It has to be taken into account that the hierarchy has not always been depicted and represented directly as a pyramid being the natural or at least the most popular shape for hierarchical subordination of people, office holders, institutions, legal norms or whole institutional or normative orders. In many cases it has been demonstrated in the mediated forms of attribution, ascription or deduction of authority. The authority is deduced from the God, the sovereign, the supreme ruler, the natural order of things and—at a much later stage—from the Kelsenian Grundnorm. It is induced from the will of the people based on their collective rationality in the context of national or the people's sovereignty. Thus it takes the presumed shape of a deductive or inductive hierarchy.

So far, the development of the hierarchy as fundamental concept of Westphalian statehood and constitutionalism with its roots in the pre-constitutional age and with its strategic importance for maintaining the order of modern complex societies has been traced down. The hierarchy has been explored as normative paradigm and as dominant form of constitutional geometry with historical, socio-legal and theoretical implications. Now let us turn to some of the most important examples of the application of the hierarchy and the pyramid as both ordering and representation schemes of Westphalian constitutional geometry. They concern the hierarchical structure of the normative order, the institutional order in general and some of its branches in particular. More concretely they have formative influence and visualising function with regard to the system of sources of law, the territorial structure of the state, the general structure of the executive power,[30] the system of the state administration, the court's system and the state prosecutor's system.

[30] According to Jean Blondel the concept of government is usually related to the ideas of hierarchy and pyramid. See J Blondel, above n 6, 271.

The organisation of the system of sources of law as hierarchy and its visual representation as hierarchical pyramid is a universal model for all modern constitutional systems. The pyramid as constitutional geometric form for representation of the system of sources of law was introduced by Hans Kelsen. However, it has gained universal recognition in modern constitutionalism even without explicit recourse to legal normativism. This is for two main reasons.

First, the hierarchy is the clearest and most efficient way for the resolution of conflict of sources of law. It assures predictability and consistency of the application of law by the institutions that perform law-implementing and conflict-resolution functions—the courts, the administration etc.

Second, the pyramid reflects the hierarchy of the substantial and political importance of the sources of law produced by both the socio-political relevance of the legally regulated social relations and the legitimacy of the state institution to regulate them through their institutionalisation in sources of law. In other words the superiority of the constituent over the legislative and of the legislative over the executive power and of the will of the sovereign over the will of the parliament and the will of the government are reflected by the normative pyramid of the sources of law. Thus the institutional hierarchy is reflected in the hierarchy of the sources of law visually represented as a pyramid.

The pyramid is also used for explanation of the system of sources of law of multilevel constitutional systems. In the multilevel context the system of sources of law is usually represented as a system of subordinated and interrelated pyramids. The lower pyramid which denominates the system of sources of law of the federated units is semi-autonomous from the pyramid of the national or federal law but is inferior to it. Indeed even in classical nation-state multilevel systems such as the federations the pyramid metaphor cannot easily give explanations to two main questions. The first concerns the way the national and the subnational pyramids are linked whereas the second is related to the appropriate allocation of the subnational constitutions presumed as the top of the subnational pyramid in relation to the national or the upper pyramid of sources of law.

The organisation of the territorial structure of the state—the form of territorial distribution of power—is built around two main forms of constitutional geometry. These are the hierarchy, conceived usually as a pyramid, and the polygon, perceived as a container. A classical paradigm of Westphalian statehood is the conception of the state as 'closed territorial container'.[31] The territoriality of the state is an invented theoretical and normative category which did not exist in the empirical realm. Thus the territoriality of the state

[31] N Brenner, 'Beyond state-centrism? Space, Territoriality and Geographical Scale. Globalization Studies' in 28 (1999) *Theory and Society* 55.

became a legal and constitutional quality of the state preconditioned upon the existence of the territory as a fact. Consequently territoriality became in a sense a legal and ideal quality of the territory, which is itself a physical-geographical notion,[32] and usually goes together with several other normative ideas. These are the linear character of the state borders,[33] the existence of 'perfect territory' in which the elements of the statehood pertaining to Jellinek's theory—the nation, the territory and the public power—quasi-naturally coincide and the spreading out of the borders of territoriality to other spatial dimensions such as the air, water and subterranean spaces.

Hence the polygon is the initial and in some sense the preliminary form of constitutional geometry of Westphalian statehood. This is due to the fact that it precedes the structuring of the territorial dimension of the public power in other forms and especially in hierarchies. Moreover the polygonal preliminary shaping of the state territory is of essential importance for the Westphalian statehood since it delimits the sovereign space from the other sovereign spaces, tries to exclude or at least to limit extraterritorial and aterritorial 'cross-cutting' jurisdictional claims[34] and serves as a natural precondition for further structuring of the territorial jurisdictions of the different state layers and state institutions. To a certain extent the polygon is the typical shape in which the modern territorial state gains its territoriality.

The geometry offers also many insights for structuring the territorial dimension of the state, especially when it comes to multilevel constitutional systems such as federations, confederations or decentralised unitary states. However, the predominant form of Westphalian constitutional geometry with regard to the territorial structure of the public power is the hierarchy and the pyramid as its more concrete visual representation.

The pyramid and the hierarchy are used as general models for the territorial structure of the state. They offer the principal constitutional framework of the territoriality of the Westphalian state. The pyramid and the hierarchy visualise and order the number of public power levels and their interrelation. They also allow for the recognition of the existence of exceptions from the general pyramidal model of constitutionalised territoriality such as territorial or national-cultural autonomies, federal territories, associated territories, capital city territories etc. The hierarchical model of shaping the territorial structure of the Westphalian state is objectively predetermined by the need to organise large territories with complex societies and wide-ranging public functions accomplished by institutional actors on

[32] JG Ruggie, above n 15, 139–74.

[33] D Newman, 'Boundaries, Borders and Barriers: Changing Geographic Perspectives on Territorial Lines' in M Albert, D Jacobson and Y Lapid (eds), *Identities, Borders, Orders: Rethinking International Relations Theory* (Minneapolis, University of Minnesota Press, 2001) 137–51.

[34] S Sassen, above n 17, 21–45.

different levels and in different spheres of government. The power spatiality of the Westphalian state cannot be organised either in alternative forms of constitutional geometry, for example in a circular or networked way or in non-territorial models for public power accomplishment.

Apart from their use as general models for ordering the sources of law and for organisation of the territorial structure of the state the pyramid and the hierarchy are also employed to structure and visualise the specific institutional design related to the different branches of state power. Thus the hierarchy organises the general structure of executive power, the system of state administration, the court system and the state prosecutor system.

Typically the executive power of the state in the context of Westphalian constitutional law is structured as a pyramid with two main layers—the government at the top and the administration at the bottom. The most comprehensive concept of this hierarchical model based on the principle of the hierarchy of the political government, the civil service and administrative levels has been provided by Max Weber.[35] That is why it is also known as the Weberian model for the structuring of executive power. On the other hand, the model was first put into real practice in nineteenth-century British constitutionalism, which is why it is also known as the Westminster model.

According to the Weberian or Westminster model for organising executive power the government is the party political top of the pyramid. It is elected on party political lines by the people, which allows the democratic control and the arbitration of the political elites by the electorate via ascription of political responsibility to the government. The government must be a party government in order to be democratic and responsible. On the other hand, the administration or state bureaucracy is the non-political and apolitical expert fundament of the executive power which is placed below the government at the bottom of the hierarchical pyramid. The staff of the administration has to be recruited on the basis of education, expertise and duration of service and not on party political lines. The administration should be immune from direct democratic control because the latter requires elections or recall which are by necessity grounded on party political influence.

The balance between governmental party political democratic leadership and administrative technocratic capacity is actually a balance between the principles of democracy and rule of law. The appropriate equilibrium between these two constitutional principles and functional aims which is reflected in the pyramidal structure of the executive power is of crucial importance for safeguarding that the efficiency of the Westphalian executive is not to the detriment of the democratic legitimacy and the legality of its functioning.

[35] M Weber, *Wirtschaft und Gesellschaft* (Tübingen, Mohr Siebeck, 2002).

The hierarchical pyramidal structure of the executive not only concerns the relationship between the government and the administration. It is also reproduced and reflected in the organisation of the government itself and in the structure of the different branches of the executive power encompassing the most important socio-political fields.

The typical primacy of the prime ministerial principle over the collegiate and resort principles for organisation of the government which reflects the domination of the will and the competences of the Prime Minister over the governmental collegium and the distinct ministers is again based on hierarchy. It can be visually represented as a pyramid topped by the Prime Minister where the government is placed on the intermediate layer and the ministers at the bottom.

Moreover, each minister heads a separate power pyramid framing the policy making and institutional design of the specific policy field. The instruments for administrative control achieved by the ministers over their administrations and by the Prime Minister and the government over the ministers are based on the hierarchical and pyramidal structure of the executive. The competence of the Prime Minister to determine and impose the guidelines of the policy to the government and the responsibility of the Prime Minister for the whole governmental activity and of the ministers for their subordinate administrations are also preconditioned upon the hierarchy and pyramid as ordering schemes of Westphalian constitutional geometry in the executive power domain.

Indeed the hierarchy and pyramid are the universal forms of constitutional geometry of the executive power in modern constitutional systems. However, their application is not limited to the executive branch alone. The hierarchy and the pyramid are also the ordering schemes and forms of constitutional geometry for judicial power. The subordination of the courts is structured in a pyramidal way. This also holds true in the case of specialised courts since they are also organised in a pyramidal shape. The existence of specialised courts only introduces plurality of pyramids in the institutional design and constitutional geometry of the judiciary.

The pyramid is even the explanatory paradigm in the constitutional geometry of the legislative power in relation to the bicameral structure of a parliament. The interrelation between both chambers is usually depicted as a pyramid. This is also the case when the second chamber is weaker than the first or is even nominal. The very terms 'lower' and 'upper' chamber, which are frequently used for denomination of the houses of parliament, demonstrate their pyramidal and hierarchical exposure in the constitutional geometry of Westphalian constitutional law.

The intermediate conclusion is that the hierarchy is the widespread, dominant and almost universal model of the constitutional geometry of Westphalian statehood. It has shaped the institutional and normative systems of the Westphalian constitutional order and has predetermined the territorial structure of the state. The hierarchy as the key modernising ordering concept and most central form of the constitutional geometry of Westphalian constitutional law has been objectively predetermined by the territoriality of power relations, by the emergence of mass society and the establishment of the national territorial state as the universal model for organising the economy, finance and politics. The hierarchy as macro model and general constitutional geometric shape has been reproduced and replicated in the different branches of state power and thus has become the matrix for organising Westphalian constitutional design.

Finally it has to be mentioned that the power concentration or the power polycentrism of the modern constitutional systems legally defined as monism, corporatism or pluralism, or as unity or separation of powers, is also related to constitutional geometry. The degrees of concentration or dispersion of public power is reflected in the different schemes and models for shaping the institutional design of the constitutional systems. The system of constitutional relations stemming out and concretising the above-mentioned basic principles for organisation of the public power in general and the state power in particular are rather complex. That is why they are usually reduced to general schemes for institutional design such as the different models for horizontal and vertical separation of powers. Thus Westphalian constitutional law typically provides for theoretically elaborated and constitutionally enshrined models for the relations between state institutions belonging to different branches or levels of state power while the models for societal power unity or power polycentrism based on the principles of monism, corporatism and pluralism remain to a high degree under-institutionalised in written constitutional law.

Constitutional and political theory also makes an attempt to use constitutional geometry as an explanatory paradigm of the inter-institutional relations with regard to both the constitutional statics and the constitutional dynamics by virtue of classifying them in institutional axes, triangles or rectangles. The institutional triangle is frequently used to explain the most important features of the relationships between parliament, government and head of state. Sometimes it turns into an institutional rectangle due to the inclusion of the Constitutional Court or the Supreme Court in the analysis. These forms of constitutional geometry are indeed theoretical constructs which, however, have a solid basis in written constitutional law. This is due to the fact that they actually consist in theoretical typologies which have to visually represent in order to better analyse and explain the systemic relations between the most important constitutional institutions on the basis of interpretation of the constitutional provisions. The increasing dysfunctionality of these analytical shapes of Westphalian constitutional geometry in the early post-Westphalian context caused by several complex but to a large extent objective factors related to the emerging supranational and even global constitutionalism will be explored in the next section.

III. POST-WESTPHALIAN CHALLENGES OF SUPRANATIONAL CONSTITUTIONALISM, GLOBAL GOVERNANCE AND INFORMATION REVOLUTION TO THE CONSTITUTIONAL GEOMETRY OF WESTPHALIAN CONSTITUTIONAL LAW

The explanation of constitutional geometry as an analytical and constructive concept, the tracing down of its historical development and its most important shapes and forms established and sustained during the Westphalian Modernity is the background against which its structural changes produced by several key phenomena of the post-Westphalian age should be exposed and analysed. The challenges to constitutional geometry—initially a modern and thus constructive phenomenon based on rationality and aimed at rational simplification of the constitutional and political world—which are produced by the emergence and development of post-Westphalian, post-national, supranational and even global constitutionalism and constitutional law are in great need of explanation.

Several processes and phenomena emerged and started to evolve during the last decades of the twentieth and the beginning of the twenty-first centuries. They pose a considerable challenge to the classical constitutional geometry of the Westphalian state and Westphalian constitutional law and theory. These phenomena are globalisation, global governance, supranational and global constitutionalism and the information revolution.

The challenges are deep and structural and not just functional. The current early post-Westphalian situation in which we live not only produces new shapes and forms, thus enriching traditional constitutional geometry; it also shakes the structural foundations on which modern constitutional theory and theory of the state are built. It is not only a matter of new rectangles, triangles, pyramids and hierarchies that emerge and have to be taken into account: the whole conceptual system of modern constitutional theory—constitutional geometry included—has to be redefined, restructured and adapted to this new socio-political reality. This is necessary in order to keep it capable of retaining its explanatory force and to allow for further shaping of both the normative dimension of the written constitution and the collective political and constitutional imaginary of the people enshrined in the ideal constitution of the state and society. Hence the above-mentioned factors produce structural changes in the ordering and organising schemes of the public power and in its constitutional design and start to change the constitutional geometry of modern statehood.

The structural changes in Westphalian constitutional geometry can be ordered in three main groups. The first group encompasses challenges to constitutional geometry imposed by the constitutionalisation of international and EU law that led to the emergence of supranational and global constitutionalism.[36] The second group includes changes in constitutional geometry produced by global governance as a broader governance paradigm that takes into account both the supranationalisation and globalisation and the privatisation of public power. The third group concerns the emergence of the Internet as a global virtual reality which fosters the 'time-space compression',[37] produces territorial detachment of the people and the elites, contributes to the global mobility of information and thus to the global mobility of social power resources, establishes global deliberative and participatory networks and provides for both a new structure and new context of the public power. Thus the Internet as the most important result of the information revolution both creates perils to democracy and the rule of law and brings new opportunities for global re-democratisation and re-establishment of the global rule of law.

Global constitutionalism is not a monolithic concept.[38] In its narrowest meaning coinciding with the supranational constitutionalism of the EU it is focused on EU integration.[39] Thus it denominates the transformation of the European communities into the European Union with the Maastricht Treaty and its constitutionalisation by virtue of the Amsterdam, Nice and especially the Lisbon Treaties as well as by the case law of the CJEU and secondary EU legislation.

The broader concept of global constitutionalism also encompasses the emergence of other supranational regimes which provide for human rights or contain a developed institutional system capable of governing constitutional or quasi-constitutional issues in an autopoietic[40] or semi-autonomous way from the Member States' governmental systems. Apart from the EU, which is the most important supranational constitutional system, there are also other sector-specific forms of supranational constitutionalism in the spheres of human rights (the Council of Europe), public finance and economy management (the World Trade Organisation) etc. Prominent authors

[36] For the 'external' challenges to the hierarchy generated by the influence of the international on the national law see F Ost and M van der Kerchove, above n 7, 10.

[37] For the concept of time-space compression see TH Eriksen, *Globalization. Key Concepts* (London, Bloomsbury, 2014).

[38] CM Amhlaigh even stipulates that there is a 'constitutional cacophony' in the theoretical proposals aiming to propose definitions of the global constitutionalism. See CM Amhlaigh, 'Harmonizing Global Constitutionalism', (2016) 5 *Global Constitutionalism* 173–78.

[39] Some authors consider supranational constitutionalism not as a framework concept with different degrees of specificity but as one of the three main versions of the broader paradigm of 'constitutionalism beyond the state'. See G Anderson, 'Beyond 'Constitutionalism Beyond the State' (2012) 39 *Journal of Law and Society* 359–83.

[40] G Teubner, *Law as an Autopoietic System* (Oxford, Blackwell, 1993).

suggest that 'global constitutionalism is an agenda that identifies and advocates for the application of constitutionalist principles in the international legal sphere'.[41]

In its broadest meaning global constitutionalism includes also the eventual emergence and development of a global government system capable of safeguarding human rights and providing for an institutional infrastructure able to produce sustainable legislative solutions, to accomplish policy management and to resolve conflicts through the global courts system. The UN is the closest example of such a global constitutional regime which is obviously sufficiently remote from that ideal model.

There are many theories which try to explain supranational and global constitutionalism. Two of them may be defined as predominant in the current constitutional discourse. These are multilevel constitutionalism[42] and constitutional pluralism.[43] They both make use of different arsenals of constitutional geometrical forms.

Multilevel constitutionalism uses the classical shapes of Westphalian constitutional geometry as organisational and analytical schemes of the emerging supranational constitutionalism. It provides for federalist solutions to supranational constitutional problems and uses the achievements of the federalist constitutional and political theory in order to explain the constitutionalisation of the EU and to a lesser extent also of other supranational regimes. Thus multilevel constitutionalism uses the hierarchy and the pyramid as ordering paradigms and as visual analytical and organising forms. It applies it to systems such as the EU that do not match the characteristics of the territorial nation state in which these forms have emerged and evolved.

Many EU legal and political scholars who are not limited only to the proponents of multilevel constitutionalism use the triangles and rectangles as explanatory and visualising schemes when analysing the inter-institutional relations between the EU institutions or between them and the institutions of the Member States. Thus they follow a durable tradition established in the context of Westphalian constitutionalism. The problem is that these constitutional geometric forms are frequently put in practice uncritically and without taking into account the specifics of the supranational context in which they are applied.

[41] A Peters, The Merits of Global Constitutionalism (2009) 16 *Indiana Journal of Global Legal Studies* 397.

[42] I Pernice, 'The Global Dimension of Multilevel Constitutionalism. A Legal Response to the Challenges of Globalization' in *Völkerrecht als Wertordnung. Festschrift für Christian Tomuschat* (Engel Verlag, 2006).

[43] N Krisch, *Beyond Constitutionalism. The Pluralist Structure of Postnational Law* (Oxford, Oxford University Press, 2011); A Stone Sweet, 'Constitutionalism, Legal Pluralism and International Regimes' (2009) 16 *Indiana Journal of Global Legal Studies*, 631 et seq; M Avbelj and J Komarek (eds), *Constitutional Pluralism in the European Union and Beyond* (Oxford, Hart Publishing, 2012).

Hence multilevel constitutionalism tries to transplant[44] the ordering schemes of Westphalian constitutional geometry which are adequate for the territorial nation state in a post-national, non-state and even in a post-territorial context. Basic normative ideologies of Westphalian constitutionalism such as the state as territorial container[45] composed of public power, territory and people,[46] representative democracy, parliamentarism, the existence of a fully fledged, politically active, integrated community with solidarity and mutual commitment among its members capable of sustaining territorial democracy, the hierarchical structure of the system of sources of law and the multilevel structure of the supranational and national institutions of the legislative, executive and judicial power are all transplants of the nation-state constitutional law in the supranational constitutional context of the EU.

The rather mechanical and artificial way that these concepts, principles and institutions are superimposed on the EU as an unprecedented supranational and post-national regime in human history without taking into account both its institutional design and socio-political context logically leads to democratic deficit and inefficiency. The 'tree of representative democracy' described above and exemplified by the already-mentioned decision of the German Constitutional Court faces several challenges in serving as a constitutional geometric form of EU constitutionalism. This tree has multiple roots—28 if the 'peoples of Europe' are counted or 29 if the democratic legitimacy of the EU can be grounded on the European citizens and the people of the 28 member states. Moreover, the European Parliament does not possess any monopoly over the input democratic legitimacy so as to serve as a source for its distribution to other EU institutions.

The same problems stemming out of the direct transplantation of the nation state constitutional geometry to the EU and its transposition as constitutional geometry of the EU can also be detected regarding the hierarchy, the pyramid and the triangles and rectangles. These modern forms of constitutional geometry are frequently misleading in a supranational and post-national context. They do not constitute sufficiently adequate ordering and explanatory schemes in the case of the EU. This is due also to the lack of a clear concept of territoriality of the EU produced by the inexistence of clear limits of its territorial expansion and by the emergence of networked atteritorial power structures and schemes in the European construction as a result of the information revolution and the crisis of territoriality.

44 A Watson, *Legal Transplants: An Approach to Comparative Law*, 2nd edn (Atlanta, University of Georgia Press, 1993).

45 N Brenner, above n 31, 55.

46 G Jellinek, above n 12.

The constitutional geometry provided by the multilevel constitutionalism theory has two main deficiencies when explaining the ordering of the legal orders[47] of the EU and its Member States. They clearly demonstrate the increasing dysfunctionality of the hierarchy and the pyramid as normative ordering concepts of Westphalian constitutional geometry applied to the post-Westphalian constitutional law and socio-political context.

First, the use of the hierarchy and pyramid as ordering schemes requires either clear subordination of EU law under the constitutions of the Member States or the undisputed supremacy of EU law over the whole domestic law including the constitution. Since the abandonment of the absolute supremacy of the EU law doctrine developed by the CJEU in its earlier case law[48] the clear subordination of the national constitution under EU law is impossible. Since the development of the latest doctrine of relative supremacy of EU law safeguarding and respecting the constitutional identity of the Member States,[49] the absolute supremacy of the Member States' constitutions is also rather problematic and questionable.

Second, there are several systems for linking the national with the supranational legal systems or for 'ordering of constitutional orders'.[50] Usually modern constitutions provide for either a monistic or a dualist system for implementation of international treaties in the domestic legal order and for linking national with international and supranational legal systems. The monistic and the dualist systems predetermine the structural exposure and the modes of opening of domestic to supranational and international law. Thus they produce different institutional results moulded in divergent constitutional geometric forms. The monistic system allows for shaping a common hierarchy and pyramid of the sources of law which also includes international law. The dualist system preserves the formal closure of the domestic pyramid of sources of law. Thus it provides for two semi-independent hierarchies of sources of law—the international law pyramid and the domestic law pyramid.

Both monism and dualism seem to be increasingly dysfunctional in the context of constitutionalisation of international law which has led to the

[47] For the concept of 'ordering of constitutional orders' see E Tanchev, 'The Contemporary Supranational Constitutional Pluralism or the Ordering of Constitutional Orders' in P Kirov (ed) *Constitutional Studies 2012–2013* (Sofia, 'St Kliment Ohridski' University Press, 2014), 171–98 (in Bulgarian).

[48] See Case C-6/64 *Flaminio Costa v ENEL* [1964], Case C-26/62 *NV Algemene Transporten Expeditie Onderneming van Gend en Loos v Nederlandse Administratis der Belastingen* [1963], Case C-11/70 *Internationale Handelsgesellschaft mbH v Einfuhr- und Vorratsstelle für Getreide und Futtermittel* [1970].

[49] See Case C-36/02 *Omega Spielhallen- und Automatenaufstellungs-GmbH v Oberbürgermeisterin der Bundesstadt Bonn* [2004] and Case C-208/09 *Ilonka Sayn-Wittgenstein v Landeshauptmann von Wien* [2010] etc.

[50] E Tanchev, above n 47, 171–98 (in Bulgarian).

establishment of EU constitutionalism and other less developed forms of supranational constitutionalism and eventually may cause the emergence of global constitutionalism. They have both conceptual and practical difficulties in explaining several key concepts of post-Westphalian constitutional and international law: the relationship between the EU law and the constitutions of the Member States; the functionality of the *pacta sunt servanda* principle in the context of activist supranational courts and national constitutional courts; the integration of the case law of the supranational courts in the domestic legal orders; the relationship between the UN Charter, EU law and the European Charter of Human Rights in the context of the case law of the CJEU[51] and the case law of the European Court of Human Rights;[52] the increasing importance of soft law etc.[53]

Constitutional pluralism is among the few post-Westphalian paradigms provided by constitutional theory at the beginning of the twenty-first century. It aims to explain supranational constitutionalism from a pluralistic and polycentric point of view by virtue of applying the network and the circle as normative ordering and explanatory shapes of the post-Westphalian age and its constitutional geometry. Moreover, it goes beyond the network and the circle as shapes which have also been known to Westphalian constitutionalism although being underestimated and used scarcely by applying a pluralist approach. It consists in mapping the supranational and global constitutional reality by using no single ordering and explanatory scheme, for example the (territorial) polygon, the hierarchy, the pyramid, the circle and the network, but through a mixture of the above-mentioned shapes.

This mixing of constitutional geometric forms better reflects the plurality of organising models for the public power. It takes into account the existence of global and regional plurality of legal orders, some of which are organised in a hierarchical way whereas others resemble much more a network or circle. Moreover, there are inter-institutional triangles which are cross-cutting the territorial polygons and the jurisdictional hierarchies and ignore the initially layered structure of the Westphalian organisation of the supranational legal order. A clear example of such a 'jurisdictional cross-cutting inter-institutional triangle' is the so-called 'Troika' composed by the European Commission, the European Central Bank and the International Monetary Fund which has played a central role in financial crisis management in the EU since 2009.

[51] See Case C-402/05 *Yassin Abdullah Kadi and Al Barakaat International Foundation v Council of the European Union and Commission of the European Communities* [2008].

[52] See *Nada v Switzerland* [GC], no 10593/08, Judgment, 12.09.2012 and *Al-Dulimi and Montana Management Inc v Switzerland*, 5809/08, Judgment, 26.11.2013.

[53] For both conceptual and comparative analysis of some of these issues see A Albi and S Bardutzky (eds), *National Constitutions in European and Global Governance: Democracy, Rights, the Rule of Law* (TMC Asser Press, forthcoming 2018).

Consequently constitutional pluralism takes into account the plurality of levels of public power both on a national and subnational level as well as the emergence of networked systems of private actors performing public functions. It preserves the hierarchical, pyramidal and layered Westphalian structure of power where appropriate while admitting the structural changes of the institutional design and constitutional geometry of the post-Westphalian age.

The ordering code of constitutional pluralism is toleration, differentiating mutual recognition and peaceful co-existence.[54] It combines the nation states' hierarchies and pyramids with the networks which are typical for the private actors of global governance and for the global civic society and public sphere players. Hence constitutional pluralism takes into account the mixture of circular, networked and hierarchical ways and matrixes on the basis of which the national, sub-national and supranational constitutional regimes and quasi-public power schemes are currently (re)organised.

Last but not least, constitutional pluralism allows for visual and analytical recognition of the existence of mutually supportive, parallel but sometimes also contradictory jurisprudence of the supranational and the national courts. The jurisprudential activity of the supranational courts in combination with the case law of the national constitutional and supreme courts regarding EU and international law matters led to the emergence of asynchronous and asymmetric supranational constitutionalism. It shapes the visual map of global constitutionalism as a realm of dots and spots marking the jurisprudential activity of the supranational and national courts which may be coordinated and systematically linked but also may emerge as non-synchronised and even opposing responses to the same or common constitutional issues. In other words the case law of the supranational and national courts and especially the judicial dialogue in which they engage with increasing intensity can only be partially explained by judicial hierarchies, judicial networks and judicial inter-institutional triangles. It much more resembles a scheme mapping different dots, spots and circles which visually depict the divergent 'epicentres' of jurisprudential activity. The courts' jurisdiction and the convincing power of their decisions determine the range of the circles and thus the 'magnitude' of their case law.

This polycentric case law is structured not in hierarchies but actually in constellations resembling star systems in which the planets are gathered around its sun—the key decision forming the centre of consequent judicial doctrine. In some cases these constellations co-exist in a dynamic equilibrium but in other cases they collide leading to the establishment of radically new trends, doctrines and case-law constellations or producing black holes as radical escapes from the established legal order. These phenomena might

[54] E Tanchev, above n 47, 172 (in Bulgarian).

have been explained in Kelsenian terms as a replacement of the Grundnorm or in Schmittian terms as a new supreme decision taken in the situation of anomy (the 'Ernstfall'). However, this is less and less possible due to the lack of clear and monolithic hierarchy based on a single Grundnorm as well as because of the lack of supranational sovereignty and the increasing dysfunctionality of state sovereignty in the context of supranational constitutionalism.

Consequently the asymmetric and asynchronous character of global and supranational constitutionalism is produced to a great extent by the divergent case law of the supranational courts and the national constitutional courts. Although constitutional pluralism seems a less clear concept than multilevel constitutionalism, in fact it better reflects the current post-Westphalian constitutional situation. For example, the asymmetric character of the concept of constitutional identity[55] as key concept of the current EU constitutionalism debate and the existence of mutual cross-fertilisation of the jurisprudence of the different supranational and national courts based on vertical and horizontal judicial dialogue[56] leading to migration of constitutional ideas can be better explained by the theory of constitutional pluralism than by multilevel constitutionalism.

To sum up, constitutional pluralism is to a certain extent a postmodern concept since it does not try to provide for a holistic model or for a fully fledged and internally coherent and uncontroversial paradigm. Constitutional pluralism is much more a reflection of the plurality of legal orders. It emerged during late Modernity in the context of globalisation, which has produced the current asymmetric, multilayered and polycentric texture of the global legal order. Constitutional pluralism is much more a *modus vivendi* of shapes and forms with divergent ontology, teleology, pragmatics and institutional outlook rather than an elaborated scheme for uncontroversial 'ordering of constitutional orders'.

Constitutional pluralism explains the constitutional nature and features of the EU in an asymmetrical way combining hierarchical with networked and circular constitutional geometric paradigms. The pyramid and hierarchy remain important ordering schemes of the EU constitutional design. They organise the principal type of interrelation between the supranational, national and subnational levels of the institutional and normative systems of the EU and its Member States.

The circle is the constitutional geometric shape in which 'Europe *à plusieurs vitesses*' is structured. The existence of the Eurozone as the hard

[55] A Saiz Arnaiz and C Alcoberro Llivina (eds), *National Constitutional Identity and European Integration* (Mortsel, Intersentia, 2013).

[56] D Law and W C Chang, 'The Limits of Global Judicial Dialogue' (2011) 86 *Washington Law Review*; M Walters, 'The Future of Transnational Judicial Dialogue' (2010) 104 *Proceedings of the Annual Meeting (American Society of International Law)* 465 et seq.

core and internal circle of the EU is supplemented by the Schengen circle. The Member States which are neither part of the Eurozone nor of Schengen are included in the most external circle of the European construction.

The network is an appropriate geometric form for visualising the interrelation between the Member States' parliaments while performing controlling functions for the principles of subsidiarity and proportionality according to Protocols No. 1 and 2 to the Lisbon Treaty. It can be applied also to the judicial dialogue among the CJEU and the national constitutional courts producing the aggregate effect of both networked and multilevel constitutional jurisdiction. Here the network is both a complementary and concurring visual explanatory and ordering paradigm to the asymmetrical totality of dots and spots framed by jurisprudential circles. Moreover, the experts and activists in the EU are linked in pan-European networks. The European citizens' initiative and the European political parties as the key forms of participatory democracy in the EU also require the network as organising form of the constitutional geometry of the European public sphere.

Hence the federalist, institutionalist and multilevel vision of 'Europe of hierarchies' is paralleled and sometimes challenged by the pluralist visions of 'Europe of circles' and 'Europe of networks'. Thus the constitutional pluralistic version of the post-Westphalian constitutional geometry of Europe in general and of the EU in particular seems to really produce a 'Kandinsky painting'.[57]

The circular and pluralistic shapes of constitutional geometry are applicable also for the explanation of the parallel membership of the states in different but partially mutually supportive forms of pan-European integration, such as the EU, the Council of Europe and the OSCE, based on partially coinciding ontology and teleology. The lack of a clear and predominant centre of the network of pan-European circles produces coordination and coherence issues which result again in a pluralistic constitutional design of pan-European constitutional geometry.

The theory of constitutional pluralism is one of the important attempts at creating a theory of post-Westphalian and globalised constitutional law. However, its main issue is that it does not provide for sufficiently clear and practicable criteria for giving preference to supranational sources of law and for solving of normative collisions. This is especially problematic when such activity is expected to be performed by the ordinary courts or administrations in their everyday praxis. From the point of view of constitutional geometry constitutional pluralism is a major novelty since it breaks with the monopoly of hierarchy and pyramid and introduces the circle and the network as explanatory and ordering paradigms of post-Westphalian

[57] I borrow the 'Kandinsky painting' metaphor from the keynote speech of Martti Koskenniemi at the 22nd IACL World Congress in Oslo, Norway.

supranational and global constitutionalism. However, the 'Kandinsky painting' produced as a result of the application of constitutional pluralism to the global and EU constitutional context is neither sufficiently clear and structured nor sufficiently emotionally and visually convincing, nor adapted for giving practicable solutions to the everyday legal and political praxis. The constitutional pluralism's deficiencies demonstrate how far we are from having a coherent theory of supranational and global constitutional law in general and of its constitutional geometry in particular which is adequate to the challenges of the post-Westphalian situation and at the same time is applicable in legal and political practice.

Global governance is a socio-political phenomenon and theoretical paradigm which profoundly changes modern understanding of constitutional geometry. It reflects the privatisation and supranationalisation of the public power as processes which run in parallel since the last decades of the twentieth century. Taken in combination they lead to the outsourcing of public power to supranational and global actors, some of which are not public institutions but private entities. Global governance presumes that the main public functions are performed by a set of public and private, national, subnational and supranational actors. Thus global governance challenges the territoriality of the public power and the limitation of its institutional design to public institutions. What is more, global governance implies the use of networks and circles not only as a supplement but also as central ordering and explanatory schemes of the constitutional geometry of post-Westphalian constitutionalism. The constitutional geometry of the global governance cannot be reduced to either hierarchies and pyramids or levels and lines. It requires by necessity the introduction of new forms of constitutional geometry which can better represent the polycentric and complex order of the globalised world.

Global constitutionalism may be eventually reduced to hierarchies if it is explained in the multilevel constitutionalist trend of thought without recourse to constitutional pluralism. However, global governance, like constitutional pluralism, is an essentially non-hierarchical concept. It is based on the network, the circle and the asynchronous and asymmetrical realm of dots and spots as visual explanatory codes of the global constitutional order and its post-Westphalian constitutional geometry.

The most important difference between global governance and constitutional pluralism with regard to their constitutional geometry is that constitutional pluralism is much more diverse as regards its ordering schemes. Thus constitutional pluralism presupposes the existence of a constitutional dimension which implies the use of hierarchies but denies the possibility of transforming them into global or regional universally applicable supranational hierarchical and pyramidal models. It is based on the presumption that public functions are performed by constitutional and thus public actors. Global governance presumes the networked organisation of supranational power relations as well as the existence of cross-cutting jurisdictions, some of which are performed by private actors.

The constitutional impact of global and territory-detached global governance actors implicitly brings to the fore the network and the circle as visualising schemes of its post-Westphalian constitutional geometry. Hence the visual world of global governance is much more focused on networks and circles than is constitutional pluralism. They indicate the increased political and thus constitutional importance of global religions,[58] transnational corporations,[59] global interest groups and lobbies and the global networks of experts and civic activists. The networked and circular visual world of global governance also demonstrates the diminishing importance of states visually defined as power pyramids.

The de-territorialisation of public power is one of the most important novelties produced by the information revolution. It constructs new power realities such as the Internet and deconstructs the monopoly of the territorial state over the governance of the policy processes framed by its territorial polygon, governed by its pyramidal normative order as applied by its hierarchical institutional system. Moreover, it reconstructs power relations on non-territorial and frequently on a global basis in circles and networks as shapes of the post-Westphalian constitutional geometry adequate to the emerging global constitutionalism.

The Internet produces several challenges to Westphalian constitutional law and its constitutional geometry. It establishes a new power reality which fosters the emergence and proliferation of deliberative and participatory forums and opportunities for political networking on a global scale. At the same time the Internet weakens the control of territorial power structures over the different policy fields and policy processes by raising the information independence—and consequently, the overall independence—of the virtually and thus globally acting local players. Thus the Internet increases power polycentrism, reorganises the global and virtual accomplishment of power not only in hierarchies but also in circles and networks and reduces the control of territorial power hierarchies and pyramids which leads to their increasing dysfunctionality. The malfunctioning of the hierarchical structure of public order and state power results in the general dysfunctionality of Westphalian constitutional law which is in dire need of new supportive ideologies, explanatory and ordering paradigms.

[58] M Saporiti, 'The Concept of Sovereignty and the Transnational Challenge of Global Religions. A Theoretical Framework' in M Belov (ed), *Global Governance and Its Effects on State and Law* (Frankfurt am Main, Peter Lang, 2016) 97–115.

[59] C Good, 'Corporate Human Rights Initiatives—From International Law to Global Governance and Back?' in M Belov (ed), *Global Governance and Its Effects on State and Law* (Frankfurt am Main, Peter Lang, 2016) 149–65.

The power reality created by the Internet as well as the deliberative and participatory networks and circles established by it are territory-detached and territory-independent as well as simultaneous, thus being also time-independent. Consequently the Internet profoundly changes the information context of public governance and policy making, which affects the activity of both the state institutions and the actors of civic society and the public sphere.

What is especially important is that the Internet emerges not only as an alternative power reality but also as a 'cross-cutting jurisdiction'.[60] It is a de-territorialised and time-independent network of networks and circles that penetrates in the hierarchies and pyramids of state jurisdictions. Thus it contributes to the de-territorialisation of the public power and to the destruction of the 'territorial container'[61] of the nation state. Hence the Internet boosts the importance of networks and circles and diminishes the role of the pyramid and the hierarchy as ordering and explanatory schemes of constitutional geometry.

In other words, the Internet provides for the first time since Early Modernity a power model that can compete with the domination of the territorial state as a universal model for organising, institutionalising and shaping the public power. The Internet challenges the territoriality of statehood and establishes a platform for development of virtual global constitutionalism based on information as a distinct power resource and on specific ordering and visual schemes of this immaterial global power reality. Hence it also brings with it alternative forms of constitutional geometry that compete and challenge the constitutional geometry of Westphalian statehood.

The Internet has an important constitutional dimension due to the fact that it directly concerns constitutionally enshrined human rights, produces the demand for the constitutional provision of new human rights, challenges the efficiency of the existing territory-defined safeguards of human rights and introduces structural changes in the functioning of state institutions as well as of the institutions of supranational constitutionalism. The problem is that the Westphalian constitutional law is rather insensitive to aterritorial power realities and to constitutional issues stemming out of non-territorial power orders. The territorial entrenchment of Westphalian constitutionalism and its structuring in polygonal territorial forms and in hierarchical and pyramidal institutional and normative orders prevents national constitutional law from giving adequate responses to both the issues and the opportunities created by the emergent aterritorial global Internet-based power reality structured in networks and circles and less frequently in hierarchies.

[60] S Sassen, above n 17, 21–45.
[61] N Brenner, above n 31, 55.

Hence the clash between the aterritoriality of the virtual polyphony and polycentrism of networks and circles which are frequently sector-specific and the territoriality of the hierarchically and holistically structured Westphalian statehood creates fields of anomy which can be visually represented as holes of disorder or as spheres of clashing orders. That is why one of the main challenges to the Westphalian constitutional law is to provide for constitutional answers to the Internet-based power reality thus constitutionalising it also with the help of the visual world of constitutional geometry.

In fact the Internet can be conceptualised and organised as the first genuinely aterritorial form of global constitutionalism. The question is whether its constitutionalisation is possible on a national or even a regional level through national or regional institutional and normative hierarchies or can be fully accomplished only on a global level in the shape of global constitutional networks and circles. This is another aspect of the broader issue of how can we capture, organise and explain the emerging supranational and global constitutional reality—through multilevel constitutionalism resting upon hierarchy or via constitutional pluralism based on polycentric and networked analytical and ordering schemes.

The constitutional shape of the public sphere of Westphalian statehood has been broadly structured in the geometrical framework provided by the territorial nation state. Thus it has been defined as a system of forums for public deliberation, political engagement and civic participation in the political process limited by the territorial polygon of statehood and the hierarchy and pyramid of the territorial power unit composed by the subordinated levels of civil society, public sphere and state institutions. The territoriality of the nation state framed the forms of political communication on a macro level in the classical shapes and forms of Westphalian constitutional geometry even though the concept of public sphere[62] allowed for non-hierarchical and polycentric engagement structured in networks and circles.

The technology and information revolution triggered by and based on the Internet allowed for the emergence for the first time in human history of essentially global forms of political communication which are structured in networked, polycentric and not only in hierarchical ways. The Internet itself is conceived as a network. Its network character and its territorial detachment and independence predetermine the communication and sociopolitical participation opportunities which it offers to its users. Thus the Internet emerges as a new type of 'cross-cutting jurisdiction'[63] exempted from the hierarchical burden of territoriality and producing networked communities and networked forms for accomplishment of public governance and thus of public power.

[62] J Habermas, *Strukturwandel der Öffentlichkeit* (Frankfurt am Main, Suhrkamp, 1999).
[63] S Sassen, above n 17, 21–45.

The Internet serves as a platform for pluralistic and networked political deliberation and participation. Thus it creates new opportunities for the development of global deliberative and participatory democracy. It allows for the territorial detachment of information and communication rights, for inclusion in networked forms of global democracy and for the emergence of aterritorial deliberative citizenship.

The new social media such as Facebook, Twitter, Google + etc. have proved to be not only platforms for information exchange and public opinion formation but also devices for policy making. They change the structure not just of the vertical political communication between politicians and the people and the horizontal political communication between the people themselves but also serve as instruments for public governance and social change that predetermine key political decisions and even produce or foster revolutions. Thus the Internet and Internet-based platforms and networks challenge the territoriality of public power, the possibility for polygonal closure and hierarchical accomplishment of policy making and restructure the territory-based deliberative and participatory democracy framed in polygonal and pyramid forms. They enhance the emancipation of symbolic policy from substantial policy and communication power from overall state power and profoundly change the information context for policy making.[64] That is why in the context of the Internet the network challenges both the hierarchy and the polygon as shapes for framing the constitutional geometry of the public sphere and introduces structural changes in the modes for the accomplishment of state power.

The Internet creates threats to the Westphalian outlook of the constitutional principle of democracy. According to S Benhabib, democracy requires closure[65] whereas the Internet dismantles the territorial closure of the demos and public power. Hence the Internet erodes the preconditions for democracy in its only known form so far, namely as territorial democracy. However, in the current context of crisis of the representative democracy, the emergence of networked sector-based civic society and territory-detached deliberative and decision-making circles of experts, citizens and activists may commence to serve as a functional equivalent of the missing supranational, European and global demos.

The European or global nation is impossible. However, European or even global networked communities of sector-based activists checking both the public power and the private actors which accomplish public functions and

[64] M Belov, 'Separation of Powers reconsidered: a Proposal for a New Theoretical Model at the Beginning of the 21st Century' in A Geisler, M Hein and S Hummel (eds), *Law, Politics and the Constitution. New Perspectives from Legal and Political Theory* (Frankfurt am Main, Peter Lang, 2014) 54–59.

[65] S Benhabib, 'Borders, Boundaries and Citizenship' (2005) 38 *Political Science and Politics* 673–77.

publicly exposing the malfunctioning of government and governance may serve as a remedy for the democratic deficit of supranational and global constitutionalism. Hence the emergence of global networked communities shaped as an atteritorial and networked system of networks and circles and serving as a supplement to the territorial democratic communities and as a functional equivalent to territorial democracy may increase public control over the global forms of public power.

IV. CONCLUSION

Several conclusions can be drawn up regarding the legal institutionalisation and theoretical explanatory power of the constitutional geometry of post-Westphalian constitutional law. The hierarchy and the pyramid as natural shapes of Westphalian constitutional geometry are questioned, challenged and in some cases even partially dismantled by the network and the circle as ordering schemes of post-Westphalian constitutionalism. The emergent scheme of the global constitutional geometry resembles, in the words of Martti Koskenniemi, a 'Kandinsky painting' in which the hierarchies, pyramids and polygons co-exist and compete with the circles, networks, lines, dots and spots thus producing global asymmetric constitutionalism.

The hierarchy, the pyramid and the polygonal 'territorial container' were objectively produced by the emergence of the territorial nation state, by the need to govern mass society on a large territory based on developed separation of public functions and social labour and by the emergence of the national legal order. The industrial revolution, which itself produced the emergence of the mass society and triggered urbanisation and modernisation and later, with the emergence of the bourgeoisie, also constitutionalisation, have been the objective determinant of the establishment of the hierarchy as ordering scheme of Westphalian statehood. The hierarchy was needed in order to establish national, universal, formalised and hierarchical modern law reflecting the principle of sovereignty and safeguarding the rule of law.

In the same way, the information revolution and globalisation produced the rise of the importance of the network and the diminishing role of the hierarchy as ordering scheme of post-Westphalian supranational and global constitutionalism. The structuring of the public power exclusively in national power pyramids linked to the supranational legal order via the dualist or monist system is put in question. The international legal order gets fragmented into plurality of legal orders which co-exist without being hierarchically intertwined. Thus the fragmentation and the constitutionalisation of international law[66] and the emergence of constitutional or

[66] A Peters, 'On the Interaction of Constitutionalization and Fragmentation in International Law' (2015) *Working Paper 2 Centre for Global Constitutionalism St Andrews*, 1–42;

quasi-constitutional supranational regimes limit the explanatory and ordering power of the classical forms of Westphalian constitutional geometry.

In a world without a single power centre in which the hierarchically organised state power is partially dismantled and deconstructed whereas no new global or even regional hierarchy is reconstructed, the network and the circle start to seem more adequate ordering schemes for the supranational constitutional order than the pyramid and the hierarchy. They are objectively predetermined by the information and mobility revolution, by globalisation and the emergence of supranational constitutional regimes.

Post-Westphalian global constitutionalism is not always organised exclusively in territorial forms of public power. Thus the partial territorial detachment of the public power and the emergence of aterritorial forms of supranational and global governance are a product of globalisation and the information revolution. They are objectively produced by them in a comparable way as the hierarchy and the pyramid have been objectively put into practice by the rise of the territorial nation state, the industrial revolution and the emergence of the mass society.

The hierarchy diminishes in importance with the rise of supranational and global constitutionalism based on constitutional pluralism and with the emergence of global governance. However, it will not perish since it is needed as an ordering and explanatory scheme of the territorial state which preserves key and strategic functions even during the current phase of globalisation.[67]

The post-Westphalian situation produces several pressing issues. The giving of proper and adequate answers to them is the key for putting global governance on constitutional roots and for restoring the constitutional government on a global scale. The adjustment of the national institutional pyramids and hierarchical constitutional and legal orders to the networked, circular and asymmetric character of supranational and global constitutionalism should reinstall some mechanisms for prevention of normative and institutional collisions and anomies. The adaptation of the constitutional ideology and the constitutional geometry to the asymmetric, polycentric and partially aterritorial post-Westphalian world order is an important step towards regaining the functionality of the national constitution which was

J G van Mullingen, 'Global Constitutionalism and the Objective Purport of the International Legal Order' (2011) 24 *Leiden Journal of International Law* 285; Fragmentation of International Law: Difficulties Arising From the Diversification and Expansion of International Law. Report of the Study Group of the International Law Commission finalised by Martti Koskenniemi, United Nations, Geneva, 2006; M Koskenniemi and P Leino, 'Fragmentation of International Law? Postmodern Anxieties' (2002) 15 *Leiden Journal of International Law* 553–79; and J Klabbers, A Peters and G Ulfstein (eds), *The Constitutionalisation of International Law* (Oxford, Oxford University Press, 2011).

[67] S Sassen, *A Sociology of Globalization* (New York, WW Norton & Company, 2007) 45–97.

born in the context of the territorial entrenchment of public power and the hierarchical Westphalian national order.

The rise of the constitutional relevance of the Internet and the need for its constitutionalisation also brings new challenges to the traditional constitutional geometry. The existence of semi-institutionalised intergovernmental networks such as G-7 and G-20 increases the importance of the network and the circle and at the same time reintroduces the hierarchy into global political relations. This is also a phenomenon that needs some constitutional response. The eventual ratification and entering into force of trade agreements with huge structural constitutional implications such as the TTIP and CETA profoundly challenges the structuring of the constitutional reality, the key distinction between public and private, supranational, national and subnational spheres thus challenging also the constitutional geometry on global, supranational and national levels. Last but not least, the White Paper on the Future of Europe issued by the European Commission in 2017 demonstrates the competition of hierarchical, networked, circular and polycentric forms of constitutional geometry aimed at reorganising the EU on the basis of multilevel constitutionalist, functionalist, sovereigntist or constitutional pluralist basis.

3

Overcoming False Dichotomies: Constitutionalism and Pluralism in European and International Studies

GIUSEPPE MARTINICO

I. AIMS AND STRUCTURE

RECENT STUDIES[1] DESCRIBE constitutionalism and pluralism as antithetical options and often speak of the former as something holistic and closed, with pluralism to be preferred, at the post-national level, because of the flexibility and openness that it could ensure.

The aim of this chapter is to offer reflection on the relationship between openness and constitutionalism by looking at some constitutional experiences, primarily (but not exclusively) the Italian constituent process, taken as interesting case studies to explore the origin of constitutional openness.

The Italian constitution belongs to the group of constitutions that Mortati called 'constitutions born from the Resistance',[2] as they were forged with the clear intent to deny and overcome the whole of the 'values' (or anti-values) that had characterised the totalitarian era.

By 'constitutions born from the Resistance', Mortati also referred to other documents, for instance, the French (Fourth Republic) and German constitutions. As Carrozza[3] recently noticed, today, we could include within this group the Portuguese, Spanish and Greek constitutions that were promulgated during the 1970s.

Openness is precisely one of the most evident features that characterise these texts, and it is possible to find the roots of this phenomenon even earlier, looking back at what, in the 1930s, Mirkine-Guetzévitch called

[1] N Krisch, *Beyond Constitutionalism. The Pluralist Structure of Postnational Law* (Oxford, Oxford University Press, 2010).

[2] C Mortati, *Lezioni sulle forme di governo* (Padua, Cedam, 1973) 222.

[3] P Carrozza, 'Constitutionalism's Post-modern Opening', in M Loughlin and N Walker (eds), *The Paradox of Constitutionalism: Constituent Power and Constitutional Form* (Oxford, Oxford University Press, 2007) 169 et seq, 180.

the 'internationalisation of modern constitutions'.[4] In other words, openness seems to belong within the core of the 'nouvelles tendances du droit constitutionnel'.[5] Something similar might be argued with regard to the connection between flexibility (in this context understood as ability to adapt) and constitutionalism, as I have tried to argue elsewhere (especially looking at what scholars term 'evolutionary constitutionalism').[6]

By openness, in this chapter, I mean the constitutionally established friendliness towards legal sources that are, from a formal point of view, external to those governed by the national system, or, in other words, that are not produced by the national actors (and, as such, are not traceable to the general will of the people) in charge of the law-making functions according to the constitution.

As for the structure of this chapter, in the initial section I shall set forth the main arguments employed by Krisch in his book *Beyond Constitutionalism: The Pluralist Structure of Postnational Law*. His book has been a turning point in the discussion between constitutional and public international lawyers, and, as such, it is an important contribution to the discussion.

At the same time, Krisch's view on constitutionalism is emblematic of a certain idea of constitutionalism that has been spread in the studies on the fragmentation of public international law. Krisch's book is part of a broader phenomenon of intellectual resistance and reaction against a certain idea of constitutionalism which was conceived at that time as the dominant narrative.[7] Second, I shall emphasise the ambiguities of this view by stressing the continuity that exists between his concept of pluralism and another idea of constitutionalism: the common element between the two is precisely expressed by the idea of openness. Against this background the purpose of this chapter is to show how a comparative law based analysis

[4] B Mirkine-Guetzévitch, *Les Nouvelles tendances du droit constitutionnel* (Paris, Giard, 1931) 48 et seq.

[5] ibid.

[6] G Martinico, *Lo spirito polemico del diritto europeo. Studio sulle ambizioni costituzionali dell'Unione* (Rome, Aracne, 2011) 27 et seq.

[7] Another example of this intellectual resistance is given by P Lindseth, *Power and Legitimacy: Reconciling Europe and the Nation-State* (Oxford, Oxford University Press, 2010). Lindseth always starts his pieces by saying the European constitutional law is still the mainstream. I do not think so, actually nowadays those who believe in European constitutional law have been under siege over the last years, and Lindseth—metaphorically of course—is one of those who led the troops to the constitutional citadel; see P Lindseth, 'The Perils of "As If" European Constitutionalism' (2016) 22 *European Law Journal* 696 and P Lindseth, 'Constitutionalism Beyond the State? The Administrative Character of European Governance Revisited' (2012) 33 *Cardozo Law Review* 1875 (where he argues that the constitutional reading is not even plausible). For a different view of European administrative law see E Chiti, 'Is EU Administrative Law Failing in Some of Its Crucial Tasks?' (2016) 22 *European Law Journal* 576.

Now, while I see their point and generally I like the emergence of new counter-narratives, I am a bit concerned about this way of presenting the constitutional and administrative options as alternative rather than mutually supportive.

can be helpful to overcome this false dichotomy (that between pluralism and constitutionalism[8]) presented by this literature.[9]

II. CONSTITUTIONALISM ACCORDING TO KRISCH

Krisch's reflections on the relationship between pluralism and constitutionalism are developed in the context of a 'post-national society'. By post-national law, Krisch means all legal phenomena that are not entirely interpretable, either in light of the traditional categories of international law or those of constitutional law:[10]

> Constitutionalism is struggling because international law and global governance have become increasingly effective, thus removing key issues from the reach of national constitutions and domestic political processes. International law, on the other hand, experiences problems because its thin, consent-oriented legitimacy base no longer appears adequate to the task. Now that international law has grown in importance, it is seen as overly formalistic and undemocratic, and a thicker, more substantive foundation seems called for. Constitutionalism stands ready to fill this gap, but to many, it appears as unsuited for this expansion and also as too emblematic of a particular political tradition.[11]

Another feature of post-national law is the interpenetration of different levels of governance—the domestic and international—due to the crisis of the traditional distinction between these two spheres.[12] For Krisch there are two grand approaches that might be used to read the structure of post-national law ('frame comprised of different orders and their norms ... overcome[ing] the categorical separation between the spheres, without however merging them fully or necessarily defining the degree of authority

[8] 'Pluralism and constitutionalism should not be seen as antithetical, but as complementary': C Eckes and S Hollenberg, 'Reconciling Different Legal Spheres in Theory and Practice: Pluralism and Constitutionalism in the Cases of Al-Jedda, Ahmed and Nada' (2013) 20 *Maastricht Journal of European and Comparative Law* 220, 222.

[9] For a similar methodological perspective see F Fabbrini, 'The Constitutionalization of International Law: A Comparative Federal Perspective' (2013) 6 *European Journal of Legal Studies* 7.

[10] 'Domestic constitutionalism, which places the national community at the centre of the legal and political universe by giving it control over its commitments, cannot reflect this broader constituency—on transboundary issues, it re-mains underinclusive. Domestic constitutionalism not only fails to include but also fails to deliver', Krisch (above n 1) 20–21.

[11] Krisch (above n 1) 3–4.

[12] 'The classical distinction between the domestic and international spheres that had sustained them is increasingly blurred, with a multitude of formal and informal connections taking the place of what once were relatively clear rules and categories. In this sense, law has become 'postnational'—the national sphere retains importance, but it is no longer the paradigmatic anchor of the whole order'. Krisch, *Beyond Constitutionalism* (above n 1) 3–4.

their different norms possess'[13]): Pluralism and constitutionalism, and the entirety of Krisch's book (and other writings by the same author[14]), are based on the distinction between these two paradigms.

In a nutshell, while for Krisch, constitutionalism is a concept that is structurally hierarchical and holistic, pluralism would be more apt and respectful of the identities that characterise the post-national context. Holism is the term employed by Krisch himself[15] with regard to the claim of constitutionalism—according to his reconstruction—that would be building a 'comprehensive, justified political order'.[16]

Against this background, holism (from Ancient Greek ὅλος—all, whole, entire) seems to refer to a whole that is closed and hierarchical, in opposition to pluralist openness:[17]

> Pluralism's openness may bring with it certain risks, but it also has significant advantages over more rigidly constitutionalised structures, especially as regards the processes of adaptation and change so pervasive in postnational politics. It also has important strengths in democratic terms not only because it gives contestation greater space but also because it reflects social indecision about which polity should govern transboundary issues. National, regional, and global polities often compete here, all with strong normative grounding and significant loyalties. Pluralism, unlike constitutionalism, does not need to decide hierarchies between them; it can grant them space for competition, mutual accommodation, and perhaps eventual settlement. Pluralism's institutional openness thus corresponds with the openness and fluidity of postnational society in a way constitutionalism, tailored to less heterogeneous societies, does not.[18]

When dealing with the polisemy of formulae like 'constitutionalism' and 'constitutionalisation', Krisch identifies at least three different meanings: constitutionalisation as the legalisation of the European political space, constitutionalisation as the progressive hierarchisation of supranational law and, lastly, constitutionalisation (and constitution) as process[19]—rather

[13] Krisch (above n 1) 12.

[14] eg N Krisch, 'Global Administrative Law and the Constitutional Ambition' in P Dobner and M Loughlin (eds), *The Twilight of Constitutionalism?* (Oxford, Oxford University Press, 2010) 245; N Krisch, 'The Case for Pluralism in Postnational Law', in G de Búrca and JHH Weiler (eds), *The Worlds of European Constitutionalism* (Cambridge, Cambridge University Press, 2003) 203.

[15] Krisch (above n 1) 305.

[16] Krisch (above n 1) 253.

[17] Krisch (above n 1) 303–04. For a different concept of holism in this ambit see N Walker, 'Beyond the Holistic Constitution?' (2009) *University of Edinburgh School of Law Working Paper* No 2009/16, <papers.ssrn.com/sol3/papers.cfm?abstract_id=1393867>.

[18] Krisch (above n 1) 26.

[19] On the constitution as a process see A Spadaro, 'Dalla Costituzione come 'atto' (puntuale nel tempo) alla Costituzione come 'processo' (storico). Ovvero dalla continua 'evoluzione' del parametro costituzionale attraverso i giudizi di costituzionalità' (1998) *Quaderni costituzionali* 343; A Spadaro, 'Il caso esemplare della Costituzione Europea come 'insieme di atti' (puntuali nel tempo) e 'insieme di processi' (storici): dalle C.E.E. (Comunità Economiche Europee), alla

than as punctual act—based on participatory and dialogical-inclusive practices.[20]

Krisch openly writes of a constitutional failure[21] and conceives the European context as part of his post-national scenario. The second chapter of his *Beyond Constitutionalism* is about the possibility of transferring what he means by 'domestic constitutionalism' to the global level, conceiving 'myriad jurisdictional regimes, including national constitutional orders and international legal sectors, as components of an integrated global legal order guided by constitutional values'.[22] When doing so, Krisch deeply analyses the concept of modern constitutionalism and stresses what are, in his view, the risks of this transplant. In the third chapter, he reconstructs his concept of pluralism; after having recalled the several types of pluralism that are present in legal philosophy, he presents the so-called 'systemic pluralism'.[23] In his effort, he starts from an idea of pluralism that is characterised by a coexistence of different orders, each of which claims supremacy over the others and their autonomy, with no submission to what he calls an 'overarching framework'.

Krisch acknowledges a preference for pluralism over constitutionalism for a series of reasons (which correspond to the exclusive virtues of pluralism in his view): adaptation,[24] openness,[25] checks and balances[26]

C.E. (Comunità Europea), all'U.E. (Unione Europea), agli U.S.E. (Stati Uniti d'Europa)', in L Leuzzi and C Mirabelli (eds), *Verso una Costituzione europea* (Cosenza, Publié, 2003) 621.

[20] 'Three main understandings of 'constitution' and 'constitutionalism' dominate this debate. The first equates constitutionalization with the increasing legalization of the European political order, the gradual submission of politics to a process of law. This understanding, however, was not alone in Stein's account. For him, the making of a transnational constitution was not only about increasing legalization, but also about the creation of a unitary, hierarchically ordered political structure in Europe—a structure he regarded as 'federal-type' already at that point ... A third main strand of constitutionalist thinking, a more discursive one, has arisen mainly since the late 1990s. Dissatisfied with classical models of constitutionalism and their potential for European governance arrangements, some authors have sought to construct alternative visions, based on the idea of a constitution as process rather than as a particular institutional form or structure.' Krisch (above n 1) 29–31.

[21] Krisch (above n 1) 30.

[22] M Sung Kuo, 'Beyond Constitutionalism by Nico Krisch' (2011) *Law and Politics Book Review*, 247.

[23] Krisch (above n 1) 71–78.

[24] 'As any order based on law, constitutionalism is in a constant tension with changing social circumstances ... Whether in a stronger or weaker form, a constitution always ties a polity to its past and thus creates tensions in the present. Pluralism promises to relax such ties, to allow for adaptation to new circumstances in a more rapid and less formalised way: by leaving the relationships between legal sub-orders undetermined, it keeps them open to political redefinition over time.' Krisch (above n 1) 78–79.

[25] 'If the argument from adaptation is based on an optimistic view of the social environment and its trajectory, that from contestation starts from a more pessimistic one. It assumes that constitutional frameworks are typically elite products, expressions of power and social hegemony, and that the element of disruption and openness in a pluralist order may provide greater contestatory space for weaker actors.' Krisch (above n 1) 81.

[26] 'The resulting picture of postnational governance would then be one of a constant potential for mutual challenge: of decisions with limited authority that may be contested through diverse

and, above all, public autonomy,[27] whose founding element is seen in the principle of free association and which is defined as the 'right to self-legislation', in which 'the element of will has to be complemented by a specification of the conditions under which it can coincide with everybody else's self-legislation'.[28] This conclusion derives from the principle of 'equal autonomy' and transforms public autonomy into one of the two pillars of his pluralist global law, together with the principle of toleration.[29]

The pluralism *à la* Krisch is grounded on participatory and pluralist dynamics that, in theory, should be neutral from a substantive point of view (because they are based on merely procedural principles that are analysed in his studies concerning 'global administrative law', that is, procedural fairness, accountability and transparency requirements[30]), without affecting the values and the post-national society that would result, and in a way, would be strangled by the holistic character of constitutionalism. According to this reconstruction, the myriad of legal orders in the post-national context might be preserved only by the pluralist paradigm due to its openness, dynamicity and elasticity, and the equidistance that it would guarantee.

III. QUESTIONING THIS RECONSTRUCTION

After having recalled Krisch's view, it is possible to mention some points to question his conclusions.[31] In this section I shall limit myself to some theoretical considerations while in the rest of the chapter I shall look at some concrete constitutional experiences to reinforce my argument.

First, the kind of constitutionalism that Krisch has in mind is the so-called *foundational constitutionalism*, a type of constructivist and revolutionary constitutionalism that claims to break the previous chains of validity[32] that

channels until some (perhaps provisional) closure might be achieved. It would be a picture of checks and balances that result in a form of systemic pluralism.' Krisch (above n 1) 85–88.

27 'Pluralism is also closer to foundational ideals of political order—namely public autonomy—than rival approaches: the plural, divided identities, loyalties, and allegiances that characterize postnational society are better reflected in a multiplicity of orders than in an overarching framework that implies ultimate authority.' Krisch (above n 1) 103–04.

28 Krisch (above n 1) 99.

29 See also P Capps and D Machin, 'The Problem of Global Law' (2011) 74 *Modern Law Review* 797–98.

30 See, eg, B Kingsbury, N Krisch and RB Stewart, 'The Emergence of Global Administrative Law' (2005) 68 *Law and Contemporary Problems* 15; N Krisch and B Kingsbury, 'Introduction: Global Governance and Global Administrative Law in the International Legal Order' (2006) 17 *European Journal of International Law* 1.

31 For another critical reconstruction of his thought, see Sung Kuo, 'Beyond Constitutionalism', above n 22.

32 H Kelsen, *General Theory of Law and State* (New York, Russell and Russell, 1945) 115; H Kelsen, *The Pure Theory of Law* (Berkeley, University of California Press, 1970) 208. On Kelsen and revolution see G Maher, 'Analytical Jurisprudence and Revolution' (1981) <www.bibliojuridica.org/libros/1/468/33.pdf>.

characterised the previous regimes in order to build a new legal order, by producing a revolution in the technical sense of the word:

> And the revolutions were dependent on constitutions. They sought to establish new systems of government, a new basis of legitimacy, and also effect fundamental changes in society, in the French case the abolition of the feudal system, in the American the establishment of a more virtuous, less corrupted polity. Constitutions were the perfect instruments for this ... It [constitutionalism] embodies a peculiarly modern trust in the ability of humankind to rationally govern itself, in the power of reason in the design of political institutions, and in the strength of those institutions in realising a common good. Pluralism eschews the hope of building one common, overarching legal framework that would integrate postnational governance, distribute powers, and provide for means of solving disputes between the various layers of law and politics. It is based instead on the heterarchical interplay of these layers according to rules ultimately set by each layer for itself. In pluralism, there is no common legal point of reference to appeal to for resolving disagreement; conflicts are solved through convergence, mutual accommodation—or not at all.[33]

However, Krisch acknowledges the existence of a form of *thin constitutionalism*[34] that might be theoretically applied to *post-national law*; in the end, he seems not to conceive it as constitutionalism *stricto sensu*, and when he recalls the reasons why pluralism would be preferable to constitutionalism, he seems to have in mind only the foundational version of constitutionalism. In conclusion it can be seen as a first proof of the unclear distinction between pluralism and constitutionalism as pointed out, more recently, by Shaffer.[35]

As mentioned above, Krisch conceives constitutionalism as hierarchical, holistic, revolutionary and constructivist, but when doing so, he reveals a

[33] Krisch (above n 1) 47.

[34] 'Constitutionalism in this reading represents a strong candidate for guiding our inquiry about the structure of postnational law, if only because of its thick domestic pedigree. Alternative, especially pluralist approaches would have to show why we need a break with key national traditions; why the structural implications of constitutionalism cannot carry over into the postnational realm. Yet some would argue that this contrast is overdrawn in the first place—that constitutionalism makes more limited demands, substantive rather than formal ones, that might even allow for a combination with pluralist ideas. In this reading, constitutionalism would simply reference a set of values democracy, rights, the rule of law—and would be thin enough to be translated into the postnational sphere'. Krisch (above n 1) 28.

[35] G Shaffer, 'A Transnational Take on Krisch's Pluralist Structure of Postnational Law' (2012) 23 *European Journal of International Law* 565. However, Shaffer's criticism is based on the 'state-centric' approach of postnational law: 'Most importantly, states remain central to these transnational processes since most legitimate authority remains within the state. It thus seems misleading to use the term post-national to describe the current context, especially outside Europe. In fact, in Krisch's study, states are more central than in most studies of transnational legal ordering. Although Krisch notes, at the book's start, the importance of 'international institutions, multilateral companies and transnational non-governmental organizations' (at 5), his case studies 'are not only court-centric, but also state-centric' (Shaffer, 578).

failure to consider another important constitutional tradition in his reconstruction: the so-called evolutionary constitutionalism.[36]

It is necessary here to recall what constitutional lawyers mean by the distinction between evolutionary and revolutionary constitutions. 'These revolutionary constitutions tend to have a blueprint character, wishing to invent the design for a future which is different from the past ... Old fashioned historic constitutions are, to the contrary, evolutionary in character'.[37] When observing the evolutionary/historical constitutions one realises that 'Codification, consolidation and adaptation are more predominant motives than modification. The constitution reflects historical movements outside itself.'[38]

The idea of constitution mentioned by that body of literature which defines itself as 'pluralism' (distinguishing itself from what some authors mean by 'constitutional pluralism'[39]) implies a 'constructivist' nature in every 'real' constitutional moment. Constructivism is 'a conception which assumes that all social institutions are, and ought to be, the product of deliberate design'.[40] The dualistic structure of Hayek's thought links the idea of constructivism to that of order, which can be conceived in two different ways: order[41] as κόσμος (spontaneous order) and order as τάξις (constructed order). For many scholars in Continental Europe,[42] to be binding and normative (and not merely descriptive), constitutions are supposed to be 'constructivist', since they are directed at the achievement of an ideal society characterised by those values deemed fundamental. For instance, the concept of constitution (and constitutionalism) inferred from Article 16 of the Declaration of the Rights of Man and of the Citizen[43] is to pursue the division of powers and the protection of rights, strive for change and address the social forces that lead to a common goal.

However, without endorsing this or that reconstruction, Krisch makes his argument by taking into account just one of the possible understandings

[36] Martinico (above n 6) 27 et seq.

[37] L Besselink, 'The Notion and Nature of the European Constitution after the Reform Treaty' (2007) *Working Paper*, <papers.ssrn.com/sol3/papers.cfm?abstract_id=1086189>.

[38] ibid.

[39] Krisch (above n 1).

[40] FA Hayek, *Law, Legislation and Liberty*, vol 1, *Rules and Order* (Abingdon, Routledge, 1973) 5.

[41] '... the situation where one author could argue with regard to a given phenomenon that it was artificial because it was the result of human action, while another might describe the same phenomenon as natural because it was evidently not the result of human design.' ibid, 20.

[42] On the development of legal doctrine in Europe (and beyond) see A von Bogdandy, 'The Past and Promise of Doctrinal Constructivism: A Strategy for Responding to the Challenges Facing Constitutional Scholarship in Europe' (2009) 7 *International Journal of Constitutional Law* 364.

[43] Declaration of the Rights of Man and of the Citizen, Art 16: 'A society in which the observance of the law is not assured, nor the separation of powers defined, has no constitution at all.'

of constitutionalism, by reducing it to its revolutionary version. This is crucial in the sense that many of those (alleged) exclusive features that he seems to attribute to pluralism are actually compatible with the evolutionary strand of constitutionalism. Moreover, pluralism does not present itself as necessarily more open than constitutionalism; here, it is sufficient to recall massive studies that have emphasised how pluralisms are actually closed in their last instance, in the sense that they are characterised by a limited openness, and they are also based on a kind of hidden hierarchy of values, as happens in the case of constitutionalism.[44] This point has been used to criticise Schiff Berman's version of pluralism.[45] This means that they are not exempt from the same criticism.[46]

However, 'while Berman's proposal is still attached to some form of liberal constitutionalism, the case of Nico Krisch's work on pluralism appears as partially different. At a certain level, Krisch's understanding of pluralism is definitely more radical than Berman's. He embraces and supports a normative perspective on systemic pluralism'.[47] Krisch's pluralism does not depart from the other pluralisms in this respect, and what he seems to advocate is just a light type of constitutionalism, which is not so different from what he calls thin constitutionalism. Even pluralisms imply a hierarchy of values and suffer from 'the paradox of drawing the limits',[48] an argument frequently used with regard to toleration.[49] This point has been stressed by Galan and Patterson, according to whom 'Krisch's principles in ordering pluralism, contrary to Krisch's own intention, lead him to a hierarchical position in which the principle of toleration takes precedence over the principle of public autonomy'.[50]

[44] This is also the case of the idea of comprehensive pluralism in Rosenfeld (M Rosenfeld, *Just Interpretations: Law between Ethics and Politics* (Berkeley, University of California Press, 1998). On Rosenfeld, see F Viola, 'La ragionevolezza politica secondo Rawls', in C Vigna (ed), *Etiche e politiche della post modernità* (Milan, Vita e Pensiero, 2003) 163–65 and A Schiavello, 'Interpretazioni corrette? Riflessioni critiche sul pluralismo comprensivo di Michel Rosenfeld' (2001) *Diritto e società* 245.

[45] P Schiff Berman, *Global Legal Pluralism: A Jurisprudence of Law Beyond Borders* (New York, Cambridge University Press, 2012).

[46] M Sung Kuo, 'On the Constitutional Question in Global Governance: Global Administrative Law and the Conflicts-law Approach in Comparison' (2013) 2 *Global Constitutionalism*, 2013, 437, 440 et seq.

[47] M Goldoni, 'The Politics of Global Legal Pluralism' (2014) *Jura Gentium* 104.

[48] 'This paradox is inherent in the idea that toleration is a matter of reciprocity and that therefore those who are in-tolerant need not and cannot be tolerated, an idea we find in most of the classical texts on toleration' F Rainer, 'Toleration' in EN Zalta (ed), *The Stanford Encyclopedia of Philosophy* (summer 2012 edn) <http://plato.stanford.edu/archives/sum2012/entries/toleration/>.

[49] eg J Locke, *A Letter Concerning Toleration* (1689). On this see A Tuckness, 'Rethinking Intolerant Locke' (2002) 46 *American Journal of Political Science* 288.

[50] A Galán and D Patterson, 'The limits of normative legal pluralism: Review of Paul Schiff Berman, Global Legal Pluralism: A Jurisprudence of Law beyond Borders' (2013) 11 *International Journal of Constitutional Law* 783, 797.

More generally, any scholar who is interested in constitutional law or constitutional theory would hardly accept his conception of constitutionalism, recognising his reconstruction as something very far away from the 'conventional definitions'. My intuition is that Krisch's idea of constitutionalism does not correspond with what we constitutional lawyers mean by the same word. This can probably be explained in light of the context in which Krisch's view has developed, by taking into account the origin of the debate at the international level, where constitutionalism has been seen as an antidote to the issue of international fragmentation:[51] something that may create (in the long run) unity, coherence and 'order'.[52]

As Dunoff and Trachtman recalled:

> To the extent that fragmentation arises due to the lack of centralised legislative and adjudicative institutions, constitutionalisation can respond by providing centralised institutions or by specifying a hierarchy among rules or adjudicators. That is, constitutionalisation can be seen as a way of introducing hierarchy and order, or at least a set of coordinating mechanisms, into an otherwise chaotic system marked by proliferating institutions and norms. Hierarchically superior norms and coordinating mechanisms can manage or resolve legal conflicts and thereby produce greater predictability and certainty for actors subject to the rules.[53]

Against this background, 'constitutionalism may be conceived as an autonomous concept of international law rather than a concept derived by analogy from the domestic conception of constitutionalism'.[54]

[51] R Deplano, 'Fragmentation and Constitutionalisation of International Law: A Theoretical Inquiry' (2013) 6 *European Journal of Legal Studies* 67, 69: 'Although there is no universally accepted definition, international legal scholars maintain that fragmentation consists of the development of highly specialised fields of international law.'

[52] J Klabbers, 'Back to Front: Positivism, Constitutionalism, and Accountability', in J d'Aspremont and J Kammerhofer (eds), *International Legal Positivism in a Post-Modern World* (Cambridge, Cambridge University Press, forthcoming): 'Constitutionalization aims to provide an answer to the fragmentation of international law resulting from increased specialization: if trade lawyers only communicate with trade lawyers, and security specialists only with security specialist, then the system requires some glue to hold it together. The putative constitutionalization of international law then provides the glue, suggesting that after all there is some system to what appears to be chaos … the vocabulary of constitutionalization suggests a vision of unity that the earlier international law vocabulary, with its insistence on sovereignty and independence, could never provide.' See also J Klabbers, 'Setting the Scene' in J Klabbers, A Peters and G Ulfstein (eds), *The Constitutionalization of International Law* (Oxford, Oxford University Press, 2009) 1, 18.

[53] JL Dunoff and JP Trachtman, 'A Functional Approach to Global Constitutionalism' in JL Dunoff and JP Trachtman (eds), *Ruling the World? Constitutionalism, International Law, and Global Governance* (Cambridge University Press, 2009) 3, 8. On constitutionalism in international law see M Koskenniemi, 'The Fate of Public International Law: Between Technique and Politics' (2007) 70 *Modern Law Review* 1, 15.

[54] Deplano (above n 51) 68.

The problem is that some scholars in this field have too heavily emphasised only the connection between hierarchy and constitutionalism. Therefore, what Krisch calls constitutionalism does not belong to the realm of constitutional law scholars. As we will see, the point of openness is crucial. Nobody would define constitutionalism as a 'closed phenomenon'; indeed, when looking at many contemporary constitutions, one can easily note that they are open texts in at least two senses, as I am going to argue in the next section. In order to do so I shall focus on openness, understood by Krisch as an essential feature pluralist paradigm. As will be clear, I maintain that openness is actually a pillar of the so-called post-totalitarian constitutionalism. Italian constitutionalism is relevant to detect the main features of post-totalitarian constitutionalism and an evidence of its importance is the interest that the Italian constitutional experience has received from eminent (non-Italian) scholars in this field (among others, Eric Stein and Vereshchetin).

IV. ITALIAN CONSTITUTIONALISM BETWEEN RESISTANCE AND OPENNESS

Openness and resistance are essential keywords to understand the essence of the so-called post-totalitarian constitutionalism. Indeed, according to Carrozza, there are at least three central points in the evolution of Western constitutionalism: the distinction between constituent power and constituted power, the affirmation of the idea of the constitution as 'higher law' and its combination with the discovery of the judicial review of legislation and, finally, the tension between universal aspiration (inherited from the rationalism of the Enlightenment) and national—territorial identity. In light of these three central points, Carrozza introduced what he called the open nature of the Western (especially European) constitutions:

> This new 'openness' in Western, and in particular European constitutionalism, is well described by Zagrebelsky. For him, the mildness and softness of the constitution is explicable in terms of its determination to express the aspiration of living together—to arrange the cohabitation of principles and values, which, if conceived in an absolutist way, would be irreconcilable. In order to lend concreteness to these sentiments, we must reintroduce two distinctions that twentieth-century Western constitutionalism sought to elide: the separation between the law meant as the narrow legal rule 'posited' by the legislator and human rights as inherent in individuals and the separation between the law and justice, the latter conceived of as an aspiration based on the reconciliation of deep principles of political morality.
>
> The 'openness' in post-modern constitutionalism may be intended, according to Spadaro, as precisely the re-awakening and re-sensitisation of the legal/political system to a superior human aspiration to justice, one that challenges the closure of

> a positivist legal/political system in which justice is reduced to formal legality. Not relativism, but reasonableness and proportionality, is the leitmotif of post-modern constitutionalism.[55]

It is possible to find this element in many constitutions born from the Resistance, which were the product of a political compromise among very different democratic forces. These forces had, as their only common point, the rejection of the totalitarian experiences. This explains why these constitutions are inspired by the sincere denial of the features of the previous regime and by the need for an entirely different society.

Some of these constitutions (including the Italian constitution) claimed the need for new societal models and were very rich in declarations of principle, reflecting a wish to produce a break with the past. In some cases, these so-called announced revolutions[56] have remained solely on paper, as one of the most influential members of the Italian Constituent Assembly, Piero Calamandrei, bitterly acknowledged with regard to many provisions of the Italian constitution a few years after it came into force.[57]

This programmatic character implied the need for a real turning point in the ways of conceiving not only the values and premises of the social life within the national boundaries, but frequently, they induced the founding fathers of these constitutions born from the Resistance to hazard the codification of the values that should inspire the life and contribution of their nations to the international arena and community (external openness). The continuity between the domestic and international sides of the societal project, which was designed in these constitutions, explains another type of openness that is crucial in questioning the idea of constitutionalism that Krisch has in mind.

V. THE ITALIAN CONSTITUENT PROCESS AND ITS RELEVANCE

To understand the content of the principle of constitutional openness it is necessary to devote a few words to the origin of the Italian constitutional process. As written above, this experience is emblematic of a broader

[55] Carrozza (above n 3) 182.

[56] Calamandrei wrote about a 'promised revolution' in exchange for the failed revolution that had been sought by the Leftist forces, ie a rupture with the past that had to be even more radical than it was at that time. P Calamandrei, 'Cenni introduttivi sulla Costituente e i suoi lavori' in P Calamandrei and Alessandro Levi (eds), *Commentario sistematico alla Costituzione italiana* (Florence, G Barbèra, 1950), now in P Calamandrei, *Scritti e discorsi politici* (Florence, La Nuova Italia, 1966) vol II, 421.

[57] P Calamandrei, 'La Costituzione e le leggi per attuarla', in AA.VV., *Dieci anni dopo: 1945–1955* (Rome- Bari, Laterza, 1955) now in *Opere giuridiche* (Naples, Morano, 1965) III, 553.

phenomenon and had a certain influence over other constitutional processes that will be recalled in the next section.

Usually, it is said that the Italian constitution is the result of a political compromise ('compromesso') among the three most important forces that acted as the engine of the constituent phase: the liberal, the Christian democratic and the Social-Communist (Left-wing) traditions. They gathered in the National Liberation Committee (CLN), and the 'glue' of this compromise was their shared anti-fascism. The Italian Resistance began after the armistice of Cassibile dated 8 September 1943 (declaring the end of the hostilities between the Italian Kingdom and the Anglo-American Allies), and it ended in the early days of May 1945, a few days after Italy's 'liberation day', dated 25 April 1945. The activity and the personalities of those who worked at the CLN had a fundamental impact on the Italian constituent Assembly.

Indeed, the Italian case is very interesting in studying the constitutional openness that is understandable as a product of that anti-fascism,[58] which had a crucial role in unifying the leading forces of the CLN. The fascist 'parenthesis'[59] resulted in a crisis (from Greek *κρίσις*, judgement, decision, election, choice) in the deepest etymological sense of the word, as it implied an important moment of reflection regarding the very nature of the whole constituent process. Unlike the German case, the Italian constituent experience is less known abroad and, at the same time, it is probably a more genuine case of a constituent phase because of the lesser impact of foreign influences, at least in the writing of the constitution. This does not mean that there was no foreign influence on the Italian constituent process,[60] but scholars have shown that the Italian constituent Assembly was really free to write a new constitution that was an 'autogenous product' of the Assembly:[61]

> On the whole, the influence of foreign models operated through Italian political parties and the personal beliefs and expertise of the members of the Constitutional

[58] M Luciani, 'Antifascismo e nascita della costituzione' (1991) *Politica del diritto* 191. See also G Delledonne, 'La Resistenza in Assemblea costituente e nel testo costituzionale italiano del 1948' (2009) 10 *Historia Constitucional*, <www.seminariomartinezmarina.com/ojs/index.php/historiaconstitucional/article/view/231/204>.

[59] On fascism as a mere 'parenthesis' in Italian history see B Croce, *Per una nuova Italia. Scritti e discorsi (1943–44)* (Naples, Ricciardi, 1944).

[60] See, eg, the activity of the *Postwar planning committee of the interdivisional committee*. See also the document entitled: Italy: Reconstruction of Local Government—views of the interdivisional committee, PWC, 25 September 1944 (RG 59, Box 144) cited by S Volterra, 'La Costituzione italiana e i modelli anglosassoni con particolare riguardo agli Stati Uniti' in U De Siervo (ed), *Scelte della Costituente e cultura giuridica. I: Costituzione italiana e modelli stranieri* (Bologna, Il Mulino, 1980) 117, 224. See also DW Ellwood, *L'alleato nemico. La politica dell'occupazione* (Milan, Feltrinelli, 1977) 263.

[61] F Bruno, 'I giuristi alla Costituente: l'opera di Costantino Mortati' in U De Siervo (ed) *Scelte della Costituente e cultura giuridica. II: Protagonisti e momenti del dibattito costituzionale* (Bologna, Il Mulino, 1980) 59. On the contrary, there was an evident American influence in

> Assembly and did not take the form of a direct foreign imposition of constitutional solutions, as happened to the other defeated States in World War II (the case of Japan is the more evident in this sense, but also the influence of the Allied Powers on the framing of the German fundamental Law of 1949 was far larger than the 'direct' influence on the Italian constitutional Assembly). The attempts to influence the solution of the Italian political crisis at the end of the war (sometimes trying to save the monarchic government) were made (in different directions from the English, the Russian and the American government) in the period between 1943 and 1946. But after the decision of the Italian government to call a referendum on the choice between Monarchy and Republic and the election of the Constitutional Assembly, those move ended. The Treaty of peace of 1947 included some 'general political clauses', according to which Italy was bound to take the necessary measures in order to grant civil rights and fundamental freedoms, such us freedom of expression, of the press, of religion, of political opinions, of assembly in public (art. 15). Italy was also bound to forbid the creation of fascists militias and organisations (art. 17). But the country was let free in the choice of the institutional device through which it could assure the implementation of a liberal democratic order.[62]

Moreover, despite the existence of a Ministry for the Constituent Assembly, the government never submitted a project, or something like that, to the Assembly, but limited itself to some preparatory documents that were important, but not really crucial, to the work of the sub-committees of the Assembly.[63] It is necessary to say something about the origin of the Constituent Assembly. After the liberation of Rome, under the Government of Ivanoe Bonomi, with the Legislative Decree of the Lieutenant of the Realm No 151 of 25 June 1944, it was stated that the choice between a republic and a monarchy had to be made by a Constituent Assembly; also, its task was to give a new constitution to the Italian country. Later, with the Legislative Decree of the Lieutenant of the Realm No 98 of 16 March 1946, the first decree was amended, and it was decided that the question of the form of the state would be left to a popular vote. Finally, the Legislative Decree of the Lieutenant of the Realm No 99 of 16 March 1946 proclaimed that both the referendum and the elections of the Constituent Assembly would take place on 2 June 1946. The Italian People opted for the Republic and elected the Constituent Assembly, which was composed of 556 members.

the following years which generated the beginning of what Elia called the 'conventio ad excludendum', a non-written practice which excluded the Communist party from the government and which made the alternation s in Italy. L Elia, entry 'Governo (forme di)', *Enciclopedia del Diritto* (Milan, Giuffé, 1970) vol XIX, 657.

[62] M Olivetti, 'Foreign influences on the Italian Constitutional System', Paper submitted to the 6th World Congress of the International Association of Constitutional Law, on Constitutionalism; old concepts, new worlds, Santiago do Chile, 12–16 January 2004, for the workshop n. 2, on Foreign Influences on National Constitutions, <www.giurisprudenza.unifg.it> (footnotes omitted).

[63] Bruno, 'I giuristi alla Costituente', above n 61, 60.

A committee of 75 deputies (chosen among the members of the Constituent Assembly and chaired by Meuccio Ruini) had a primary role in the preparation and writing of the constitutional text.[64] This Committee was then divided into three sub-committees: the first was chaired by Umberto Tupini and worked on the 'Rights and Obligations of the Citizens'; the second was chaired by Umberto Terracini and worked on the 'Constitutional Organisation of the State'; finally, the third was chaired by Gustavo Ghidini and worked on the 'Economical and Social Relationships'. There was then another committee (the so-called 'Committee of 18'), which drafted the constitution in accordance with the activity of these three sub-committees. The Italian constitution came into force on 1 January 1948. The quality of the members of the Constituent Assembly was excellent:[65] some of them were mainly technicians (Costantino Mortati, for instance: the best constitutional law scholar in Italian history), some of them were politicians (Palmiro Togliatti, for instance), and some of them had a mixed background (Vittorio Emanuele Orlando, the father of Italian studies in public law, but also a former prime minister and important statesman).

All of these figures, so different in their cultural and political backgrounds, were gathered around the memory of the past, as Calamandrei powerfully recalled:

> If you want to go in pilgrimage to the place where your constitution was born, you should go to the mountains where the resistance fighters were killed, to the prisons where they were jailed, to the fields where they were hanged. Wherever an Italian died trying to win back the freedom and dignity of our nation, there you should go, young Italians, because it was there that your constitution was born.[66]

All of the constitutional provisions that govern the foreign relations of the Italian Republic are the direct offspring of this idea, starting with Article 11, which is devoted to the pacifist principle and states: 'Italy rejects war as an instrument of aggression against the freedom of other peoples and as a means for the settlement of international disputes. Italy agrees, on conditions of equality with other States, to the limitations of sovereignty that may be necessary to a world order ensuring peace and justice among the Nations. Italy shall promote and encourage international organisations furthering such ends.'

[64] On this, see L Elia, 'La commissione dei 75, il dibattito costituzionale e l'elaborazione dello schema di costituzione', in AA.VV. *Il parlamento italiano 1861–1988* (Milan, Nuova Cei, 1989) vol XIV, 128.

[65] E Cheli, 'Il problema storico della Costituente' (1973) *Politica del diritto* 485.

[66] P Calamandrei, 'Discorso sulla Costituzione', speech given at the Salone degli Affreschi della Società Umanitaria (Milano, 26 January 1955) <www.calamandrei-vc.it/web/index.php?option=com_content&task=view&id=233&Itemid=124>.

VI. EXTERNAL OPENNESS

After having recalled the Italian experience it is now possible to extend these considerations to other legal systems. What is the connection between this internationalisation of constitutions and the phenomenon of the Resistance? This internationalisation should be seen as a direct reaction to the legal nationalism that had characterised the totalitarian regimes. This should not be surprising; as Bobbio pointed out in his essays,[67] law and politics can be considered as two sides of the same coin, with politics as the dynamic side of political power. If the prevalent ambit of the policies after the seventeenth century was the nation-state, then the law can be regarded as the main expression of such a political power, and this explains the importance that was given to the Civil or Penal Codes, which were conceived as an important attempt to rationalise and govern the life of polities, hence the many preoccupations of political historians and scholars about the link between codification and absolutism, for example.[68]

As recalled at the beginning of this chapter, by openness, I refer to the constitutionally established friendliness towards legal sources that are, from a formal point of view, external to those governed by the national system, or, in other words, that are not produced by the national actors empowered to produce legal norms according to the constitution. This kind of openness might present different forms. It can be limited to what we call general public law (international customary law) or even extended to international treaties. Within this last group, there are constitutions that present a wider openness with regard to human rights treaties, because of the continuity that exists between their axiological contents and the substance of these treaties. Spain and Portugal, as we will see, are good examples.

This kind of openness, as has been studied by several scholars,[69] may perform a double function of constitutional relevance. On the one hand, it may reinforce the original pact codified in the constitution, that is by providing new instruments to guarantee those rights enshrined in the *Verfassung*. The Dutch case is emblematical from this point of view. There the constitutional reform of 1953 introduced, among other things, Article 94[70] of the

[67] N Bobbio, entry 'Diritto', in N Bobbio, N Matteucci and G Pasquino (eds), *Dizionario della Politca* (Turin, UTET, 1976) 334.

[68] See, eg, G Tarello, *Storia della cultura giuridica moderna. Assolutismo e codificazione del diritto* (Bologna, Il Mulino, 1998).

[69] A Peters, 'Compensatory Constitutionalism: The Function and Potential of Fundamental International Norms and Structures' (2006) 19 *Leiden Journal of International Law* 579.

[70] 'Statutory regulations in force within the Kingdom shall not be applicable if such application is in conflict with provisions of treaties that are binding on all persons or of resolutions by international institutions'. On constitutional openness in the Netherlands see B Oomen, 'Strengthening Constitutional Identity Where There Is None: The Case of the Netherlands' (2016) 77 *Revue interdisciplinaire d'études juridiques* 235; G Betlem and A Nollkaemper, 'Giving Effect to Public International Law and European Community Law before Domestic

Grondwet, which empowers national judges not to apply national law in conflict with international treaties, primarily the ECHR. This is what I mean by providing new instruments to guarantee constitutional rights.

On the other hand, constitutional openness might also perform a transformative function, by giving new blood to the constitutional text (for instance, serving to update the list of rights included in the original text) and by making it more adaptive to the new needs of the society. Again the Dutch example is crucial and the openness of the *Grondwet* has been recalled to justify the unnecessity of new amendments to its first part.[71]

This elasticity of the original text knows some limitations, of course, because many of these constitutions are also characterised by the existence of a group of principles that may not be jeopardised, because their violation would imply the denial of the axiological bases on which their legal orders are founded. At the national level, constitutional law scholars describe this set of principles in different ways, for example, the 'republican form' (*forma repubblicana*[72]) in Italy and the eternity clause (*Ewigkeitsklausel*[73]) in Germany.[74]

This openness is represented by some constitutional provisions that govern not only the effects of external norms in the local territory, but also the national participation in and contribution to the international community. All of these norms are based on the existence of an axiological continuity between the principles and values that govern the life of a given polity within its own boundaries and those that should characterise the international community. In other words, these constitutions have never accepted the limitation of the promotion of their values to the domestic boundaries, and indeed, even when the wording of their provisions refers to 'citizens', their constitutional courts have frequently extended the substance of these norms to non-citizens, at least in the field of fundamental rights.[75] These constitutions seek to govern the activity of domestic actors even beyond the national territory, promoting their values even in the post-national arena. The Italian experience is emblematic from this point of view, but is also part of a broader trend.[76]

Courts. A Comparative Analysis of the Practice of Consistent Interpretation' (2003) 14 *European Journal of International Law* 569.

[71] See Oomen (above n 70) 245 and J Gerards, 'The Irrelevance of the Netherlands Constitution, and the Impossibility of Changing It' (2016) 77 *Revue interdisciplinaire d'études juridiques* 207.

[72] Art 139 of the Italian constitution.

[73] Art 79 para 3 of the Basic Law (Grundgesetz-GG) for the Federal Republic of Germany.

[74] For an overview of these clauses, see F Palermo, *La forma di stato dell'Unione europea. Per una teoria costituzionale dell'integrazione sovranazionale* (Padua, Cedam, 2005).

[75] This is the Italian case—for instance, see decision No 432/2005, <www.cortecostituzionale.it>.

[76] See A Cassese, 'Modern Constitutions and International Law' (1985) *Recueil de Cours* III, 331.

Nowadays, national constitutions do not provide an exhaustive list of fundamental rights as a consequence of that constitutional openness, which, according to Saiz Arnaiz,[77] causes these constitutions to make reference to international and supranational law to ensure the protection of certain constitutional goods. For instance, with regard to the Italian case, it was said that the general clause of protection of fundamental rights that is contained in Article 2 of the constitution is to be considered an 'open' norm.[78] This reading of Article 2 has allowed the Constitutional Court to recognise and guarantee the so-called new rights (the right to know, the right of privacy, environmental rights) and to keep the constitution up to date with respect to the need to protect the 'person' (*principio personalista*). In the 1990s, when commenting upon some of the provisions of the Central and Eastern European constitutions, Eric Stein stressed the existence of a 'paradigm of progressive internationalisation of constitutions'.[79] However, those provisions represented only a fifth stage[80] of this process that was connected, in that case, with a broader phenomenon of mixed or (partially) guided domestic constituent processes due to the influence of the international Community,[81] which was the origin of what Cope now terms 'intermestic constitutionalism'.[82]

The case of the Central and Eastern European constitutions and the cases of the German and Italian constitutions share the same spirit of openness, as recalled, among others, by Cassese and Stein.[83] In this process of

[77] A Saiz Arnaiz, *La apertura constitucional al derecho internacional y europeo de los derechos humanos. El artículo 10.2 de la Constitución Española* (Madrid, CEPC, 1999).

[78] Art 2 of the Italian constitution: 'The Republic recognises and guarantees the inviolable rights of the person, both as an individual and in the social groups where human personality is expressed.'

[79] E Stein, 'International Law in Internal Law: Toward Internationalization of Central-Eastern European Constitutions?' (1994) 88 *American Journal of International Law* 427, 429.

[80] ibid, 429.

[81] A Lollini and F Palermo, 'Comparative Law and the "Proceduralization"' of Constitution-Building Processes' in J Raue and P Sutter (eds), *Facets and Practices of State-building* (Leiden and Boston, MA, Brill/Martinus Nijhoff, 2009) 301.

[82] 'Intermestic constitutionalism demonstrates how international and domestic constitutionalism can exist side-by-side, that is, how a single constitution can be at once transnational and indigenous. More important, intermestic constitutionalism shows that under certain conditions, these dual influences will methodically impact the two main components of constitutions—human rights provisions and structural/institutional framework; transnational forces tend to affect human rights, and indigenous influence tends to dominate structural arrangements. The idea that both international and domestic forces can influence constitutions is hardly new, but the notion that these forces simultaneously impact constitutional components in predictably distinct ways is novel'. KL Cope, 'The Intermestic Constitution: Lessons from the World's Newest Nation' (2013) 53 *Virginia Journal of International Law* 667, 670.

[83] Cassese (above n 76), 351. In the words of Stein: 'Antonio Cassese conjures up another, related correlation between the efforts to establish democracy following the defeat of an authoritarian system in a war and revolution, on the one hand, and what he terms "the opening of state constitutions" to the international community generally and international law in particular, on the other. Writing in 1985, he perceived four historic stages: the first extending from

internationalisation of modern constitutions the Republic of Weimar represented an important starting point. That Weimar constitution originated from the acknowledgment of the atrocities of World War I as can be inferred when looking at its Preamble ('The German people, united in its tribes and inspirited with the will to renew and strengthen its Reich in liberty and justice, to serve peace inward and outward and to promote social progress, has adopted this constitution') and at Article 227 of the Treaty of Versailles, the wording of which spoke of 'a supreme offence against international morality and the sanctity of treaties'.[84]

This combination of factors generated a series of norms aimed at taking the internal and external dimensions together in the constitutional discipline. On the one hand, Article 4 acknowledged that 'the generally recognised rules of international law are valid as binding elements of German Reich law'. Another relevant provision is Article 162, which states that: 'the Reich advocates an international regulation of the rights of the workers, which strives to safeguard a minimum of social rights for humanity's working class'. Provisions such as Article 162 are based on the attempt to create parallelism of values between the domestic and international spheres.

Another important novelty that will be regained, also employed later by the Spanish constitution of 1931, was the progressive involvement of the parliament in foreign affairs.[85] Indeed, the Spanish constitution of 1931 contained

1787 to World War I; the second, from the Weimar Constitution of 1919 to World War II; the third, from the French Constitution of 1946 to the late 1950s; and the fourth starting in the early 1960s. The United States Constitution of 1789, written after a revolutionary war against a monarchy, was the first milestone on this historic continuum … After more than a century, and another war and revolution against a monarchy the short-lived democratic Weimar Constitution of 1919 made 'generally recognised rules of international law' a part of federal law. This formula was extended (after still another war) in the 1949 Basic Law of the Federal Republic of Germany so as to make general international law superior to legislation and directly invocable by individuals … The 1931 Constitution of the democratic, socialist Spanish Republic took the lead by establishing for the first time in history the precedence of treaties over ordinary legislation, enforceable by a Constitutional Court—a solution embraced in substance after almost half a century of war and dictatorship by the new Spanish constitution of 1978. The constitutions of 1946 and 1958 restructuring post-World War II democratic France carried on the idea of treaties' superiority over legislation, subject, however, to the perplexing new requirement of reciprocity—a pattern followed by the Francophone countries of Africa'. Stein (above n 79) 427–29.

[84] The Versailles Treaty, 28 June 1919: Part VII, Art 227, <avalon.law.yale.edu/imt/partvii.asp>.

[85] A Cassese, 'Politica estera e relazioni internazionali nel disegno emerso alla Assemblea Costituente' in U de Siervo (ed), *Scelte della Costituente e cultura giuridica. I: Costituzione italiana e modelli stranieri* (Bologna, Il Mulino, 1980) 505, 519. See Art 35: 'Reichstag establishes a standing committee for foreign affairs, which also meets when Reichstag is not in session, after the term is expired or after Reichstag has been dissolved, until a new Reichstag meets for the first time. Their sessions are not public, unless two thirds of its members vote to hold a public session. Reichstag furthermore establishes a standing committee to safeguard the rights of parliament juxtaposed Reich government, for the time when parliament is not in session [or], after a term has expired or Reichstag has been dis-solved, until a new Reichstag has assembled. These committees have the status of inquiry committees'.

a number of interesting provisions, starting with Article 7 ('The Spanish State shall abide by the universal norms of international law, including them in its positive law'[86]) and, above all Article 65, which considered 'all international conventions ratified by Spain and registered in the League of Nations and in the nature of international law' as 'a constitutive part of Spanish legislation'. This way, the Spanish constitution created a clear obligation for the national legislature to act in compliance with international law and this resulted, as Cassese stressed,[87] in transforming a possible violation of international law into a breach of the constitution (a constitution guaranteed by the establishment of a constitutional court—the 'Tribunal de Garantías Constitucionales'). Finally, another series of provisions accorded an important series of competences to the Spanish parliament in the field of foreign affairs (authorisation of the ratification of international treaties, declaration of war[88]).

Another example of the external openness of modern constitutions is obviously given by the German Basic Law. Its preamble opens by acknowledging the responsibility of the German people 'before God and man' and affirming 'the determination to promote world peace as an equal partner in a united Europe'.[89] Its Article 25 recognises the primacy and precedence of the general rules of international law over the national norms. Also in practice, thanks to techniques like the famous 'völkerrechtsfreundliche Auslegung'[90] the German legal system has shown itself to be very open to the influence of international law.

A third wave of constitutional internationalisation is represented by the Spanish and Portuguese constitutions. These constitutions introduced a fundamental distinction: that between the general category of international treaties and that particular group of international treaties devoted to human rights. As for Portugal, the fundamental provision is Article 16 of the constitution,[91] which recognises that international human rights treaties have a complementary role to the constitution. This provision accords an

[86] Spanish constitution of 1931. An English version is available here: <http://production.clinecenter.illinois.edu/REPOSITORYCACHE/30/Q5yIX5tC8600tRU2W626ZMl50lZBw60L-h1f87D7C8Pw62oP797cB900ax15KOQ4USxKCS3zEFI97LguMwL8S8IIKWOR8nd2cUcu-NyiAvp33_19231.pdf>.

[87] Cassese (above n 76) 510–11.

[88] See Art 77.

[89] German Basic Law, Preamble: <www.btg-bestellservice.de/pdf/80201000.pdf>.

[90] 'According to this technique, any German law should be construed as far as possible in conformity with international law, parallel to the established method of interpretation to comply with EU law ('europarechts konforme Auslegung'). This mode concerns any norm in national law, since any norm must be in conformity with the international law obligations of Germany.' P Dann and M von Engelhardt, 'The Global Administrative Order Through a German Lens: Perception and Influence of Legal Structures of Global Governance in Germany' (2011) 12 *German Law Journal* 1371, 1386.

[91] Art 16 Constitution: '1. The fundamental rights enshrined in this Constitution shall not exclude such other rights as may be laid down by law and in the applicable rules of international law. 2. The provisions of this Constitution and of laws concerning fundamental rights shall be interpreted and construed in accordance with the Universal Declaration of Human Rights.'

interpretative role to the Universal Declaration of Human Rights, seemingly excluding other conventions like the ECHR, but the Portuguese Constitutional Court often used the ECHR as an important auxiliary hermeneutic tool for interpreting the constitution, leaving the matter unresolved.[92]

A similar provision is Article 20, paragraph 1 of the Romanian constitution: 'Constitutional provisions concerning the citizens' rights and liberties shall be interpreted and enforced in conformity with the Universal Declaration of Human Rights, with the covenants and other treaties Romania is a party to.'

Finally, the most important confirmation of human rights treaties' special ranking in Spain is Article 10.2,[93] acknowledging that they provide interpretive guidance in the application of human rights related constitutional clauses (even if the Constitutional Court specified that this does not imply that human rights treaties have a constitutional status[94]).

An example which is particularly interesting in the study of the openness of these constitutions to international human rights treaties is given by the Czech case. Before the Czech Euro amendment, Articles 10 and 87 of the constitution[95] distinguished between international treaties in general and international human rights treaties, giving the latter a super-primary rank and leaving unanswered the question of whether international human rights treaties belonged to the constitutional block. At the same time Article 87, paragraph 1[96] of the constitution empowered the constitutional court to declare the unconstitutionality of laws conflicting with the constitution but also those conflicting with international human rights treaties.

After the Czech Euro amendment,[97] the new Article 10 of the constitution abandoned such a distinction and now grants all international treaties a super-primary but still sub-constitutional rank,[98] at least, from a formal

[92] On Portugal see F Coutinho, 'Report on Portugal', in G Martinico and O Pollicino (eds), *The national judicial treatment of the ECHR and EU Laws: A Comparative Constitutional Perspective* (Groningen, Europa Law Publishing, 2010) 351, 360.

[93] Art 10 Constitution: (2) 'The norms relative to basic rights and liberties which are recognised by the Constitution shall be interpreted in conformity with the Universal Declaration of Human Rights and the international treaties and agreements on those matters ratified by Spain.'

[94] Tribunal Constitucional, Judgment 30/1991, <www.tribunalconstitucional.es>.

[95] Art 10 (previous version) of the Czech constitution: 'Ratified and promulgated international accords on human rights and fundamental freedoms, to which the Czech Republic has committed itself, are immediately binding and are superior to law.'

[96] Art 87, para 1 (previous version) of the Czech constitution: '(1) The Constitutional Court resolves: (a) the nullification of laws or their individual provisions if they are in contradiction with a constitutional law or an international agreement under Article 10 [international human rights treaties].' O Pollicino, *L'allargamento ad est dell'Europa e rapporti tra Corti costituzionali e Corti europee. Verso una teoria generale dell'impatto interordinamentale del diritto sovranazionale?* (Milan, Giuffrè, 2010) 104.

[97] Constitutional Act 395/2001 Coll.

[98] See M Bobek and D Kosař, 'Report on the Czech Republic and Slovakia' in G Martinico and O Pollicino (eds), *The national judicial treatment of the ECHR and EU Laws: A Comparative Constitutional Perspective* (Groningen, Europa Law Publishing, 2010) 133.

point of view. The Czech constitutional court has also adopted a very broad reading of the ECHR and considers it, and other human rights treaties, as different from and superior to the other international treaties.[99]

In fact, the Czech constitutional court has given a very creative reading to new constitutional provisions, *de facto* rewriting them, since it considers itself empowered to review the validity of national legislation in light of the ECHR[100] in spite of the new text of the constitution. In 2002 the Czech constitutional court said that: 'The inadmissibility of changing the substantive requirements of a democratic state based on the rule of law also contains an instruction to the [CCC], that no amendment to the Constitution can be interpreted in such a way that it would result in limiting an already achieved procedural level of protection for fundamental rights and freedoms'.[101] This way, therefore, the constitutional court concluded that 'the international human rights treaties have retained their constitutional status'.[102]

VII. FINAL REMARKS

In this chapter I tried to question the dichotomy pluralism versus constitutionalism as presented by Krisch. In order to do so I demonstrated that openness, described as one of the pillars of the pluralist paradigm, can also be seen as one of the building blocks of the post-World War II constitutionalism. In order to do that I looked at the Italian constitutional experience first, and then I moved on to other relevant legal contexts.

The constitutional openness described by Cassese has produced a turning point, even in the way of conceiving the function of the general principles in these legal orders. If they were seen before as the moment of closure for a legal system (nothing out of the code, no reference to natural law was allowed), today, the principles are perceived as the moment of openness for a legal order that connects internal and international law, favouring the transformation or the updating of the former (within the previously mentioned limits).

The comparative context described in this chapter is open and represents something very far from the idea of constitutionalism that is imagined by Krisch. If this is true, constitutionalism has favoured the emergence of a kind of 'osmotic law'[103] or, as I have tried to explain elsewhere, 'complex'

[99] Judgment of 15 April 2003 (I. ÚS 752/02).

[100] Judgment of the CCC of 30 November 2004, Pl. ÚS 15/04; Judgment of the CCC of 22 March 2005, Pl. ÚS 45/04.

[101] Judgment of the CCC of 25-06-2002, Pl. ÚS 36/01, <http://www.usoud.cz/en>.

[102] Bobek and Kosař (above n 98) 135.

[103] A Ruggeri, 'Dimensione europea della tutela dei diritti fondamentali e tecniche interpretative' (2009) *Federali-smi*, <www.federalismi.it/ApplMostraDoc.cfm?Artid=14806&

(because it is based on a constitutional synallagma[104]). How is this possible, and how is this related to that openness (or opening[105]) described by Carrozza? A possible explanation is offered by the axiological (desired) continuity that exists between the domestic and the international levels, and by the efforts made to construct a better society, even at the international level.

This double orientation (internal and external) of the constitutional project was crystal clear to the members of the Italian constituent Assembly. There are, for instance, at least three reasons for the codification of the pacifist principle in the Italian constitution. The first is connected to political realism: Italy could not be considered a military power, so the constitutionalisation of an imperialistic foreign policy was not an option.[106] The second reason was, in a manner of speaking, ethical, and finds expression in the words used, among others, by Don Luigi Sturzo, who defined war as 'immoral, illegitimate and prohibited'.[107] But the main reason for it was the intent 'to transfer, on the international level, those principles of freedom, equality and substantive respect for the human person that were to be affirmed and implemented in the domestic order.[108]

Here again, the choices made at the Italian constituent Assembly responded to a broader openness that had been experimented with even in other countries.[109] This emphasis on internal-external continuity, and these efforts to project the values of constitutionalism, even towards post-national society, show that constitutionalism has never accepted a conception of itself as a phenomenon that had been limited by national boundaries many years ago, and it offers new grounds to question Krisch's conclusions and does not exclude the suitability of the constitutional paradigm for the new challenges of the global governance.

content=Dimensione+europea+della+tutela+dei+diritti+fondamentali+e+tecniche+interpretative&content_author=Antonio+Ruggeri#.U-yBp-N_s44>.

[104] G Martinico, *The Tangled Complexity of the EU Constitutional Process: The Frustrating Knot of Europe* (Abingdon, Routledge, 2012).

[105] He seems to use these two words in a fungible manner: Carrozza (above n 3) 182.

[106] See P Nenni, *Una battaglia vinta* (Rome, Leonardo, 1946) 104.

[107] L Sturzo, 'La guerra, l'Italia e l'intervistato' in L Sturzo, *Politica di questi anni. 1957–1959* (Bologna, Zanichelli, 1954), 144.

[108] A Cassese (above n 85) 519. The translation is mine.

[109] 'Hence, it is not incidental that far-reaching provisions on the status of international law within national legal systems were introduced in the German Constitutions after World Wars I and II, in the Italian and Japanese Constitutions after the Second World War, and in the Russian Constitution after the end of the "cold war". Article 28(1) of the 1975 Greek Constitution, Article 96 of the 1978 Spanish Constitution, Article 8 of the 1976 Portuguese Constitution and corresponding articles in some other constitutions may also be viewed as a product of the reaction by the legislature and public of these countries to their former totalitarian or authoritarian regimes, which had often defied international obligations and betrayed common human values.' VS Vereshchetin, 'New Constitutions and the Old Problem of the Relationship between International Law and National Law' (1996) 7 *European Journal of International Law* 29, 31.

Part II

Limits to Global Constitutionalism

4

Counter-developments to Global Constitutionalism

KONRAD LACHMAYER

> '… it is not just constitutional ideas that migrate, but it may well be anti-constitutional ideas as well.'
>
> Kim Lane Scheppele[1]

I. THE ROAD TOWARDS CONSTITUTIONAL AUTHORITARIANISM

A. The Hungarian Government's Attack on Academic Freedom

IN 2017, AN amendment to the national higher education law (Act No 204 of 2011),[2] changing the possibilities for 'foreign' (non-EU) universities to operate in Hungary, was drafted by the Orbán government and enacted by the Hungarian parliament. This amendment requires that such universities offer a campus in the country in which they are accredited. As is widely known, the amendment was not designed to address general concerns held by the Hungarian government, but was instead an attack on democratic structures, because the act's primary purpose was to close down the Central European University (CEU). The CEU has a very specific function within the university landscape in Hungary. It is not only an institution of the highest excellence, but also an academic stronghold, which has not shied away from intellectual disputes concerning political (especially authoritarian) developments in Hungary over the last seven years.[3]

[1] KL Scheppele, 'The migration of anti-constitutional ideas: the post-9/11 globalization of public law and the international state of emergency' in S Choudhry (ed), *The Migration of Constitutional Ideas* (New York, CUP, 2006) 347, 373.

[2] See R Uitz, 'The Return of the Sovereign: A Look at the Rule of Law in Hungary—and in Europe', iconnectblog.com/2017/04/the-return-of-the-sovereign-a-look-at-the-rule-of-law-in-hungary-and-in-europe/.

[3] See GA Tóth (ed), *Constitution for a disunited nation: On Hungary's 2011 fundamental law* (Budapest, CEU Press, 2012); R Uitz, 'Can you tell when an illiberal democracy is in

The political and legal developments in Hungary since the election to power of Victor Orbán in 2010 include various attacks against the country's constitutional structure including imposing limitations on the media, making changes to the court system or restricting, opposing and influencing the constitutional court.[4] Opposition to the Hungarian government has been systematically shut down and this applies to civil society[5] as well as universities. During the last year the University of Public Service has been strengthened while all other state universities have been financially starved.[6]

First of all, the attack against the Central European University represents a disproportionate limitation on academic freedom in Hungary. While it is not, as already mentioned, the only negative change to academia in Hungary, it is perhaps the most significant one since it illustrates the decline in compliance with human rights by an illiberal government. Second, however, it is relevant to much more than just a rights perspective; it is also crucial to the maintenance of overall democracy in Hungary. As mentioned, the Hungarian government has been attacking all pillars of democracy in Hungary to create a semi-authoritarian regime, which uses guided democracy as a façade to control governmental power. The destabilisation of democracy has already affected all democratic institutions in the country, and the governmental rejection of democracy is a systematic attempt to destroy them all, one after another.

The Hungarian example is by no means an isolated development, however. On the contrary: after 25 years the rise of global constitutionalism[7] is coming to an end while the counter-developments are gathering momentum. This affects not merely those countries which only started their narratives of constitutional democracy 25 years ago, but also countries with a culture of long-lasting democracies, those formerly understood as strongholds of constitutionalism.

the making? An appeal to comparative constitutional scholarship from Hungary' (2015) 13 *International Journal of Constitutional Law* 279; P Bárd, 'The Hungarian Fundamental Law and related constitutional changes 2010–2013' (2013) *Revue des Affaires Européennes* 457.

[4] M Bánkuti, G Halmai and KL Scheppele, 'From Separation of Power to a Government without Checks: Hungary's Old and New Constitutions' in GA Tóth (ed), *Constitution for a Disunited Nation: On Hungary's 2011 Fundamental Law* (Budapest, CEU Press, 2012) 237, 253–59.

[5] While the parliament was passing the law against CEU (Lex CEU), another bill was drafted to limit foreign funding of NGOs, which is crucial to civil society in Hungary. See R Uitz, 'The Return of the Sovereign: A Look at the Rule of Law in Hungary—and in Europe', iconnectblog.com/2017/04/the-return-of-the-sovereign-a-look-at-the-rule-of-law-in-hungary-and-in-europe/.

[6] See, eg, <http://www.universityworldnews.com/article.php?story=20130220151416428>; B Magyar, *Post-communist Mafia State: The Case of Hungary* (Budapest, CEU Press, 2016) 153.

[7] WC Chen and SC Chu, 'Taking Global Constitutionalism Seriously: A Framework for Discourse' (2016) 11 *National Taiwan University Law Review* 383; DS Law and M Versteeg, 'The Evolution and Ideology of Global Constitutionalism' (2011) 99 *California Law Review* 1163–1257.

This chapter focuses on these counter-developments to global constitutionalism, distinguishing between anti-globalisation developments (II.A) and anti-constitutionalism developments (II.B), but also uncovering the links between the two. The Hungarian example clearly illustrates both elements. The vicious attack on the CEU can be understood as an anti-global and thus nationalistic action on the part of the Hungarian government. Besides these obvious elements, the chapter delves into the anti-constitutionalism approach, as already mentioned above. Both approaches (anti-globalisation/anti-constitutionalism) play an important role and their interrelation ultimately characterises the overall developments which can be observed all around the globe.

Over the centuries, the aim of constitutionalism has been the establishment of constitutional documents, followed by the creation of constitutional institutions and culminating in the spread of constitutional law based on the texts of the constitutional documents and their interpretations by constitutional institutions in the light of constitutionalism.

Nowadays, we are faced with a contrasting movement. Constitutional documents have long been enacted, constitutional institutions are—seemingly firmly—in place and constitutional law as a whole is well-established. What is emerging, however, is not constitutionalism but illiberalism and authoritarianism. These developments show how strongly constitutional law depends on an intact constitutional culture based on constitutionalism. The question still remains, however, how we can fight for constitutionalism if its ideals can no longer be protected by constitutional documents, constitutional institutions and constitutional law.

B. The Migration of Anti-constitutional Ideas

More than 10 years ago, at a time when comparative constitutional law as well as the internationalisation of constitutional law was on the rise, Kim Lane Scheppele identified that the migration of constitutional ideas is not only a positive dynamic, but can also be reversed into negative developments.[8] She focused on certain questions of counter-terrorism, which limited rights protection and circumvented standards of the rule of law.

Scheppele identified how especially international law laid down by the UN Security Council led to new legislation on counter-terrorism around the world, which affected constitutional principles, such as the separation of powers, the rule of law and human rights.[9] She focused on two particular

[8] KL Scheppele, 'The migration of anti-constitutional ideas: the post-9/11 globalization of public law and the international state of emergency' in S Choudhry (ed), *The Migration of Constitutional Ideas* (New York, CUP, 2006) 347–52.

[9] ibid.

phenomena that limited procedural fairness: '(a) the requirement of clarity in the prohibitions of criminal law so that people know precisely which actions would generate criminal penalties'[10] in the context of criminalising terrorism in many countries around the world and '(b) the requirement that individuals be given a hearing and an opportunity to confront the evidence against them before they are deprived of their rights'[11] in the context of freezing assets of suspected terrorists. In her analysis, she concluded that 'many states have stepped outside constitutionalist principles in the name of following a newer, higher law—the new international security law'. But the new international security law had produced a 'state-by-state invocation of emergency powers that tends to limit individual rights and to concentrate powers in the executive'.[12]

Since 9/11, the counter-terrorism measures around the world have already created manifold negative effects on constitutional orders, undermining any number of constitutional principles. These measures include, for example, the imprisonment of individuals without procedure in extraterritorial, secret prisons,[13] the attempt to legitimise torture ('waterboarding'),[14] the extrajudicial killings of individuals by drones without any form of proper judicial proceedings,[15] new forms of mass surveillance and intrusion into the privacy of many,[16] intensified discrimination based on religion,[17] the freezing of bank accounts and other financial assets,[18] the obligations imposed on many professional groups to report any suspicious activity to the police, secret (military) tribunals, etc. Counter-terrorism has since separated from the concept of 'state of emergency'. While the 'state of emergency' argument is still regularly used,[19] the intensity of international terrorism continues to

[10] ibid, 360.

[11] ibid.

[12] ibid, 371.

[13] J Steyn, 'Guantanamo Bay: The Legal Black Hole' (2004) 53 *International and Comparative Law Quarterly* 1.

[14] J Waldron, 'Torture and Positive Law: Jurisprudence for the White House' (2005) 105 *Columbia Law Review* 1681.

[15] D Cole, *The Drone Presidency*, NY Rev Books, 18 August 2016, 19–22; D Cole, 'How We Made Killing Easy' on NYRblog, The New York Review of Books, *NYRblog* (6 February 2013) <http://www.nybooks.com/blogs/nyrblog/2013/feb/06/drones-killing-made-easy>; JL Kleidman, 'The Constitutionality of the Predator Drone Program' (2010) 4 *Vienna Journal on International Constitutional Law* 359.

[16] K Lachmayer and N Witzleb, 'The challenge to privacy from ever increasing state surveillance: A Comparative Perspective' (2014) 37 *University of New South Wales Law Journal* 748; K Lachmayer, 'Rethinking Privacy Beyond Borders' (2015) 20 *Tilburg Law Review* 78.

[17] J Cesari (ed), *Muslims in the West after 9/11: Religion, Politics and Law* (London, Routledge, 2010).

[18] CC Murphy, *EU Counter-terrorism Law: Pre-emption and the Rule of Law* (Modern Studies in European Law) (Oxford, Hart Publishing, 2012) 115–46.

[19] See, eg, in France (<https://www.hrw.org/news/2017/03/13/breaking-frances-addiction-its-state-emergency>).

be very high, and counter-terrorism measures are so well established that the effects on constitutional law are already permanent. This understanding of counter-terrorism has become the end to justify a whole array of anti-constitutional means.

Constitutional and supreme courts are still trying to restrict and abolish attempts to extend counter-terrorism measures,[20] but their powers to do so have always been limited. As a consequence, the damage to the concept of constitutional democracy can no longer be denied and it must be acknowledged that the extension of counter-terrorism measures is a permanent process without any limitations in time.

Ten years on from Scheppele's observations, the world has changed again. A dramatic financial and economic crisis, the tragic developments of the constitutionally driven Arab Spring, the constant increase in climate change, the negative effects of free global trade[21] and overall population growth[22] have led to different forms of migration all around the world. Although not the only reasons, the overall intensity of migration and certain economic decline are crucial factors in the new developments of nationalism, radicalism and illiberalism in Western liberal constitutions, developments which are threatening the very foundations of global constitutionalism. Around the world, the rise of anti-constitutional ideas is affecting ever more countries that are already struggling in their attempts to establish liberal democracies. These dynamics have started a negative spiral of events, reducing the power and effectiveness of constitutional concepts.

History provides ample illustration of the unfortunate results of such developments. The decline of a liberal democracy usually starts with the suppression of certain elements of the system of checks and balances, often including the critical public (especially the media) and independent courts (above all the constitutional or supreme courts); it creates new ways of keeping power for governments (for example by changing electoral law) and fosters an ever-increasing lack of transparency. Uncontrolled governmental activities lead to a significant rise in corruption and the suppression of minorities. The increasing surveillance of the population is often accompanied by the establishment of the idea of an enemy. The power of the police,

[20] F Fabbrini, 'The Role of the Judiciary in Times of Emergency: Judicial Review of Counter-Terrorism Measures in the United States Supreme Court and the European Court of Justice' (2009) 28 *Yearbook of European Law* 664; K Lachmayer, 'Constitutional and Anti-Constitutional Responses to Terrorism: The Difficulty of Removing Exclusions from Constitutional Law' (2010) 2 *Hong Kong Law Review* 5–18.

[21] U Mattei and L Nader, *Plunder: When the Rule of Law is Illegal* (Malden, Mass, Blackwell, 2008).

[22] B Opeskin and E Nwauche, 'Constitutions, populations and demographic change' in M Tushnet, T Fleiner and C Saunders (eds), *Routledge Handbook of Constitutional Law* (Hoboken, Taylor and Francis, 2013) 455–68.

the military and other similar bodies is steadily increased. Finally, a culture of violence, especially state violence, emerges. When violence becomes the preferred problem-solving strategy, and fear the steering instrument, internal suppression of the people paves the way for new wars externally.

C. Constitutional Authoritarianism, not Authoritarian Constitutionalism

In these times of re-emerging illiberalism, populism and authoritarianism, there is an increasing need for us to attempt to find new academic concepts to describe the phenomena that are arising. These efforts can also help to redefine existing forms of constitutional developments. One increasingly common term used is authoritarian constitutionalism,[23] which seems to fit into the debates of the last decades like global constitutionalism or international constitutionalism and appears to describe new developments in constitutionalism.

The use of the term authoritarian constitutionalism in an academic or public debate is, however, misleading, conceptually wrong and politically dangerous. It is therefore necessary to respond to an attempt to conceptualise authoritarian constitutionalism, as suggested by Roberto Niembro Ortega.[24] Niembro defines authoritarian constitutionalism as 'a concept that refers to a very sophisticated way in which ruling elites with an authoritarian mentality exercise power in not fully democratic states. In this case, the regime's liberal democratic constitution, instead of limiting the power of the state and empowering those who would otherwise be powerless, is used for practical and authoritarian ideological functions.'

Although Niembro concedes that there is a contradiction contained within the concept ('At first glance, authoritarian constitutionalism appears absurd and nonsensical'), he justifies the concept as 'a perplexing category, but not absurd', saying that it 'emphasises the tension between the exercise of power within ill-defined limits, lack of accountability, and how the ruling elite executes and masks its violence under the forms of the constitution, and the

[23] M Tushnet, 'Authoritarian Constitutionalism' in T Ginsburg and A Simpser (eds), *Constitutions in Authoritarian Regimes* (New York, Cambridge University Press, 2013) 36–50; see also T Isiksel, 'Between text and context: Turkey's tradition of authoritarian constitutionalism' (2013) 11 *International Journal of Constitutional Law* 702; A Somek, 'Authoritarian Constitutionalism: Austrian Constitutional Doctrine 1933 to 1938 and its Legacy' in M Stolleis, NS Ghaleigh and C Joerges (eds), *Darker Legacies of Law in Europe: The Shadow of National Socialism and Fascism over Europe and its Legal Traditions* (Oxford, Hart Publishing, 2003) 361.

[24] See R Niembro, Conceptualizing authoritarian constitutionalism. A Latin American view, *Völkerrechtsblog*, 17 July 2017, doi: 10.17176/20170717-082012, see R Niembro, 'Conceptualizing authoritarian constitutionalism' (2016) 49 *Verfassung und Recht in Übersee* 2016, 339–67.

idea of constitutionalism'. He ultimately wants to establish this concept 'not to hide or justify these authoritarian functions', but to use it as 'a tool that helps us understand, uncover, and critique those functions. In this sense, authoritarian constitutionalism is normatively attractive as a critical tool'.

Niembro is not disputing the classic concept of constitutionalism, which serves the ideas and ideals of a liberal democracy, the rule of law and the protection of human rights. Constitutionalism as a concept is therefore a liberal ideology, a political programme and a normative concept.[25] Authoritarianism is very much the opposite of the concept of constitutionalism, arguing in favour of illiberalism, limiting democracy, extending the power of the government, rule by law and restricting the rights of individuals.

Niembro develops a concept of authoritarian constitutionalism that primarily describes how authoritarianism is spreading in constitutional legal systems.[26] Upon close inspection of his argument, namely that he wants to conceptualise these developments, it becomes apparent that these developments do not fit into the normative concept of constitutionalism. On the contrary, these tendencies oppose the very ideas of constitutionalism. It is not sufficient to point out paradoxes to overcome the contradictory nature of the two normative concepts.

Niembro does not distinguish between the different layers. Constitutionalism is a normative concept which summarises the core ideas of a liberal democracy, while the developments which can be summed up as authoritarian constitutionalism are factual ways of dealing with constitutional law in (semi-)authoritarian regimes. When it comes to conceptualising these developments, it becomes clear that the concept is not one of authoritarian constitutionalism (which would mean constitutionalism no longer taking itself seriously), but much rather of constitutional authoritarianism. Constitutional authoritarianism is a conceptual category of authoritarianism which uses constitutional law (not the normative concept of constitutionalism) to give governments political stability and which misuses and distorts certain constitutional institutions (without giving them full powers). It creates the semblance of constitutionalism, while undermining the concept.

It is important to stress that constitutional authoritarianism and authoritarian constitutionalism are not at all similar. While the first reveals an authoritarian government's ways of using constitutional law for its own purposes, the latter is a contradiction of the concept.

It should also be pointed out that, in liberal democracies, the ideas of constitutionalism are never realised 100 per cent. However, acting in accordance with the values of constitutionalism is not only mentioned in

[25] ibid, 342–47.
[26] ibid, 347–61.

the constitutions of liberal democracies, but is also a leading principle for the overall legal and political culture. Although politicians, groups and individuals might try to change the overall setting, the conceptual perspective is clear. Developments of a constitutionally authoritarian nature are never geared towards the ideals of constitutionalism. On the contrary, they stabilise certain authoritarian approaches.

It is also necessary to distinguish between authoritarian constitutions and authoritarian constitutionalism. While concrete constitutions can neglect the ideas of constitutionalism and include authoritarian provisions, interpretations or institutions, this does not mean that the normative concept of constitutionalism is realised by these authoritarian constitutions. Finally, authoritarian regimes might be masked by an uncontroversial constitutional text, which resembles those of liberal democracies, but has no relevance at all to the legal culture of the country.

Obviously, a concrete constitutional system or the different actors in a constitutional system can give rise to different normative concepts when it comes to different constitutional questions. Certain legal systems might promote the rule of law (for example, independent courts), but still not guarantee democratic elections or civil participation. It is, however, still important to distinguish the different developments in any particular legal system from the conceptual level. Thus, a constitutional system can head in different conceptual directions at the same time. Niembro suggests that his concept serves a critical function, but the important goal of critical analysis can be realised much better by not using the term 'authoritarian constitutionalism'.[27] A critical constitutional theory fits perfectly into the concept of traditional constitutionalism and can show how elites hold and use authoritarian practices.

It should have become clear that all developments that are circumscribed by the phenomena of authoritarian constitutionalism (examples from Niembro: ill-defined limits, lack of accountability, execution and concealment of violence by the ruling elite) belong to the conceptual category of 'authoritarianism' and not to the category of 'constitutionalism'. Insofar as constitutional law is used to pursue these authoritarian ideas, it is plausible to use the term constitutional authoritarianism.

But why is it so necessary to distinguish between authoritarian constitutionalism and constitutional authoritarianism? Besides the importance of terminological clarity in a constitutional discourse, I have already attempted to illustrate why the idea of authoritarian constitutionalism is conceptually wrong. 'Authoritarian' is not a characteristic of constitutionalism. Constitutionalism is also not a characteristic of authoritarianism, but authoritarianism can be constitutional, in the sense that it applies the

[27] ibid, 339–67.

strategy of (mis-)using constitutional law to pursue authoritarian ideas. Although authoritarian developments in Eastern Europe cannot be compared to the constitutional dilemmas faced for decades by states in Latin America,[28] this does not change the conceptual problem of authoritarian constitutionalism.

A concept of authoritarian constitutionalism is also misleading, because it creates the possibility for constitutionalism to be understood as authoritarian. Thus, the term not only fails to help clarify current developments, but unfortunately also confuses the constitutional discourse, both in academia and in the public domain. It is at this point that the term 'authoritarian constitutionalism' becomes politically dangerous. It enables authoritarian governments to claim that their approach of authoritarian constitutionalism is at least an approach of constitutionalism. This issue has become even more important, because nowadays terminology and concepts are rhetorically used to refer to the opposite of their real meanings (in a twenty-first century version of Orwell's Newspeak[29]).

II. THE THREATS TO GLOBAL CONSTITUTIONALISM

A. Anti-global Constitutionalism

The rise of global constitutionalism is the dominant narrative of the last 25 years in comparative constitutional law. Recent years, however, have given reason to believe that this success story is coming to an end before fulfilling its mission. Although processes of constitutionalisation are still progressing in certain parts of the world,[30] new nationalistic concepts are seeping more and more into the political mainstream. Even countries with a long and successful history of supporting global constitutionalism are now finding themselves struggling with the ideas of constitutionalism in their territory.

The developing theories of anti-global constitutionalism are criticising the globalisation of constitutional ideas and topics and the politics of nationalism are re-emerging after lying dormant for decades. The developments of EU constitutionalism, on the rise in the 1990s, reached their peak with the debate about a European constitution at the beginning of the new millennium.[31] The failure of the Constitutional Treaty, the dynamics of the

[28] See R Gargarella, *Latin American constitutionalism, 1810–2010: The engine room of the constitution* (Oxford, Oxford University Press, 2013).

[29] G Orwell, *Nineteen eighty-four* (London, Penguin, 2008).

[30] Such as—until recently—Myanmar; see M Crouch and L Tim (eds), *Law, Society and Transition in Myanmar* (Oxford, Hart Publishing, 2017).

[31] R Schütze, *European Constitutional Law* (Cambridge, Cambridge University Press, 2012) 37–44.

enlargement in Eastern Europe, the economic crisis and the refugee influx of recent years all led to new forms of nationalism, which can be observed in many European countries ranging from France to Hungary, from Poland to Austria.[32]

These developments have found their culmination in the Brexit, the biggest political earthquake in the European process of constitutionalisation so far, but definitely not the last. The concept of stopping the development of global constitutionalism by opposing legal globalisation is not limited to the European Union, but can be observed in many ways. The 2016 US presidential election also illustrates how new forms of nationalism may emerge.

The traditional understanding of the methodology of comparative constitutional law as prominently described by Mark Tushnet[33] mirrors the range of positions concerning global constitutionalism. The binary code applied in comparative (constitutional) law refers to similarities and differences.[34] Four positions can be distinguished on the line between the highest similarity and highest difference: universalism, functionalism, contextualism and expressivism.[35]

The strongest position on similarity is universalism, which claims that 'constitutionalism itself entails everywhere some fundamental principles'.[36] If one applies this methodological universalism to global constitutionalism, it refers to a position in which global constitutionalism is heading towards one global constitution to unify the different national constitutions on a global level. In this context, one might argue—like Bardo Fassbender[37]—that the UN Charter could serve as a constitution for the international community. A unified global constitution creates the strongest form of global constitutionalism.

The most common methodological approach in comparative (constitutional) law refers to functionalism. Although the understandings of functionalism can be manifold,[38] we will stick to Tushnet's understanding in the context of constitutional law. In his words, functionalism 'tries to identify things that happen in every constitutional system that is the object

[32] J-W Müller, *What Is Populism?* (Philadelphia, University of Pennsylvania Press, 2016).

[33] M Tushnet, *Weak Courts, Strong Rights: Judicial Review and Social Welfare Rights in Comparative Constitutional Law* (Princeton, Princeton University Press, 2008) 5–15.

[34] G Dannemann, 'Comparative Law: Study of Similarities or Differences?' in M Reimann and R Zimmermann (eds), *The Oxford Handbook of Comparative Law: Oxford Handbooks in Law* (Oxford, Oxford University Press, 2008) 383–419; M Siems, *Comparative Law* (The law in context series) (Cambridge, Cambridge University Press, 2014) 302.

[35] M Tushnet, above n 33, 5.

[36] ibid.

[37] B Fassbender, 'The United Nations Charter as Constitution of the International Community' (1998) 36 *Columbia Journal of Transnational Law* 531–619.

[38] See R Michaels, 'The Functional Method of Comparative Law' in Mathias Reimann and Reinhard Zimmermann (eds), *The Oxford Handbook of Comparative Law: Oxford Handbooks in Law* (Oxford, Oxford University Press, 2008) 339–82.

of study'; 'Functionalists believe that examining the different ways in which democratic nations organise [themselves] can help us determine which are better and which are worse processes'.[39] If we apply this perspective of similarities to global constitutionalism, it creates a unifying and harmonising process of constitutional values around the world. It reflects how global constitutionalism was applied over the last 25 years by implementing global values of constitutionalism in constitution-making processes. The migration of constitutional ideas[40] led to the spread of constitutional values around the world by creating common standards of (global) constitutionalism on a national level. In this sense, global constitutionalism does not create a unified global constitution, but fosters the unification of global values, ideas and standards of constitutionalism.

The traditional methodology of functionalism is confronted with the critique of the third method of contextualism, which 'emphasises the fact that constitutional law is deeply embedded in the institutional, doctrinal, social, and cultural contexts of each nation, and that we are likely to go wrong if we try to think about any specific doctrine or institution without appreciating the way it is tightly linked to all the contexts within which it exists.'[41] If we transfer this concept to global constitutionalism, the critique of the harmonising project furthered by global constitutionalism becomes dominant. Global constitutionalism can create a Western, US-European perspective of constitutional values, which does not consider other approaches to constitutionalism that still adheres to the constitutional values of democracy, rule of law and human rights, but with different emphases.[42] An example might be the role of social rights,[43] minority rights or group rights as well as the participation of indigenous groups in legislation or the consideration of legal pluralism[44] in a rule-of-law-based constitutional system. The differences between the various constitutional orders still serve the idea of constitutionalism, which must not create neo-imperialistic effects in global constitutionalism. Contextualism addresses the plurality to make constitutionalism work in different cultures and societies.

The fourth and final method in Tushnet's overview refers to expressivism. 'Expressivism suggests that a nation has a (single) self-understanding that

[39] M Tushnet, above n 33, 8.

[40] S Choudhry, 'Migration as a new metaphor in comparative constitutional law' in S Choudhry (ed), *The Migration of Constitutional Ideas* (Cambridge, Cambridge University Press, 2006) 1–35.

[41] ibid, 10.

[42] See, eg, Asian constitutionalism or constitutionalism in Latin America.

[43] X Contiades and A Fotiadou, 'Social rights in the age of proportionality: Global economic crisis and constitutional litigation' (2012) 10 *International Journal of Constitutional Law* 660.

[44] See P Schiff Berman, *Global Legal Pluralism: A Jurisprudence of Law beyond Borders*, 1st paperback edn (Cambridge, Cambridge University Press, 2013).

its constitution expresses.'[45] 'An expressivist approach to comparative constitutional law would contrast the self-understandings found in the constitutional documents of different nations.'[46] Applying expressivism to global constitutionalism means to give up the global element in constitutionalism. Constitutionalism can then only be understood as a national agenda, which means that only a nation state within its own tradition can create constitutionalism. The expressivist version of global constitutionalism thus creates a nationalistic perspective, because it neglects the inherent transnational influence of constitutionalism.[47] The establishment, application and development of constitutionalism was and is, however, a transnational agenda, which includes different perspectives on constitutional values. In this sense, constitutional differences are not used—as, for example, in a contextualist approach—to make constitutionalism more accurate or more flexible, but rather to create a sense of national uniqueness, which excludes constitutionalism's inherent openness to transnational influences.

This overview enables us to better understand the developments of anti-global constitutionalism, which follow in the tradition of the expressivist perspective. The examples which can be cited in this context are Brexit and the developments in US politics brought on by the new US government. In both cases, it is possible to observe the different ways in which global constitutionalism is coming under pressure, which will ultimately lead to severe limitations and its destruction. At the same time, new threats are evolving, which are not limited to the transnational, international or global dimensions of constitutionalism, but affect constitutionalism itself.

Constitutional patriotism[48] has to be distinguished from constitutional nationalism. While constitutional patriotism focuses on constitutional values, which together create the identity of the state, constitutional nationalism focuses on nationalistic values, which are to be represented by the constitution. The Orbánian constitution from 2011 does not violate constitutional values in a broader sense,[49] but creates a nationalistic basis within constitutional law.

[45] M Tushnet, above n 33, 14.

[46] ibid, 12.

[47] See with regard to the different approaches to the transnational between engagement and resistance V Jackson, *Constitutional Engagement in a Transnational Era* (New York, Oxford University Press, 2010).

[48] J-W Müller, *Constitutional Patriotism* (Princeton, Princeton University Press, 2009).

[49] See A Jakab and P Sonnevend, 'Kontinuität mit Mängeln: Das neue ungarische Grundgesetz' (2012) 72 *ZaöRV* 79, but if looking at the details one can observe that there have already been anti-constitutionalist elements from the very beginning; see eg M Bánkuti, G Halmai and KL Scheppele, 'From Separation of Power to a Government without Checks: Hungary's Old and New Constitutions' in GA Tóth (ed), *Constitution for a Disunited Nation: On Hungary's 2011 Fundamental Law* (Budapest, CEU Press, 2012) 259–67; J McBride, 'Trees in the Wood: The Fundamental Law and the European Court of Human Rights' in GA Tóth (ed), *Constitution for a Disunited Nation: On Hungary's 2011 Fundamental Law* (Budapest, CEU Press, 2012) 359–78.

A nationalistic perspective challenges the transnational and pluralistic elements of constitutional law. To begin with, it is important to focus on the fact that such kinds of domestic constitutions exclude transnational and international influences. The focus on domestic constitutions, however, often creates the foundations for a re-emerging nationalistic approach with regard to foreign nationals. While at first only the underprivileged (migrants, workers, etc) might be affected, other measures (visa restrictions, further requirements for tourists) are then taken. Limiting the rights of foreigners leads to increasing discrimination against non-citizens and this usually affects the rule of law, especially the element of effective legal protection.[50] These developments of abolishing constitutional values by shutting out the international dimension of constitutional law can also be observed from a democratic perspective. Foreign sponsorship of, for example, NGOs or religious groups is limited, the rights of foreigners or citizens to engage in international or foreign political action are restricted and, in the name of militant democracy, further steps are often taken.

All of these developments have to be viewed within the context of the overall picture concerning counter-terrorism measures and the establishment of a surveillance society and Orwellian police state.[51] Big sections of societies find themselves confronted with an increasingly extensive surveillance of their private lives; terrorist suspects (not convicted murderers) are not only monitored but also detained, interrogated and threatened. The nationalistic turn in constitutionalism takes the concept perilously close to the limits of constitutionalism and creates the risk of authoritarian elements taking over in formerly constitutional systems. While at first a nationalistic approach will mostly threaten and discriminate against foreigners, further measures will invariably also affect citizens, especially activists or unwanted political groups or individuals.

The two examples which shall be mentioned here are again Brexit and the developments in the United States.

The withdrawal of the United Kingdom from the European Union followed a deeply nationalistic agenda. The influx of foreign workers (especially) from Eastern Europe, a one-sided portrait of the EU in the media and other factors combined to create a negative and nationalistic political

[50] See as a comparative analysis K Lachmayer and Z Szente (eds), *The Principle of Effective Legal Protection in Administrative Law* (Aldershot, Ashgate Publishing, 2016).

[51] D Cole, F Fabbrini and S Schulhofer (eds), *Surveillance, Privacy and Trans-Atlantic Relations* (London, Bloomsbury Publishing, 2017); F Davis, N McGarrity and G Williams, *Surveillance, Counter-Terrorism and Comparative Constitutionalism* (Hoboken, Taylor and Francis, 2014).

atmosphere, which led to the Brexit vote.[52] The most interesting aspect from a constitutional perspective relates to critical attitudes towards the European influence on British (constitutional) law. While the UK parliament has, in recent times, further constitutionalised the British system in keeping with the concept of constitutionalism, for example by creating a Supreme Court,[53] the recently displayed nationalistic tendencies to create its own Charter of Human Rights can be seen as a sharp shift of direction. These developments are not limited to the EU, but also concern the UK as a member of the Council of Europe and as a party to the ECHR.[54] The crucial questions of Brexit negotiations concern British treatment of EU citizens in the UK and the situation of UK citizens in the European Union.[55] As mentioned above, the nationalistic shift carries the risk that foreigners will be discriminated against and that all kinds of foreign 'influences' will be rejected.

Similarly, the victory of Donald Trump in the 2016 United States presidential election was made possible by nationalistic tendencies and the deployment of a nationalistic agenda ('America first').[56] While the US constitution—for historical reasons—has always been focused on a national agenda, the newly-elected US president and his government attempted to restrict foreigners' rights from the very beginning. The travel restrictions imposed have so far not been successful because of the resilience of the US courts.[57] The pressure on migrants was increased, however, and the overall political and social climate shifted to one involving more open discrimination.[58]

It is significant that, besides this anti-global approach, it is already possible to identify anti-constitutional elements in the Trump administration. The president's ever-increasing war on the media[59] has affected the US democratic system from the very beginning. Although the media still proves resilient, the president is reducing the possibilities to obtain information and to review or criticise the government's actions. This trend towards opacity

[52] K Armstrong, *Brexit Time: Leaving the EU—Why, How and When?* (Cambridge, Cambridge University Press, 2017) 33–35.

[53] P Leyland, *The Constitution of the United Kingdom: A Contextual Analysis* (Constitutional systems of the world, 2nd edn) (Oxford, Hart Publishing, 2012) 202–04.

[54] See, eg, <http://www.independent.co.uk/news/uk/politics/theresa-may-campaign-leave-european-convention-on-human-rights-2020-general-election-brexit-a7499951.html>.

[55] See, eg, <https://www.theguardian.com/politics/2017/aug/17/eu-citizens-no-visas-visit-uk-after-brexit>.

[56] See, eg, <https://www.nytimes.com/2016/03/27/us/politics/donald-trump-foreign-policy.html>.

[57] See D Cole, 'We'll See You in Court, 2.0: Once a Muslim Ban, Still a Muslim Ban', <https://www.aclu.org/blog/immigrants-rights/well-see-you-court-20-once-muslim-ban-still-muslim-ban>.

[58] <https://www.nytimes.com/2017/08/15/us/politics/trump-press-conference-charlottesville.html>.

[59] <https://www.nytimes.com/2017/07/01/us/politics/trump-tweets-stoke-voter-fraud-claim-and-attack-news-media.html>.

and the abolishment of political dialogue have reduced the potential for the necessary public exchange of ideas. The president is also putting pressure on the judicial system,[60] which is a further aspect of a classic authoritarian approach. This will be discussed in the next section.

In conclusion, the anti-global approach creates a dangerous situation from the perspective of constitutionalism. The risk that a nationalistic shift in a democratic society will affect constitutional values is very high. Constitutionalism was developed as a transnational agenda and represents not only the idea of the equality of citizens but also the plurality of humans. An inward-looking concept of constitutionalism carries a high risk of foreigners being excluded from participation, discriminated against and having their rights restricted. The more a state distinguishes between different social groups and creates second-class human beings, the more the values of constitutionalism are under threat. These nationalistic, anti-pluralistic developments will also lead to a society which itself reduces the relevance of constitutionalism.

B. Global Anti-constitutionalism

Globalisation in the context of constitutional law can not only serve to support ideas of constitutionalism, but can also spread ideas opposing the values of constitutionalism. As described above, Scheppele coined the phrase 'migration of anti-constitutional ideas' in the context of the global war on terror by Western nations. A global legal order led to the rapid migration of anti-constitutional ideas.[61]

It is important to understand that the post-9/11 anti-constitutionalism approaches are the starting point of the developments on which we are focusing today. Counter-terrorism after 9/11 legitimised, in international fora as well as in well-established liberal democracies, significant exemptions from constitutionalism,[62] causing lasting change to the constitutional world. Although the measures first taken appeared to be limited in time, they were extended year after year, and although supreme and constitutional courts have set limits and restrictions to governmental actions, the legislators have since continued to expand the possibilities of surveillance and other interference with human rights. The concept of counter-terrorism

[60] <https://www.nytimes.com/2017/02/08/us/politics/donald-trump-immigration-ban.html>.

[61] KL Scheppele, 'The migration of anti-constitutional ideas: the post-9/11 globalization of public law and the international state of emergency', in S Choudhry (ed), *The Migration of Constitutional Ideas* (New York, CUP, 2006) 347.

[62] See K Roach, *The 9/11 Effect: Comparative Counter-terrorism* (New York, Cambridge University Press, 2011).

has been functioning as a sort of legal vacuum in which constitutionalism applies only to a limited extent. The spreading of these counter-terrorism measures in a global, increasingly intensifying and relevant development can in itself be understood as a global anti-constitutionalism development.

While Scheppele focused on the context of counter-terrorism measures, the overall situation in the last 10 years has created even greater challenges to constitutionalism on a global level. Scheppele illustrated the role of international law in the spread of anti-constitutional ideas in the context of terrorism. The new forms of authoritarianism, however, are much rather a transnational than a national phenomenon, and are at least partly opposed by international law and international organisations.[63] The spread of anti-constitutional ideas is now primarily a problem of transnational migration and expansion from one country to another.

The rise of new forms of authoritarian constitutions, illiberal democracies and rule-by-law states shows that the very core of constitutionalism is under attack. Adopting a free market approach and global economic strategies does not prevent countries like Russia or Turkey from limiting, violating, reducing and mutilating the values and principles of constitutionalism step by step. New hybrid and distorted forms of constitutions are on the rise, which do not pursue ideas of constitutionalism, but rather of authoritarianism. Anti-constitutionalism creates an authoritarian approach to constitutional law, which limits democracy, undermines the rule of law and deprives individuals of the possibility to exercise their human rights. A traditional method of limiting democracy is the attempt to manipulate elections.

The process of changing constitutional law from a constitutionalism-based system towards an authoritarian system is a long (taking at least several years) and in many countries still ongoing development, which follows certain paths to distort the foundations of constitutionalism. The authoritarian shift in legal systems which are based on constitutionalism is a steady process of undermining and destruction which threatens all values of constitutionalism, including democracy, rule of law and human rights. All elements are dismantled and put together again in an authoritarian fashion.

An important feature of these developments is to stick to constitutional terminology instead of concepts of constitutionalism and operate within a superficial concept, used to create the impression that constitutionalism is still thriving. Thus, while the excavated façades of constitutionalism can still be seen standing in the Potemkin village of constitutional law, the authoritarian regime takes over and completes the transition by the elimination of the remnants of constitutionalism.

[63] For example, by the Venice Commission in a European context.

The processes of changing the Turkish political system can be used to demonstrate the ambivalence of constitutionalism.[64] Twenty years ago, the power of the Turkish military within the constitutional order was an undemocratic element in a system which did, however, provide a semi-constitutional situation including democratic elements. The extension of democracy, the reduction of military power and the granting of religious rights, however, provided more and more scope for the AKP to use democratic and rights-based privileges to limit constitutionalism.[65] The balancing act of simultaneously enabling constitutionalism and protecting it against attempts to abolish it is a difficult one and the Turkish system did not succeed in protecting constitutionalism. The attacks on Kurdish opposition and limitations imposed upon other opposition parties, as well as the destruction of public media, clearly display authoritarian and anti-democratic tendencies.[66] These developments also include the exertion of influence over the educational system and universities.[67] The attacks on the rule of law included the destruction of the independence of the judiciary (even before the attempted coup d'état) and affected the police as well as the judicial body.[68] Within these developments, human rights are limited systematically. The Gezi park demonstrations might serve as just one prominent example and can only symbolise the overall growing disregard for human rights.[69] The coup d'état attempt finally created the necessary conditions for further changes to the Turkish constitution. Nationalism was an important element in the political strategy to guarantee democratic majorities to remodel the state. Thus, nowadays, Turkey has a constitution in place and many constitutional institutions, which have, however, been distorted and contain only partial remnants of a liberal democracy.

The Hungarian elections of 2010 were the start of the authoritarian shift subsequently taken by the newly elected Hungarian government.[70] A new Hungarian constitution (Basic Law) was enacted in 2011, which integrated nationalistic rhetoric but was fundamentally (with the exception

[64] See T Isiksel, 'Between text and context: Turkey's tradition of authoritarian constitutionalism' (2013) 11 *International Journal of Constitutional Law* 702.

[65] A Acar, 'De-constitutionalism in Turkey?', *International Journal of Constitutional Law* Blog, 19 May 2016, at <http://www.iconnectblog.com/2016/05/deconstitutionalism-in-Turkey>.

[66] <https://www.theguardian.com/world/2016/nov/04/turkey-arrests-pro-kurdish-party-leaders-mps>.

[67] <https://www.nytimes.com/2017/04/13/magazine/inside-turkeys-purge.html>.

[68] <https://www.economist.com/news/europe/21722200-president-erdogans-drive-power-includes-putting-judges-under-his-thumb-turkeys-purges-are>.

[69] <https://www.amnesty.org/en/documents/EUR44/022/2013/en/>.

[70] M Bánkuti, G Halmai and KL Scheppele, 'From Separation of Power to a Government without Checks: Hungary's Old and New Constitutions' in GA Tóth (ed), *Constitution for a*

of a few particulars) in accordance with the European constitutional texts.[71] However, constitutionalism and even constitutional law cannot be understood by a written constitutional text alone. Even before the new constitution was enacted, the government started to limit the Constitutional Court in its powers to review. Another step taken concerned the Hungarian media, which was subjected to new and stricter governmental controls. The judiciary was also not spared and new organisational and institutional concepts led to a stronger influence of the government over the judiciary. Over the next few years, these developments were expanded as election laws were amended[72] and the last stronghold of constitutionalism, the Constitutional Court, again came under attack. The number of members of its judicial body was increased to create an opportunity for more governmental influence while constitutional amendments ensured that the judgments of the Constitutional Court could be obstructed.[73] An analysis of the human rights situation (for example, religious rights and the treatment of refugees) clearly showed that the importance of the concept of rights protection was dramatically decreasing. Unprofessional forms of direct democracy were and still are being used to legitimise governmental action. Theoretically, people still have the possibility to vote out the government at the next election but public debate is already strongly influenced by the government and the state of democratic opposition parties is poor.[74] But even if, in theory, a change of government is still possible in today's Hungary, the damage that Hungarian constitutionalism has suffered is severe, affects all existing law and established institutions and cannot easily be repaired.

The road of authoritarianism always includes the potential for things to change again. On the one hand, there is no compulsory logic dictating that authoritarian regimes cannot fail and that still existing or newly developed movements of constitutionalism will not be able to generate fresh momentum. On the other hand, the effects of spreading and increasing authoritarianism are foreseeable. Authoritarianism creates opacity, which

Disunited Nation: On Hungary's 2011 Fundamental Law (Budapest, CEU Press, 2012) 237, 253–59.

[71] See P Bárd, 'The Hungarian Fundamental Law and related constitutional changes 2010–2013' (2013) *Revue des Affaires Européennes* 457; P Bárd, 'The Hungarian Fundamental Law and related constitutional changes 2010–2013' (2013) *Revue des Affaires Européennes* 45; A Jakab and P Sonnevend, 'Kontinuität mit Mängeln: Das neue ungarische Grundgesetz' (2012) 72 *ZaöRV* 79; A Arato, 'Regime Change, Revolution and Legitimacy' in GA Tóth (ed), *Constitution for a Disunited Nation: On Hungary's 2011 Fundamental Law* (Budapest, CEU Press, 2012) 35–58.

[72] <http://www.spiegel.de/international/europe/hungarian-parliament-amends-election-law-a-864349.html>.

[73] See G Halmai, 'An Illiberal Constitutional System in the Middle of Europe' (2014) *European Yearbook of Human Rights* 497.

[74] <https://www.economist.com/news/europe/21723801-inspired-emmanuel-macron-momentum-wants-kick-out-old-generation-politicians-new>.

leads to a lack of governmental accountability. Usually, these developments result—despite severe penalties—in corruption. Corruption, however, tends to spread like influenza in an overheated subway carriage and affects all parts of the administration, undermining the rule of law in its core elements.

But even worse: authoritarianism must ultimately lead to violence. Usually, at the start of an authoritarian transition, violence is exercised mainly against minorities, the political opposition etc. While at first violence thus limits itself to suppressing the most vulnerable and least 'wanted', the dynamics set in motion by authoritarianism soon lead to violent tensions permeating every aspect of society until they finally spill over into wars and other forms of armed conflict against foreign nations.

The anti-constitutionalism approach also follows an anti-global, nationalistic agenda. Usually authoritarian regimes will strive to create a nationalistic atmosphere in order to legitimise the introduction of authoritarianism as a 'necessity'. International law, which promotes aspects of constitutionalism like international human rights protection, will be rejected very early on in the transitional process. Authoritarian regimes cannot avoid today's globalised dimension of trade.[75] Despite their international power, they will need to create circumstances which are favourable to them, or form new partnerships which give them the possibility to reduce their dependence on democratic countries. The anti-constitutionalism approach also significantly affects the globalised approaches to constitutionalism. However, a new transnational dimension might occur: the transnational migration of anti-constitutional ideas. Authoritarian regimes might use their international power to destabilise democratic developments in other countries, thus creating an atmosphere to establish further international law limiting constitutionalism on a global level.

C. Conclusions

The counter-developments to global constitutionalism are intensifying and have not yet reached their peak. Counter-global and counter-constitutionalism developments are linked to and influence each other.

On the one hand, the establishment of an authoritarian regime by restricting constitutional developments is usually combined with a nationalistic political agenda. Opposing constitutionalism also means reducing the openness and plurality of a legal regime, society and government policies. An authoritarian shift, however, cannot ignore (especially) economic globalisation. Although illiberal governments cater to the nationalistic feelings of the people, they are at the very same time interested in promoting

[75] Even North Korea is significantly dependent on trade with China.

a neo-liberal agenda which secures underlying economic stability.[76] Global interdependences, especially when it comes to foreign investments, natural resources and military power, will remain. This does not prevent authoritarian regimes from countering globalisation with regard to constitutional issues (prevention of international support for NGOs, fighting against refugees or the limitation of international human rights protection).

On the other hand, the anti-global developments of global constitutionalism are also affecting the constitutionalism agenda within countries themselves. When the globalisation of constitutional values is under attack, international cooperation to protect constitutional values will be neglected, opposed and restricted. This includes the international human rights protection as well as organisations aiming to guarantee democratic elections,[77] etc. Anti-global policies seem to reduce international trade and investment, but usually try to re-write existing agreements to reduce equality and to create a more favourable position for the nationalised governments.[78] A more nationalistic state will primarily affect the opportunities of ordinary people and the poor. The government will usually play off different groups of society (for example, citizens and foreigners) against each other, while at the same time decreasing the opportunities for both groups. The rise of inequalities in societies moreover creates the foundations for stronger discrimination and a potential for violence—especially state violence—against certain minorities. A nationalistic agenda will thus create a threat to constitutional values as well.

As a result, nationalistic, anti-global developments and authoritarian anti-constitutionalism have a significant influence on each other. They limit constitutionalism on a domestic level as well as reducing constitutional cooperation and control on an international level. This leads to a reduction of constitutionalism in general and causes a serious setback for global constitutionalism in particular.

These developments are a severe challenge to the success of global constitutionalism. Every generation needs to strive to uphold the values of constitutionalism. The dynamics of globalisation are rapidly transforming the world and global constitutionalism must quickly adopt new concepts fast to keep its ideas alive before global terrorism, economic crises and political instabilities re-create an authoritarian world in which the global exploitation of human beings and disregard for their most basic rights once again become a reality.

[76] As authoritarianism usually leads to corruption, it is not possible to maintain the ideals of a market economy. On the contrary: authoritarian regimes create an economic divide between the few rich and the broad majority of the poor.

[77] There are many institutions which provide international election observation. See, eg, <http://www.osce.org/odihr/elections>.

[78] <https://www.nytimes.com/2017/08/16/business/economy/nafta-negotiations-canada-mexico.html>.

III. BETWEEN SOCIETAL AND CIVIC CONSTITUTIONALISM

The analysis of these developments raises the urgent question of how to keep constitutionalism alive and well. Constitutionalism is in grave danger of losing its power across the globe and being reduced to the mere rhetoric of semi-authoritarian regimes. It seems necessary to find an adequate response to these developments in order to guarantee democracy, the rule of law and human rights in the twenty-first century. The success of global constitutionalism is seriously challenged. It appears that this generation's time has come to defend constitutionalism and uphold its values.

To begin with, it is necessary to remember the roots of constitutionalism, which means that it is necessary to create new forms of radical constitutionalism.[79] The field of constitutionalism has become very broad and diverse in recent decades. Constitutionalisation has led to the spread of constitutionalism into every part of the legal order[80] and beyond.[81]

Radical approaches to constitutionalism therefore have to focus on the very cornerstones of constitutionalism: democracy, the rule of law and human rights. This approach does not necessitate a universal understanding of these values but allows for consideration of their specific cultural contexts in the different parts of the world. Thus, it might not be possible to create a general key to solve the overall problems.

Radical constitutionalism has to go back to the people to legitimise, stabilise and re-create constitutional law. The people as such can no longer, however, be the group of reference. In a post-authoritarian and post-nationalistic understanding, the concept of 'the people' can no longer be based on citizenship, nation and state borders. It is therefore necessary to understand constitutional law in the twenty-first century in the context of pluralistic societies, and no longer following from the concept of nation states. As Gunther Teubner illustrates in his work on constitutional fragments, constitutionalism in the twenty-first century has to be based on societal constitutionalism, which brings society back into the process of constitutional law and constitutional design.[82] In a critique of legal constitutionalism, Paul Blokker develops the concept of societal constitutionalism further. While criticising Teubner's concept as an apolitical form

[79] The term 'radical' is derived from the Latin word *radix*, which means 'root'.

[80] See, eg, H Micklitz (ed), *Constitutionalization of European Private Law* (Oxford, Oxford University Press, 2014).

[81] J Klabbers, A Peters and G Ulfstein, *The Constitutionalization of International Law* (Oxford, Oxford University Press, 2009).

[82] G Teubner, *Constitutional Fragments: Societal Constitutionalism and Globalization* (Oxford, Oxford University Press, 2012) 38–41, 114–23.

of societal self-governance, he favours alternative, direct forms of democracy and the dimension of decentralised democracy.[83]

In my opinion, the potential lies in between the two positions. First, it is necessary to understand that societies are not constituted by the state alone, but in manifold ways. Constitutionalism has to approach these forms of pluralistic societies first and not the states. Second, it is necessary to develop a political process within these societies to establish their understanding of constitutionalism.

[83] P Blokker, *New Democracies in Crisis? A Comparative Constitutional Study of the Czech Republic, Hungary, Poland, Romania and Slovakia* (London, Routledge, 2014) 13–44, 42.

5

Romanian Tendential Constitutionalism and the Limits of European Constitutional Culture

MANUEL GUTAN

> Let's cherish our heroes, let's be worthy of their greatness by letting to the next generations, to all inhabitants of Romania, an united and sovereign country, marked by love to its past and culture, with self-respect, master of its land, educated and prosper, a country belonging to United Europe but having its own identity, a Romanian one.[1]

I. FAILURE OF THE EUROPEAN MODEL OF CIVIC CONSTITUTIONALISM

SINCE THE BEGINNING of the 2010s there has been an increasing amount of academic talk about the tendencies of democratic backsliding and birth of constitutional illiberalism in Central and Eastern Europe (CEE). Hungary, Slovenia[2] and, recently, Poland have been strongly criticised for rejecting the values and principles of European constitutional culture (grounded on liberal-democratic constitutionalism) which they seemed to fully assimilate, while Romania and Bulgaria are rather considered to be victims of their unaccomplished post-communist transition towards democracy and the rule of law.

However, the evaluation coming from the liberal-democratic constitutional orthodoxy could be questioned with regard to its capacity to fully capture the complex dynamics inherent to the process of constitutional

[1] Excerpt from the Romanian Academy's call to the Romanian People and the institutions of the Romanian state labelled 'Identity, Sovereignty and National Unity', 8 February 2017, www.acad.ro/com2017/apelAR/d0208-ApelAR.pdf.

[2] B Bugaric, 'A Crisis of Constitutional Democracy in Post-Communist Europe: "Lands in-between Democracy and Authoritarianism"' (2015) 13 *I.CON*, 219, 227 et seq.

change in the region. Concepts like democratic backsliding, democratic regression,[3] birth of illiberalism, rejection of liberal constitutionalism and 'legal resentment'[4] express the particular concerns of those situated between contempt for having built a common European constitutional culture, hope to have it quickly and thoroughly assimilated by the emerging democracies and the disappointment of seeing it eventually rejected. This analytical paradigm explaining the socio-political and constitutional change in CEE with the algorithm 'guided transition towards democracy—successful democratic transition—democratic backsliding' belongs to a reductionist perspective which is short of sensitivity for local peculiarities.

The intense theoretical debate on regional constitutionalism (as shared constitutional values and principles) and the overwhelming interest in European constitutional convergence is mainly focused on particular mechanisms of constitutional change, for example the transfer of particular European constitutional values and principles in the CEE countries, and particular outcomes, such as Europeanisation. But it underrated the inherent (cultural) limits to constitutional change deeply rooted in the CEE constitutional cultures.

The 'watchdogs' of European constitutionalism are measuring mainly democratic performances and compliance with the rule of law (the fight against corruption, balance and separation of powers, independency of judiciary, efficient constitutional adjudication, the respect for human rights etc). Respect for the neutral state, pluralism and multiculturalism was also considered by the scholars of the European constitutional convergence. The overall impression is that many CEE Member States are currently distancing themselves from these values and split Europe once again along the old East-West constitutional divide that existed before 1989. However, it is hardly true to say that this divide ever disappeared after the fall of communism.

In my opinion, the scholars of liberal-democratic constitutionalism underestimate the continuous presence, since the end of communism, of strong 'illiberal'[5] elements in the constitutional cultures of CEE countries. Some of these elements, such as ethnocentric constitutional identity, nationalistic symbolism of the constitution, difficulty in accommodating cultural,

[3] J Rupnik and J Zielonka, 'Introduction: The State of Democracy 20 Years on: Domestic and External Factors' (2013) 27 *East European Politics and Societies and Cultures* 3, 26.

[4] P Blokker (2014) <www.jus.uio.no/english/research/news-and-events/events/conferences/2014/wccl-cmdc/wccl/papers/ws10/w10-blokker.pdf>.

[5] I understand 'illiberal constitutionalism', in Li-Ann Thio's terms, as 'communitarian constitutionalism … where cultural and religious identities or group moral solidarity is central to the polity's character'. L-A Thio, 'Constitutionalism in Illiberal Polities' in M Rosenfeld and A Sajo (eds), *The Oxford Handbook of Comparative Constitutional Law* (Oxford, Oxford University Press, 2013), 133, 148. In my approach, the illiberal communitarian illiberalism takes the shape of ethnocentric constitutionalism, prizing the values and goals of a particular historical ethnic nation against the individual constitutional rights of the citizens.

religious or ethnic pluralism in the spirit of civic liberalism, and prevalence of communitarianism over individual autonomy have never disappeared.[6] What is more, they were never meant to completely disappear.

These illiberal elements did not go unnoticed[7] after the fall of communism, but were usually considered as a (negative) part of the post-communist transition towards democracy and the rule of law and as easily manageable, in the frame of European constitutional convergence, through more or less sophisticated political and academic strategies (for example, European conditionality). Earlier 'signals of alarm' seem to have been ignored by the very optimistic proponents of the successful European enlargement towards CEE. In 2009 J Toth was very clear about the strong anti-European impetus developed by ethnocentric constitutionalism in CEE countries:

> Enlargement has uncovered the inconsistencies affecting nationality and identity in transition societies. While these states are adapting to European standards including human rights obligations and acquis (eg EU immigration law), their modernisation is often hindered by underdeveloped political culture, weak statehood, ethnical exclusion and absence of social and cultural absorbing or integrative capacity.[8]

Other scholars even considered ethnocentric constitutionalism to have been eradicated in some CEE countries and were really surprised about the 're-traditionalisation' of the constitutional ethos and the emergence of the anti-pluralistic 'partisan state' in the new Hungarian constitutional avowal.[9] From my point of view, we should rather speak about the constitutional expression of a historically determined ethno-nationalism that constantly lay at the bottom of Hungarian modern constitutionalism and shaped the core of Hungarian contemporary political and constitutional cultures. As Jan-Werner Muller correctly emphasised, we are in the presence of a 'a deep-seated nationalism and a feeling of resentment and victimisation that goes back at least to the post-First World War Treaty of Trianon and the huge losses of territory imposed by the Allies in 1920'.[10]

[6] A Batory, Kin-State Identity in the European Context: Citizenship, Nationalism and Constitutionalism in Hungary' (2010) 16 *Nations and Nationalism* 31–48.

[7] A Sajo, Protecting Nation States and National Minorities: A Modest Case for Nationalism in Eastern Europe' (1993) 53 *The University of Chicago Law School Roundtable* 53–74; A Sajo, 'Constitution without the Constitutional Moment: A View from the New Member States' (2005) 3 *International Journal of Constitutional Law* 243–61, 258; UK Preuss, 'Constitutional Powermaking for the New Polity: Some Deliberations on the Relations Between Constituent Power and the Constitution' (1992/1993) 14 *Cardozo Law Review* 639–60.

[8] J Toth, 'The Impact of EU Enlargement on Nation Building and Citizenship Law' in E Guild, K Groenendijk and S Carrera (eds), *Illiberal Liberal States. Immigration Citizenship and Integration in the EU* (London and New York, Routledge, 2016) 111.

[9] M Dani, 'The "Partisan Constitution" and the corrosion of European constitutional culture' (2013) 68 *LEQS* Paper, 27 ff.

[10] JW Muller, 'The Hungarian Tragedy' (2011) *Dissent*, 5, 7.

The Hungarian case should be assessed against a general picture of constitutional change in the region. The above-mentioned trend not only exists nowadays but also its persistence has become more evident in the populist and nationalist European context and is amplified by the contemporary phenomenon of migration. The apparent Hungarian U-turn towards illiberalism is keeping in the headlines because Hungarian constitutional ethnocentrism is particularly proactive amidst aggressive populist governance. Less assertive, the Romanian post-communist constitutional culture, before and after EU accession, still proves that the ethnocentric constitutionalism and its core elements have always been at stake in Romanian constitutional, political and social life. Romania has a constitution which is meant to express and protect the Romanian national identity. This constitution forbids the establishment of any cultural or territorial autonomy for the national ethnic minorities. It does not offer opportunities for effective integration of Romanian society on the basis of common constitutional values and goals.

These constitutional developments seem to threaten the European project and raise questions about the existence and solidity of European constitutional culture based on tolerance, respect for human dignity and human rights. In particular, it endangers the very fabric of a European constitutional ethos rooted in the positive values of liberal individual rights-centred constitutionalism.[11]

There is an intimate linkage between intolerance and rejection of pluralism on the one hand and the old ethnocentric constitutionalism practised at different degrees in CEE on the other. The presence of the former depends on the underpinning of the latter. Conversely, the extinction of the former depends on the rejection of the latter:

> [t]he European Union has been symbolically constructed as a civil alternative to the ethnically burdened nation states and has but little chances to fulfil its mission without taming ethno-nationalism.[12]

The reality shows that ethno-nationalism was neither eradicated nor even really tamed in CEE countries. Thus, the recent nationalistic (illiberal) constitutional developments in some CEE countries should be addressed not only in terms of backsliding, regression, rejection and disappointment but, in a wider constitutional context, also in terms of continuity, persistence and organic constitutional development. In other words, we should take illiberal constitutionalism more seriously. From this point of view, enthusiastically

[11] A von Bogdandy, 'Founding Principles' in A von Bogdandy and J Bast, *Principles of European Constitutional Law* (Oxford and Portland, Hart Publishing; Munich, Verlag CH Beck, 2011) 42 ff.

[12] J Priban, 'Happy Return to Europe? The Union's Identity, Constitution-Making, and its Impact on the Central European Accession States' in W Sadurski, A Czarnota and M Krygier (eds), *Spreading Democracy and the Rule of Law?* (Dordrecht, Springer, 2006) 197–98.

discussing post-Westphalian global (European) constitutionalism while neglecting particular local constitutional developments would be like navigating at full sail on a sea of sand.

Romania could become a hard case of this particular constitutional and social evolution grounded on ethnocentric nationalism that makes a common European constitutional culture grounded on civic constitutionalism a really difficult task to fulfil. Ethnocentric nationalism may have been a post-communist tool of political legitimation in the hands of the former communist political elite but mainly it was and still is a consistent illiberal part of the Romanian constitutional culture with strong historical roots. In order to offer a relevant explanation of its persistence, I shall approach the process of European constitutional integration less as a transition of CEE EU Member States towards the European standards of liberal-democratic constitutionalism and more as a continuous and sometimes irritating constitutional transplant. Learning from the rich Romanian tradition of constitutional transplant and borrowing from the Romanian sociology of modernisation, I shall use the concept of 'tendential constitutionalism' to argue that, despite its old (pre-communist) tendency towards West-European constitutional Modernity, the present Romanian constitutional culture has inner limits that block any full and decisive constitutional Europeanisation.

As in the pre-communist period, any contemporary process of massive constitutional transplant from the Western European constitutional model(s) is consciously limited by the Romanian political and legal elites with the express goal of protecting the Romanian ethnic nation and its national identity. Paradoxically, this is happening while the Romanian elites are endorsing the individual rights-centred constitutionalism as the panacea of all social and inter-ethnic problems in Romania. Thus, the Romanian constitutional culture tends constantly towards constitutional Europeanisation but it remains perpetually tendential, as long as it has no decisive impetus to give up its ethnic-nationalistic ethos. This is clearly highlighting the limits of the European constitutional integration and the impossibility to build a common European constitutional culture.

II. THE EUROPEAN CONSTITUTIONAL CONVERGENCE AND THE LIMITS OF THE EUROPEAN CONSTITUTIONAL TRANSPLANT

This intermingling between constitutional change and constitutional continuity has been approached in different analytical frameworks, for example 'sham constitutionalism' or 'forms without substance'.[13] Their common

[13] M Guţan, *Sisteme de drept comparate. Introducere în teoria generală a dreptului comparat* (Bucureşti, Hamangiu, 2014) 302 ff.

focus lies on the limited change in the constitutional culture of the CEE states coupled with a formal-institutional constitutional change. However, their approach is more normative than explicative. Much has already been explained but there is a lot of room for additional explanatory perspectives and an interdisciplinary research should be very welcome.

At the same time, academic perspectives such as 'transitional constitutionalism' and the assessment of European Union's enlargement against the backdrop of the pre-accession conditionality have poor resources to fully explain the interplay between the desire to become European and the desire to constitutionally express and preserve the ethnic national identity in the process of European integration. They are regularly driven by institutional constructivism and are optimistically focused on positive outcomes. From my perspective, it would be necessary to elaborate a theoretical perspective capable of explaining the complex interplay between the European [constitutional] culture and constitutional cultures of the CEE countries not primarily in terms of outcomes but with regard to their inner dynamic. We rather need an explanatory perspective centred mainly on the process of constitutional change in the different CEE Member States such as Romania, capable of addressing the deep socio-cultural and historical strings, for example of Romanian ethnocentric constitutionalism.

The contribution of comparative law methodology, especially the theories of legal transplant and law as culture,[14] could add more value to this debate with the condition to mediate their optimistic and pessimistic assumptions with regard to the possibility of legal-cultural convergence. For this purpose, I am not following theoretical paths capable of teaching us how to make the European constitutional transplant (or transposition)[15] successful in the EU Member States and thus presenting Romania simply as a case of constitutional 'irritation'. Romania is generally eager to (at least) formally transplant European constitutional standards without being obsessively preoccupied by their positive adaptation to the Romanian social and political environment. At the same time, it is prone to reject any European constitutional standard which would go beyond a sensitive line of demarcation between the 'European' and the 'Romanian'. To explain this, I shall rely on the Romanian tradition of constitutional transplant which has emerged since the beginning of the nineteenth century.

[14] C Harlow, 'Voices of Difference in a Plural Community' in P Beaumont, C Lyons and N Walker (eds), *Convergence and Divergence in European Public Law* (Oxford and Portland, Hart Publishing, 2002) 199–224; P Legrand, 'Public Law, Europeanization and Convergence. Can Comparatists Contribute?' in P Beaumont, C Lyons and N Walker (eds), *Convergence and Divergence in European Public Law* 225–56.

[15] E Örücü, 'Law as Transposition' (2002) 51 *International & Comparative Law Quarterly* 205–23.

In this context, the transition from communism to liberal-democratic constitutionalism of the CEE countries in the frame of European integration could be defined as a top-down attempt at constitutional convergence. This attempt has two aspects. The first one concerns standardisation and reification of common constitutional values and principles which are formally transplanted and, it is believed, substantially assimilated by the CEE states. The second aspect is founded on the domestic compliance embedded in cultural legacies, constitutional idiosyncrasies, tolerance to external pressures, and intensity of the desire to become European. The latter represents more or less intense obstacles on the road to European constitutional convergence which frequently are impossible to overcome. Thus the poor score of CEE countries in endorsing civic constitutionalism is an example of an obstacle which is very difficult to surmount.

III. FACTORS EXPLAINING THE POOR ROMANIAN SCORE IN ENDORSING CIVIC CONSTITUTIONALISM

It is difficult to build a general explanatory pattern for all CEE countries with regard to their modest evolutions related to civism and accommodation of pluralism. Each CEE state's constitutional culture should be explored and assessed with a view to its peculiarities. In the Romanian case the poor progress towards civic constitutionalism, pluralism and multiculturalism could be explained by three factors:

1. the existence of a nation-state centred constitutional culture, deeply rooted in the ethnocentric and religious remnants of the Romanian modern constitutionalism developed in the nineteenth century;
2. the capacity of Romanians to strongly emphasise their constitutional culture and to impose limits to the protection of the national ethnic minorities in the context of the EU's standards for the protection of national minorities' group rights;
3. the interest of Romanian politicians and constitutional law scholars to endorse the Romanian nation-centred constitutional identity in the context of comparative constitutional scholarship's difficulty to theorise the national minorities' group rights.

All these could be understood as parts of an integrated dynamic of constitutional change in contemporary Romania that could explain the poor Romanian performances in recognising and protecting the minority group rights. This is a pattern of constitutional development that perpetually mediates between the need to become 'European' and the need to remain 'Romanian'.

The first factor contributing to the poor progress towards civic constitutionalism, pluralism and multiculturalism is the nation-state centred constitutional culture, which is deeply rooted in the ethnocentric and religious remnants of the Romanian modern constitutionalism developed in the nineteenth century. The debates in the post-communist constitutional assembly (1991) and in the Parliament (2003) relating to the adoption of a new constitution or to its subsequent amendment were predetermined by the need of the Romanian majoritarian ethnic group to express its national myths and symbols, its constitutional anxieties (with regard to the integrity of the state) and its (supposedly democratic) constitutional traditions in the constitutional text. This approach was a matter of both discontinuity and continuity. The pre-communist constitutional arrangement mixing ethnocentric nationalism and liberalism was reinstated. However the process of 'defrosting' the old constitutional culture was eased by the very strong ethnocentric nationalism practised by the communist regime.

In this perspective, the rise of the post-communist constitutional nationalism was not necessarily only a cohesive factor in the process of nation (re)building in the absence of alternatives.[16] It was also the natural expression of the part national ethnic identity played in the perpetual authoritarian politics and the public discourse both before and during communism.[17] After the fall of communism, the national identity as it was imagined during communism (more ethnic and less religious) changed only its political and constitutional frameworks. As in the pre-communist period, Romanian constitutional identity is primarily rooted in the national ethnic identity and the whole constitutional *ethos* is marked by Romanian moral values. The *telos* of the Romanian constitution was particularly adapted to this constitution-making approach being at the same time constitutive, expressive, partially inclusive and protective.

A. The Constitutive *Telos* of the Romanian Constitution

The Romanian constitution is neither an act of political foundation (social contract) nor does it give birth to a new political community of equal and free citizens. The constitution has created an institutional order and the juridical conditions for limiting the political power. It is, in Ulrich Preus's words, 'a mere instrument of government of a pre-existing community'.[18]

[16] W Sadurski, 'Minority Protection in Central Europe and Accession to the UE' in M Weller, D Blacklock and K Nobbs (eds), *The Protection of Minorities in the Wider Europe* (Palgrave Macmillan, 2008) 224.

[17] Radu Cinpoeş, *Nationalism and Identity in Romania. A History of Extreme Politics from the Birth of the State to EU Accession* (London and New York, Tauris Publishers, 2010) 90.

[18] UK Preuss, 'The Exercise of Constituent Power in Central and Eastern Europe' in M Loughlin and N Walker (eds), *The Paradox of Constitutionalism* (Oxford and New York, Oxford University Press, 2008) 211–28, 227.

The bloody revolution of December 1989, the fast and radical change of the constitutional order and the lack of round table talks in the constitution-making process unleashed Romanian nationalism from its communist strings and provided, inevitably, 'one of the most illiberal constitutional drafts ... in any Eastern European country'.[19] After its liberal facelift, the constitution of 1991 has remained profoundly illiberal with regard to the relationships between the Romanian ethnic majority and the national ethnic minorities, recovering the nationalistic pre-communist constitutional discourse. Its direct consequence was the uniqueness and exceptionalism of the founding nation: in the eyes of the Romanian constitutional founders, every nation state could be founded only by one entitled founding nation on its historical territory. No other nation, except the Romanian one, may claim the founding right on the same territory, neither alone nor in association with the Romanian nation. No other nation may impose its political and moral values in the new constitutional order. Every national minority should respect the Romanian nation's right to self-determination.

B. The Expressive *Telos* of the Romanian Constitution

The constitution expresses the national identity of the majoritarian national group and the homogenous values of Romanians. A peculiarity of the 1991 Romanian constitution is both the strong emphasis on the Romanian ethnic nation and the national unitary state (Romania is a *national*, sovereign and independent, unitary and indivisible state) and the very loose religious identity (the Romanian Orthodox Church lost its past constitutional primacy). However, the recent developments with regard to the constitutional definition of the family show a strong national Christian (Orthodox) identity which demands to be constitutionally expressed.

C. The Partially Inclusive *Telos* of the Romanian Constitution

The national minorities' rights are recognised only as individual rights. Besides the clause of non-discrimination, the constitution (amended in 2003) and the subsequent legislation guarantees to those people who belong to the national minorities the right to preserve, develop and express their ethnic, cultural, linguistic and religious identity, the right to use their language in education, administration and courts under specific conditions and to the national minority ethnic groups the right to be represented by one deputy if they don't pass the electoral threshold.

[19] J Elster, 'Constitutionalism in Eastern Europe. An Introduction' (1991) 58 *University of Chicago Law Review* 447, 463.

Despite the evident progress, the very active Hungarian minority constantly accuses the Romanian majority of promoting double standards in the matter of national identity. It claims that the majority is constitutionally expressing its identity as a group, but is safeguarding only individual rights to the national minorities. Under these conditions, the Hungarians are strongly demanding the recognition of particular minority group rights such as territorial and cultural autonomy (including a state university in the Hungarian language). The Romanian majority perpetually denies these requests and there is latent and ongoing tension between the ethnic majority and the Hungarian minority. To put it in Dieter Grimm's terms, there is a nice piece of disintegration by constitution in Romania.[20]

Despite the ostentatious recognition of ethnic pluralism, the Romanian constitutional culture remains essentially authoritarian and unable to completely fulfil the ends of liberal democracy.

D. The Protective *Telos* of the Romanian Constitution

The constitution safeguards the human rights of all Romanian citizens. However, it devotes special protection to the Romanian national spirit and national ethnic homogeneity against the perils coming from abroad. A very old constitutional artefact is present in Article 3, paragraph 4 of the constitution according to which 'no foreign population shall be displaced into, or colonised within the territory of the Romanian State'. This article was recently activated and referred to with a view to the protection of Romanians against the EU decision to distribute migrants among the EU Member States. Moreover, the protection of the Romanian ethnic identity inwards is intimately connected to the protection of the Romanian ethnic identity outwards. According to Article 7 of the constitution, the Romanian state protects the ethnic, cultural, linguistic and religious identity of ethnic Romanians living abroad.

The second factor contributing to the poor progress towards civic constitutionalism, pluralism and multiculturalism is the capacity of Romanians to protect their constitutional culture and impose limits on the protection of national ethnic minorities in the context of the EU's defective conditionality and standards with regard to the protection of national minorities' group rights. Neither Romania nor the EU has demonstrated remarkable and decisive progress in their constitutional cultures with regard to the protection of national minority group rights. The Romanian constitutional culture seems to have reached its very limits of adaptability and change as regards

[20] D Grimm, 'Integration by Constitution' (2005) 3 *International Journal of Constitutional Law* 193–208.

the strong demands of the Hungarian minority for protection of its group ethnic identity. At the same time the EU has a very loose and timid constitutional culture and provides for contradictory standards[21] in the matter of national minority group rights. Overall, the EU pre-accession conditionality has ignored, more or less deliberately, the very complex ethnic realities in the candidate states from CEE. In the Romanian case it has allowed the very strong demands of cultural and territorial autonomy coming from the Romanian Hungarian community to remain unanswered.[22] That approach allowed Romania to easily and rather formally comply with the Copenhagen criteria and introduce lock, stock and barrel its ethnocentric constitutional culture into the EU.

On the surface, both the Romanian and the EU constitutional cultures seem to rely on the same individualistic liberal approach to minority rights with a special touch on the principle of non-discrimination. However, they both have their 'hidden agendas'. The Romanian constitutional culture is embedded in a deep non-pluralistic and non-liberal pattern of constitutional thinking that constantly promotes the ethnic Romanian group's cultural values. Some Western EU Member States have known a gradual shift towards pluralistic liberalism, granting territorial, cultural and political autonomy to their important national minorities, while EU is 'toying' with the idea of collective or group minority rights developed by the Council of Europe.

Effectively, there are no converging patterns of constitutional thinking between Romania and the EU with regard to national minority rights. The Romanian post-communist constitutionalism is formally 'individualistic' and substantially 'collectivistic', while the Western EU Member States are balancing the individualistic and collectivistic approaches.

The lack of standardisation on the EU constitutional level has discouraged any serious top-down or bottom-up change in Romanian constitutional culture. The EU did not fully succeed in making the Romanian ethnic majority think in terms of individual rights and liberal philosophy. At the same time, Romania was not at all encouraged to change its constitutional design and constitutional culture even with in the light of the tense developments in Spain, the United Kingdom and Belgium.

Even if the situation of the Hungarian community in Transylvania is far from being the same as those of Scots and Catalans, the possible secession of Scotland and Catalonia amplifies the old Romanian constitutional anxiety relating to the integrity of the national territory. It compels Romania

[21] D Kochenov, 'A Summary of Contradictions: An Outline of the EU's Main Internal and External Approaches to Ethnic Minority Protection' (2008) 31 *Boston College International & Comparative Law Review* 1–51.

[22] E Szocsick, 'The EU Accession Criteria in the Field of Minority Protection and Demands of Ethnic Minority Parties (2013) 11 *Journal of Ethnopolitics and Minority Issues in Europe* 104–27.

to formally declare a strong commitment towards European constitutional culture and still remain outside the European constitutional mainstream of civic liberalism. To express Romanian national identity in the constitution while guaranteeing only individual rights to people belonging to national ethnic minorities was and still is the perfect solution for mimicking Europeanisation.

At the same time, it is questionable whether a strong conditionality and clear EU standards, in the matter of minority group rights, would have been efficient in reshaping the Romanian constitutional culture. Considering the recent developments in Romanian society, the answer seems to be positive. As the post-conditionality in the case of the Mechanism for Cooperation and Verification and the impressive street manifestations against corruption (2017) have proved, the EU is capable of successfully developing in the course of time a form of cultural engineering which can produce increasing social support for the anti-corruption fight, despite the resistance of the Romanian political class.

However, it is doubtful that strong conditionality in the matter of minority group rights would work as an efficient panacea in Romanian society. Romania has not only an inherently conditioned appetite to fully join European constitutionalism but also sufficient potential to fight back any attempt to equate Romanian constitutional identity with European or to build a multi-layered European identity based on common anti-ethnos (civic) values.

Until now, Romania has succeeded in ignoring the Venice Commission's opinion (2003)[23] suggesting the deletion of the word 'national' from the Romanian state's definition in Article 1, paragraph 1 of the constitution in order to eliminate the possible equation between the Romanian ethnic majority and the Romanian nation and to promote the national ethnic minorities as rightful constitutional subjects along with the Romanian ethnic group in a Romanian multinational state.

The Venice Commission's opinion was easily defeated with the 'arsenal' of the EU's constitutional culture, stressing the protection of the individual rights of people belonging to national ethnic minorities. Axiomatically, the EU and EU law have not been evaluated as turning points of Romanian post-communist constitutionalism but rather as authoritative arguments endorsing strategies of external and internal self-insulation.[24] The national

[23] Opinion on the Draft Revision of the Constitution of Romania adopted by the Venice Commission at its 54th plenary session (Venice, 14–15 March 2003).

[24] In this context it is obvious why Romania refused to give internal effect to Recommendation 1201 (encouraging the recognition of collective minority rights), which was accepted as a part of the accession to the Council of Europe (1993) and which was also included (with reserves) in the bilateral treaty with Hungary (1996).

and constitutional identities protected by the Treaty establishing a Constitution for Europe (under debate at that time) were handled so as to justify the European character and pertinence of the Romanian ethnocentric design and the right of the Romanian nation to pursue its own constitutional ideals.

The magniloquent words of the Romanian Academy quoted at the beginning of this chapter are illustrative for the Romanian perspective on European integration: 'a country belonging to United Europe but having its own identity, a Romanian one'. Here the word 'Romanian' undoubtedly expresses the commitment to ethnicity.

Romania joined the EU primarily for economic reasons. The threat to core national and constitutional ethnocentric values is capable of fostering Euroscepticism[25] more than any abstract issues such as 'limitation of national sovereignty' or 'the democratic deficit', which are in fact of completely secondary importance in Romania. This kind of instrumental approach to European integration is not expected to promote the advantages of the European values of republicanism and liberal constitutionalism among the Romanian citizens and the European pattern of social stability[26] grounded in the solidarity of peoples and citizens. Indeed at first glance Romania seems to be a case of successful EU enlargement due the formal fulfilment of the pre-accession conditionality with regard to respect for human rights and the protection of minority rights. However, a more thorough look shows that Romania represents another case where national identity matters[27] for blocking deeper and substantial constitutional integration into the EU.

The third factor contributing to the poor progress towards civic constitutionalism, pluralism and multiculturalism is the Romanian constitutional law serving as an instrument for endorsement of the Romanian nation-centred constitutional identity in the context of the difficulty of the comparative constitutional scholarship to theorise the national minorities' group rights. The mainstream comparative constitutional law theory deals with the protection of ethnic minorities following the orthodoxy of liberal constitutionalism. In the 1990s, Zakaria (1997)[28] warned against the rise of illiberal democracy and strongly urged a move towards liberal constitutionalism as

[25] It would be hazardous and out of Romanian context to claim, as Kymlicka does, that Romania would have accepted a pre-accession conditionality imposing the restauration of Transylvania's autonomy (W Kymlicka, 'Reply and Conclusion', below n 33, 370). Beyond the confusion between Transylvania and the Szekely Land (the eastern part of Transylvania inhabited by a compact mass of Hungarians), this assertion neglects the central place that Transylvania has in the Romanian national identity.

[26] A Sajo, 'Constitution without the Constitutional Moment: a View from the New Member States' (2003) 3 *International Journal of Constitutional Law* 243, 257–58.

[27] T Freyburg and S Richter, 'National Identity Matters: the Limited Impact of EU Political Conditionality in the Western Balkans' (2010) 17 *Journal of European Public Policy* 263–81.

[28] F Zakaria, 'The Rise of Illiberal Democracy' (1997) 76 *Foreign Affairs* 22–43.

a panacea for ethnic divisions. Unfortunately, this implies little interest in communitarianism. As Hirsch puts it: 'strong community and liberal constitutionalism are fundamentally incompatible'.[29] The tradition of liberal constitutional thinking, widely endorsed by European constitutional culture, treats any deviation as a matter of illiberalism.

Admittedly, liberal constitutionalism is offering an outward, standardised and individual rights oriented solution which is completely insensitive to the ethnic realities in different parts of the world, including the CEE countries. However, theoretical socio-political and constitutional perspectives endorsing group minority rights, for example pluralist liberalism[30] and mixed constitutionalism,[31] are marginal in the literature relating to the CEE constitutionalism, even if there is increasing interest in making them more visible.[32]

I have doubts that these theoretical approaches would add any impetus for change in Romanian constitutional culture. First, with the exception of some Romanian scholars, mainly of Hungarian origin, no one in the Romanian constitutional scholarship is interested in exploring theories supporting minority group rights. Eventually, these recent doctrines prizing communitarianism against individualism would only have the chance to theoretically legitimise and encourage the old ethnocentric constitutional identity underpinned by the Romanian majority.

Second, these theories would have only limited normative value in the Romanian context since they are not properly indicating how to constitutionally mediate the national identity of the majoritarian ethnic group with the ethno-cultural identities of the national minorities as long as the former and the latter are mutually exclusive.

Besides recovering the communitarian roots of classical political liberalism, Kymlicka's pluralist liberalism is unacceptable since it tries to remedy the problem of equality between the ethnic majority and minorities with the minority groups' territorial autonomy.[33] The integrity and unity of the Romanian national territory are a part of the Romanian national and constitutional identities. Any idea of ethnic territorial autonomy is doomed in the Romanian context. In the Romanian national imaginary, the national

[29] HN Hirsch, 'The Threnody of Liberalism. Constitutional Liberty and the Renewal of Community' (1986) 14 *Political Theory* 423–49.

[30] W Kymlicka, 'Multiculturalism and Minority Rights: West and East' (2002) 4 *Journal of Ethnopolities and Minority Issues in Europe* 1–24.

[31] G Walker, 'The Mixed Constitution after Liberalism' (1996) 4 *Cardozo Journal of International and Comparative Law* 311–28.

[32] W Sadurski, 'Rights Before Courts. A Study of Constitutional Courts in Postcommunist States of Central and Eastern Europe' (Dordrecht, Springer, 2005) 207 ff.

[33] W Kymlicka, 'Reply and Conclusion' in W Kymlicka and M Opalski (eds), *Can Liberal Pluralism be Exported? Western Political Theory and Ethnic Relations in Eastern Europe* (Oxford, Oxford University Press, 2002) 361 ff.

territory is intimately linked with the birth and survival of the Romanian nation. The simple idea of losing part of this territory amplifies Romanians' negative constitutional sentiments.

At the same time, any 'partial establishments' of newly 'mixed constitutionalism' enabling both the ethnic majority and minorities to benefit from the advantages of communitarianism would hardly have the chance to go beyond the historical limits of the Romanian mixed constitutionalism established in the nineteenth century. Consequently it seems that there is room only for the Romanian majority's group rights in the Romanian public space. Moreover the recent and challenging theoretical approaches dedicated to the constitutional identity, coming especially from the US constitutional scholarship, could have only short relevance in a Romanian (constitutional) cultural environment particularly concerned with the identity of the majoritarian ethnic group.

Essentially, the Romanian political and academic discourse on the protection of national ethnic minorities appreciates the 'individual rights' approach. It overemphasises the 'deeply liberal' character of the constitution and the virtues of the individual rights against the collective rights. Last but not least, it appreciates the perfection of the Romanian minority rights protection system.

Apparent signs of 'informal national pluralism',[34] such as the participation of the DUMR (the Hungarian minority political party) in different governmental coalitions, should be interpreted rather as Romanian pragmatic political strategies than as a profound change in the Romanian constitutional culture. Also pragmatic, the DUMR joined the government with the clear purpose of promoting the Hungarian minority's group rights. Any successful attempt at political bargaining between the Romanian majority and the Hungarian minority meets the unbreakable limit of the Romanian ethnocentric national identity and the Hungarian minority's interest to protect its collective identity.

The Romanian constitutional scholarship which is in favour of national minorities' group rights is marginal. It has difficulties in demonstrating how the Hungarian community's 'need to secede' or its demand for 'community privacy', endorsed by the territorial and cultural autonomies,[35] would turn the ethnic majority and minorities into a cohesive and integrated social unit. 'The normative multiculturalism' grounded on 'the realisation of a common supra-ethnic identity, equality of opportunity, and non-discriminatory treatment of the members of all ethno-cultural groups'[36] is stripped of its positive

[34] Z Csergo and K Deegan-Krause, 'Liberalism and Cultural Claims in Central and Eastern Europe: Towards a Pluralist Balance' (2011) 17 *Nations and Nationalism*, 85, 104.

[35] G Andreescu, 'Cultural and Territorial Autonomy and the Issue of Hungarian Identity' (2007) 21 *Hungarian Studies* 61, 69–70.

[36] ibid, 70–71.

finalities in the absence of effective strategies of reconciliation between the Romanian and Hungarian ethnic identities.

Both Romanian politicians and constitutional law scholars perceive the individual rights granted to members of the ethnic minorities and the system of minority groups' representation as the ultimate expression that the Romanian post-communist democracy could ever get. Any political demands to collective ethnic and cultural identity coming from the Hungarian ethnic group are labelled as 'ethnic chauvinism, civic disobedience, and incitement of violent behaviour, sometimes directed against the constitutional order'.[37]

IV. ROMANIAN TENDENTIAL CONSTITUTIONALISM

One of the main intellectual concerns of Romanian historians, economists, lawyers, political scientists, philosophers of culture and sociologists of modernisation from the end of the nineteenth century to the present day is to explain why Romania has always been and still is far behind its Western European models despite the huge interest in modernisation and aspiration towards Western European standards of civilisation and in spite of its commitment to socio-political and legal change. Different historical, geographical, cultural[38] and economic[39] explanations have been provided. They have taken into consideration a wide range of variables and explanatory contexts. Summarising, a contemporary well-known (and contested) historian bluntly concluded that Romania is simply, unavoidable and negatively 'different'.[40]

Interestingly enough, all these theories perceive Romania as different not because of its vocation to be itself but rather due to its incapacity to become a duplicate of its Western European models. Concepts like 'delay', 'retard' and 'recessive Modernity'[41] are witnessing the disappointment of those expecting to see Romania running forward on a straight path of modernisation without looking or stepping backwards. This is the image of the unaccomplished Modernity in a Romanian society doomed to perpetually parallel itself with the performances of the West and eager to conceptualise its complex of inferiority.

Borrowing from the Romanian sociology of modernisation,[42] especially from C Schifirneţ's concept of 'tendential Modernity', I shall use the concept

[37] C Ionescu, 'Conceptul de identitate etnică. O perspectivă constituţională' (2015) 25 *Revista de drept public* 25, 32.

[38] L Vlăsceanu and M-G Hâncean, *Modernitatea românească* (Bucureşti, Editura Paralela 45, 2014) 231 ff.

[39] B Murgescu, *România şi Europa. Acumularea decalajelor economice (1500–2010)* (Iaşi, Polirom, 2010).

[40] L Boia, *De ce este România altfel?* (Bucureşti, Humanitas, 2013).

[41] L Vlăsceanu and M-G Hâncean, *Modernitatea românească*, above n 38, 456.

[42] C Schifirneţ, *Modernitatea tendenţială* (Bucureşti, Tritornic, 2016).

of 'tendential constitutionalism' to describe the endeavour of constitutional change grounded on the interest of the Romanian elites in the values and principles of liberal-democratic constitutionalism as reified aims of Europeanisation and a never-ending process in between.

Unlike other Romanian theories of modernisation, the theory of tendential Modernity keeps Europeanisation of the Romanian society as a clear desirable 'tendency'. However, it does not address this process as compulsory, unavoidable, necessary organic and complete, but as a 'tendential' one. In this context the idea of a 'tendential' phenomenon does not address the failure or the backwardness of Romanian Modernity but renders the process of modernisation a problematic one.

The 'tendentiality' could be defined as 'incompleteness' or 'inconsistency' but this does not change the object of 'the tendency'. This object remains Europeanisation. However, the emphasis is no longer placed on the result, but rather on the process itself. Essential here is the idea that Modernity is tendential because 'of the interaction between internal and external contexts of a society'[43] that should be taken into account and explained.

My concept of 'tendential constitutionalism' builds upon this theory. The process of constitutional modernisation before communism and after the fall of communism tended towards constitutional Europeanisation. However, it did not become tendential during the process. It has been tendential from the very beginning.

Certain internal factors in Romanian society prevented constitutional Europeanisation from fully achieving its goals. The Romanian ruling elites have always had a clear idea about the incompleteness of the process of Europeanisation. Constitutional Europeanisation was supposed to remain only partial.

Today, the internal factors pushing Romanian constitutional tendentiality towards constitutional Europeanisation are comparable with those existing in the nineteenth century and the beginning of the twentieth. In fact, there are two main internal factors contributing to the emergence of the current version of the Romanian 'tendential constitutionalism'. The first is the identification between the Romanian ethnic nation and the Romanian state with the effect of intermingling the Romanian national and constitutional identities. The second is the wide support provided by the Romanian political, lawyers and legal science elites for this constitutional ethos and their readiness to defend it against its internal and external enemies.

Of course, it would be an exaggeration to assert that without these impediments the process of constitutional Europeanisation would have been fully successful. The internal idiosyncrasies of Romanian society, that is 'the lack

[43] C Schifirneţ, 'Tendential Modernity' (2012) 51 *Social Science Information* 22–51, 31.

of qualified labour in the administration, the lack of tradition in managing modern institutions, corruption, nepotism, bureaucracy, incapacity to understand the mechanisms of the state in a modern society'[44] have contributed to keeping Romania on the never-ending road towards constitutional Europeanisation.

Intentionally, my main focus is on Romanian deliberate constitutional tendentiality. It perfectly highlights the difficulty or even impossibility of having Romania fully enclosed in a process of European constitutional integration. It also explains why European constitutional culture built around the liberal-civic version of constitutionalism can hardly be achieved in Romania.

The concept of tendential constitutionalism is more appropriate than the concept of transitional constitutionalism. Unlike transitional constitutionalism, which implies a more or less long and difficult process of constitutional change that finally ends in consolidated democracy, tendential constitutionalism is an ongoing and permanent process. It constantly tends toward liberal-democratic constitutionalism but never fully achieves it due to the unwillingness and incapacity of Romanian society to produce substantial and not just formal reform.

The idea of tendential constitutionalism relies heavily on the past Romanian experience of social and constitutional modernisation gained, especially, in the nineteenth and the first half of the twentieth centuries. Being usually undertaken top-down through massive transplants from the Western European models, effective constitutional modernisation was the expression of the Romanian elites' interest and capacity to manage these transplants. It was always and still is constitutional modernisation having Europeanisation as its incentive, the Romanisation of the inevitable constitutional transplants as mechanism and a never-accomplished constitutional modernisation as the outcome. Thus, Romanian tendential constitutionalism has three main components.

The first of these is Europhilia. A clear idea about the need to change Romania's economic, social, political and legal backwardness has always existed among the pre-communist Romanian political and intellectual elites. For many of them the panacea resided in 'constitutional modernisation through Europeanisation'. Thus, Romanians have considered themselves not only geographically European but also Western Europeans by vocation. After the fall of communism, this paradigm of constitutional modernisation has become present again. The road to Europeanisation was opened again and, this time, it had clear and pre-determined institutionalised shapes: the Council of Europe and the European Union.

[44] ibid, 28.

The second component is the constant and massive use of and recourse to constitutional transplants. Constitutional transplantation was inevitable and the Romanian elite undertook it on a massive scale by following its sense of cultural affiliation. Thus the French and Belgian constitutional models became the main benchmarks of constitutional values, principles and institutions to be transplanted. The constitutional transplant was massive, undertaken in a short period of time and with strong effects as regards the modernisation of the constitutional texts. The constitutional change was even radical when the imported values and principles were contributing to the promotion of the national agenda as set by the national political elite.

Simultaneously constitutional modernisation through Europeanisation was constantly paralleled by a conservative and traditionalist perspective. It essentially endorsed a constitutional modernisation through organic constitutional development.

The mediation between these two extremes gave birth to a complex and particular mixture of ideas and strategies about legal modernisation resulting in a genuinely Romanian epistemology of the legal transplant. Its main assumption was the idea of a rational legal and constitutional transplant. Its core assumption consists in the desire to use transplants only when they are necessary, in the necessary amount and from the proper sources. The aim was to become part of the European constitutional civilisation, but at the same time to achieve it in the Romanian way. This idea still dominates the political and academic discourse, as demonstrated by the epigraph of this chapter.

The implementation of this strategy for managing the constitutional transplant was evident not only during the constitutional assemblies of 1866 and 1923 but also in the constitutional assembly of 1991 which adopted the current Romanian constitution. In each case, although with different particular emphasis, the constitutional transplants were balanced and evaluated against the core values of the Romanian national identity. These values are the national unitary state, the common origins and history of the Romanian nation, the homogeneity and solidarity of the national ethnic group, the national language and culture, the national symbols and the national religion (Christian Orthodoxy). These phenomena have served and still function as the limits to the process of constitution making on the road to Europeanisation.

The third component is the balance between Modernity and tradition leading to a perpetual return to the Romanian 'constitutional self'. Romanian culture in general and Romanian constitutional culture in particular have a long and rich historical experience in balancing universal and domestic paths of social change. During the nineteenth century and at the beginning of the twentieth century the key challenge has been the interrelation, interplay and sometimes clash between perpetually exogenous

Modernity and endogenous traditionality. Multiple and diverse subsequent encounters emerged out of this original clash. These were the oppositions between bourgeoisie and peasantry, capitalism and agrarianism, secularism and Christian orthodoxy, education and ignorance, European identity and national identity.

This phenomenon has also had projections on a political-constitutional level. More precisely liberalism has been opposed to 'collectivistic' nationalism, democracy to autocracy, tolerance to intolerance, individuality to community and the citizen to the ethnic nation. Overall, liberal constitutionalism has collided with ethnocentric constitutionalism giving birth to the well-known mix between liberalism and illiberalism which is specific to the CEE region.[45]

The outcome of the main and original challenge and of its derivative encounters found its expression as a process where the 'civilised' and open-minded part of the Romanian intellectual and political elites sincerely tried to bring these exogenous ideologies, values, principles, mechanisms, strategies and institutions into Romanian society. Many authors have tried to assess this process in order to understand its consequences. Thus multiple explanatory hypotheses have been proposed. Some of the most important of them are the theories about cultural synchronism,[46] cultural determinism, uncritical borrowing,[47] tendential Modernity,[48] irrational transplantation,[49] Europeanisation etc.

Notwithstanding their methodological or conceptual differences all these theories have come to the conclusion that despite the efforts of the modernising elites, this process did not end in the full modernisation of Romanian society. The final result was rather disappointing. Modernity was not able to be transplanted as a holistic phenomenon. In fact only its formal and institutionalised aspect has been more or less accommodated with domestic Romanian reality.

At the constitutional level, liberal constitutional values, principles, mechanisms and institutions belonging to Western constitutionalism have been transplanted since the nineteenth century. Two written constitutions with well-elaborated liberal architecture were adopted in 1866 and 1923. However, only limited substantial reform of the Romanian constitutional culture and socio-political conditions has been achieved. This outcome can be defined as a failure for the modernisation of political and intellectual elites, but is not necessarily a loss to Romanian society itself.

[45] B Kissane and N Sitter, 'The Marriage of State and Nation' (2010) 16 *Nation and Nationalism* 49–67.

[46] E Lovinescu, *Istoria civilizației române moderne* (București, Editura Minerva, 1997).

[47] G Ibrăileanu, *Spiritul critic în cultura românească* (Iași, Editura Junimea, 1970).

[48] Schifirneț, above n 44.

[49] Guțan, above n 14.

The explanation is twofold: on the one side, the modernisation elites themselves did not aim at the establishment of a fully fledged constitutional Modernity. At the same time, the resistance of the traditionalists against unconditioned Modernity has been widespread, strong and very well ideologically endowed.

Both the modernisation elites and the traditionalist elites believed that the Romanian ethnic nation and the preservation of its identity were at stake in the course of interplay between modernisation via Europeanisation and the preservation of the traditional political culture and institutional design. For the proponents of modernisation, this means that the process of constitutional and political modernisation should be strictly adapted to the needs of the nation. On the other hand, the traditionalists believe that the primacy of the Romanian constitutional customs and the development of the inner Romanian political and legal culture and practices should be protected.

Undoubtedly, both the traditionalists and the modernists have also launched some extreme positions and proposals. The radical modernists proposed a complete reshaping of the Romanian constitutional and political architecture by strict application of the Western prototypes of constitutional modernisation. The radical traditionalists have preached the rejection of the Western constitutional models and the elaboration of a typically Romanian genuine path of social and constitutional change.

However, both sides of the Romanian radicalism have been rejected in favour of more pragmatic and fruitful approaches. The constitutional and legal reforms have been accomplished on the basis of compromise solutions. The Romanian nation and the protection of its identity have been conceived as supreme values. Consequently the process of constitutional modernisation was supposed to be accomplished in a way capable of respecting and protecting them. Simultaneously the traditionalists have acknowledged that Romania has no sufficient internal resources for social and constitutional reform. That is why the recourse to Western prototypes and transplants has been almost compulsory.

This clash of interests and ideas has produced an interesting paradox. Romania's adherence to the process of social and constitutional modernisation has been subordinated to the preservation of the core values belonging to Romanian constitutional traditionalism such as the ethnic nation, the national and unitary state, the national spirit, Christian orthodoxy, constitutional traditions etc. Consequently, Romania's compliance with constitutional universality was turned into a strategy and path for achievement and realisation of its domestic agenda.

The illiberal, community-centred nature of the Romanian constitutional core values in the age of Modernity is easily recognisable. This should not be a puzzling surprise, as long as Romanians entered constitutional Modernity rather as a homogenous ethnic nation sharing a common language, common religious beliefs, common territory to live in, common political ideals and hopes and a common history and culture. The national identity has been tailored around these objective elements and values. Moreover, after the Romanian unitary nation state was born in 1862, romantic expectations arose with regard to the capacity of these elements and values to determine the Romanian constitutional identity. Hence the desire of some modernising reformist elites to promote human rights protection and safeguards against the abuse of political power has inevitably clashed with this traditional set of values and has achieved only secondary importance.

It must be stressed that the Romanian nation state was not only a product of the process of constitutional modernisation. It served also as the matrix of constitutional and socio-political modernisation.

The Romanian independent nation-state, established in 1877, was meant to frame the Romanian territories, to safeguard the survival of the Romanian ethnic group and to promote the Romanian path towards (constitutional) modernisation. This is why in the Romanian national narrative, national identity and constitutional identity were and still are so intimately intermingled. The national values have been expressed, more or less explicitly, in the constitutions adopted by the Romanian nation. Even in the cases when these values are not explicitly defined, due to different internal or external pressures, they are still deeply embedded in the Romanian constitutional culture. This explains why the primacy of the nation to the individuals and of the state to its citizens are important features of modern Romanian constitutionalism, even if the liberal outlook of the formal constitutional texts prevails over the illiberal elements provided by the Romanian constitutions.

This particular balance between constitutional modernisation and constitutional tradition, and between uncompleted liberalism and uncompleted illiberalism, was possible due to the massive and sometimes irrational process of constitutional transplantation. Accordingly, it was not the process of transplantation of Western (especially French and Belgian) liberal constitutionalism that was remarkable in the nineteenth century. It was inevitable and can be explained by many reasons.[50] What were particularly important were the frequently irrational results of the constitutional and legal transplantation. The lack of rational constitutional transplants or, in other words, the lack of critical assessment of the constitutional transplantation in the process of selecting the sources, object and amount of the values and institutions to be transplanted was a result of the controversies between modernisation and the traditional elites. The main object of this clash concerned the issue of which are the traditional and identitarian Romanian constitutional values which had to be enshrined and protected by the constitution. It was

[50] M Gutan, 'The Challenges of the Romanian Constitutional Tradition. II. Between Constitutional Transplant and (Failed) Cultural Engineering' (2013) 26 *Journal of Constitutional History* 217–40.

not a coincidence that the most intense debates in the constituent assembly of 1866 which adopted the first Romanian constitution were dedicated not so much to the accuracy and utility of the massive constitutional transplant from the 1831 Belgian constitution, but rather to issues such as the equation between the nation and the majoritarian ethnical group, the political rights of the Jews and the particular constitutional status of the Romanian Orthodox Church.

The first Romanian constitution has been criticised as an irrational form of transplantation also due to the fact that the traditionalists stipulated that the Romanian constitutional tradition and the 'Romanian spirit' have been underrepresented in the constitutional text. Moreover, they criticised the failure of liberal constitutionalism to make the 1866 constitution sufficiently expressive of the domestic constitutional and national values thus lacking 'constitutional expressivism'.

Modern Romanian constitutionalism has been developed on the basis of this particular symbiosis between the need to be European and the need to remain Romanian. The encounter between the European and the Romanian identity in the constitutional law domain was perfectly described and analysed by the 'form without substance' theory.[51] According to this, European constitutionalism contributed regularly with transplanted institutions and mechanisms to the development of Romanian formal law. On the other hand, Romanian constitutionalism compensated the formality of the transplanted institutions with the 'national spirit' encapsulated in traditional values and institutions.

Thus, Romanian constitutionalism has perpetually evolved with the purpose of practically filling the huge gap between the transplanted formal constitutional institutions and the Romanian constitutional tradition which was believed to be underrepresented in the constitutional text. This mediation has been accomplished less by virtue of socio-cultural engineering and more by factual ignoring of the transplanted constitutional institutions. The 'Romanian concept' of constitution and constitutionalism has been declared to be promoted as an important legitimation strategy in the course of formal constitutional amendments.

Logically, the Romanian political elite was attracted during World War II by fascism, corporatism and Nazism. The fascist, corporatist and authoritarian theories were considered to better promote and safeguard the Romanian constitutional identity. This tendency towards authoritarianism as a safeguard of the national identity explains also why Soviet constitutionalism was undermined, in a different ideological context, by the Romanian

[51] M Gutan, 'The Legal Transplant as Socio-Cultural Engineering in Modern Romania' in M Stolleis, G Bender and J Kirov (eds), *Konflikt und Koexistenz. Die Rechtsordnungen Sudosteuropas im 19. Und 20 Jahrhundert. Band I: Rumanien, Bulgarien, Griechenland* (Frankfurt am Main, Vittorio Klostermann, 2015) 481–530.

nationalism, exceptionalism (protochronism) and historicism developed under the communist dictatorship of Nicolae Ceausescu.

After the fall of the Ceausescu regime the re-emerging pre-communist constitutional tradition has naturally been counterbalanced with contemporary Universalist, European and liberal constitutional values. Once more, this has been done by recourse to a massive constitutional transplant. Again, the rationality of the constitutional transplant was assessed against its capacity to cope with the Romanian national agenda with a special emphasis on the protection of the ethnic nation, the unitary nation state and the national identity. Not accidentally, the 2003 constitutional amendment introduced into the Romanian constitution indirectly provided that the whole set of Romanian constitutional values should be interpreted 'in the spirit of the Romanian democratic traditions' (Article 1, paragraph 3).

Besides the deliberate 'Romanianisation' of the constitutional modernisation accomplished through constitutional transplantation there has been also a process of implied contextualisation of the transplanted institution and their factual adaptation to the Romanian socio-political reality. It resulted from the cultural entanglements of the Romanian political elite and of Romanian society. The massive constitutional transplant, which occurred in a society with a strong authoritarian political culture, ruled by aristocracy, with a peripheral economy, inhabited by illiterate peasants (80 per cent) and obsessed by nationhood, had only a limited and mainly formal modernisation impact. For example, the endemic corruption of the political and administrative elites systematically blocked any serious attempt to substantially change the society, the politics and the constitutional culture. Very often, the constitutional transplants were 'compromised' through distortion, ignoration or rejection.[52]

Romanian constitutional history has witnessed a tricky path towards modern and contemporary constitutionalism. The Romanians were and still are regularly eager to follow the path towards Western European constitutionalism but within the limits established by Romanian constitutional idiosyncrasy. This is the reason for the fact that while the Romanian elites were formally or sincerely striving to follow the modernisation example of the 'European West', Romanian society constantly remained anchored in the 'East'.

During the processes of institutional transplantation, rejection of transplantation or simulation of reform while avoiding its practical consequences the Romanians were always looking, more or less consciously, for their 'constitutional self'. They have constantly put in its core the ethnic nation, the nation state, the national spirit and Christian Orthodoxy. In other

[52] M Gutan, *Transplant constituţional şi constituţionalism în România modernă 1802–1866* (Bucureşti, Hamangiu, 2013) 398 ff.

words, Romanian constitutional culture demonstrated pragmatic empathy for European constitutionalism but adopted it only within the limits of its already established, undisputed and unchangeable built-in illiberal constitutional identity. This makes clear why the Romanians, due to their axiological background, have had a historically grounded constitutional difficulty in adopting and promoting supranational, European or global constitutionalism. This conclusion is valid for any attempt to substantially and not just formally adhere to any globalised plethora of constitutional values, especially pluralism, and ethnic-free constitutional arrangements. This seems also to be valid for any attempt to integrate the Romanian state in any form of global or regional governance (such as the EU) which is based on these universal constitutional values.

V. CONCLUSIONS

The process of building European liberal democratic constitutionalism grounded on a common European constitutional culture seems to be eroded by democratic backsliding and deviations from the rule of law in the CEE EU Member States. Manifestations of illiberal and ethnocentric constitutionalism, contradicting European civic liberalism, were recently reported but their presence seems to be misrepresented and underestimated. As the Romanian case demonstrates, ethnocentric constitutionalism underlines the Romanian post-communist constitutional culture. Its core elements persisted and were never meant to be replaced or reformed. This is really undermining the foundations of European constitutional culture and questions the process of European constitutional convergence.

This situation might be caused by specific factors such as the inescapable Romanian ethnocentric constitutional culture coming from the nineteenth century; the loose and unclear European standards with regard to the protection of ethnic minority rights; and the difficulty of comparative constitutional law scholarship in producing a coherent conceptual and theoretical framework with regard to the protection of group minority rights. However, only an all-encompassing perspective assessing the complex pattern of socio-legal change in Romania may claim to have full explanatory relevance. Borrowing the concept of 'tendential Modernity' from the Romanian sociology of modernisation, I have proposed the concept of 'tendential constitutionalism' in order to explain why Romanian contemporary constitutionalism is constantly situated on the road towards European constitutionalism but Romanian society neither wants to nor can achieve it. This perspective allows us to explain the persistence of illiberal elements in Romanian constitutional culture despite the fact that Romania is apparently eager to become fully European.

Thus it becomes clear that the present European constitutional convergence is nothing more than an important constitutional transplant introduced and evolving in a specific Romanian pattern of constitutional modernisation built on a very complex strategy of managing the constitutional transplants. This strategy reflects a process of constitutional modernisation which is constantly grounded and dependent on constitutional transplantation and meant to promote limited constitutional change.

The limits of constitutional change and reform were and still are the core elements of Romanian national identity which is supposed to be expressed and protected by the constitution. This fact explains why the constitutional ethos fully reflects Romanian values, why the Hungarian community will not have constitutionally recognised ethnic group rights, and why the religious identity of the Romanians will probably finally be expressed in the constitution. Despite the fact that the Orthodox identity is currently far from being reflected in the constitution in the same way it was in the pre-communist period and despite their stronger endorsement by the European Court of Human Rights, the right to family and the right to marriage will be constitutionally framed in their traditional Christian shapes.

The unclear European approach both of the EU and the Council of Europe to the problem of [ethnic] minority group rights and the hesitant academic approach to the recognition of minority group rights endorse Romanian tendential constitutionalism. They allow Romania to declare a strong commitment towards European constitutional culture and still remain outside the European constitutional mainstream with regard to civic liberalism.

The lack of both strong and clear pre-accession conditionality with regard to the protection of minority rights and clear European common standards with regard to the protection of national ethnic minorities has allowed Romania to easily and rather formally comply with the Copenhagen criteria and integrate lock, stock and barrel its ethnocentric constitutional culture in the EU. The adoption of an individual-rights perspective endorsed by the EU and the Council of Europe was a perfect constitutional strategy for Romania to achieve and promote the balancing of the Romanian national identity with European constitutional culture. Expressing the Romanian national identity in the constitution, while safeguarding only individual rights to people belonging to the national ethnic minorities, is the perfect solution for mimicking Europeanisation.

Romanian politicians and scholars of constitutional law are sticking to the individual rights-centred constitutionalism preached by the mainstream European constitutional scholarship. This is a typical intellectual attitude in the scope of Romanian tendential constitutionalism. The politicians are eager to preach the universal benefits of the individual rights against the inherent authoritarianism of the minority ethnic group. Romanian scholars are, with rare exceptions, both active proponents of the individual rights and passive supporters of the Romanian national identity as core constitutional identity. Very sensitive to foreign models of constitutional thought, this time they are not interested in the full recognition of civic liberalism and strategically reject the model of plural liberalism accommodating the majority group rights to minority group rights. The civic European constitutional culture is avoided for its anti-collectivist approach and plural liberalism is avoided for being too collectivist.

Central to Romanian tendential constitutionalism is its inherent resistance to any external pressures for constitutional change. Basically, it grew out of the free choice to follow European constitutional Modernity and to self-impose the limits of constitutional transplants. The pre-communist record of Romanian compliance with European external pressures with regard to the Romanian ethnocentric constitutionalism is poor. Thus further European pressures meant to enhance the protection of the individuals belonging to national ethnic minorities will probably be successful because they do not cross the limit of national tolerance. On the other hand, any pressures with regard to ethnic minority groups' rights such as cultural and territorial autonomy will probably fail or produce only formal constitutional change along with strong turmoil in society.

As a result, Romanians were and still are permanently on the road to constitutional modernisation through Europeanisation with only a small chance of reaching its end for two reasons. First, they do not want to reach it due to their commitment to the national identity. Second, they cannot reach it due to their cultural embedment. This situation has lasted since the beginning of the nineteenth century and has every chance of persisting into the future. Today, Romanians constantly tend towards European constitutionalism framed as EU constitutionalism and the Council of Europe's human rights constitutionalism. However, it does not seem probable that Romanian society will match these constitutional standards very soon due to the lack of both will and capability. Historical experience demonstrates that any external pressure for constitutional reform has triggered not so much strong resistance of the Romanian political elite but rather formal compliance with the transplanted legal standards.

Part III

Issues of European Supranational Constitutionalism

6

The Limits of Sovereignty Pooling: Lessons from Europe

BALÁZS FEKETE*

I. AN EVERGREEN PROBLEM RE-EXPOSED

BOTH THE ROLE and evolution of sovereignty in the constitutional order of the European Union have always been considered key questions of European integration literature.[1] Much has already been said on the possible political scenarios and several debates have emerged about the future of sovereignty during recent decades.[2] This chapter, on the one hand, subscribes to this line of thinking, but, on the other, it also tries to develop an account that at least partly deviates from the 'norm'. In essence, it submits that some classical tenets of European sovereignty discourse are in need of revision in the light of the latest, and often unfavourable, European developments.

The concept of sovereignty pooling, as elaborated by Robert Keohane, is among the key components of this discourse. It is based on a qualitatively new interpretation of sovereignty as a general political phenomenon and has a strong explanatory potential with respect to the genesis and evolution of European integration and the formation of its unique constitutional architecture. However, the recent crisis starting with the European public debt problems in 2009 and resulting in fierce political controversies over the handling of the influx of migrants uncovered the weaknesses of this

* I am very grateful to all of my friends and colleagues for their stimulating comments and help in the development of this chapter, especially to Martin Belov, Nóra Chronowski, Konrad Lachmayer, Miklós Lojkó, Márton Varju and Gábor Vető. The preparation of this chapter was supported by the HAS Centre for Social Sciences Lendület HPOPS research group.

[1] For a classic account see JHH Weiler, 'The Transformation of Europe' (1991) 100 *The Yale Law Journal* 2403.

[2] For mapping this discussion see N Walker (ed), *Sovereignty in Transition* (Oxford, Hart Publishing, 2006).

strategy. Thus, this concept—sometimes regarded as the main factor in the overwhelming success of European integration[3]—needs to be re-examined in order to better understand its very nature and inherent limits.

In order to foster a critical understanding of sovereignty pooling, this chapter argues that the operation—and, therefore, the success—of this strategy for coordinating state behaviour is strongly—and to a surprising extent—political culture dependent. That is, the more political are the goals to be achieved via sovereignty pooling, the less chance there is to realise them in a political culture that remains strongly buttressed by an overarching claim and a strong respect for sovereignty as the highest level political status of a community. Needless to say, European political culture is still heavily reliant on sovereignty at both the level of political rhetoric and that of constitutionalism.[4] Thus, sovereignty pooling seems to be inherently limited by the general settings of political culture, and, therefore, it cannot be regarded as a universal and value-neutral strategy to cope with harmonisation of various sovereignty claims in a given supranational structure. The cultural embeddedness of this idea must always be taken into account when applying it as a potential cooperation strategy for possible regional integrations.

To argue for this unconventional thesis the chapter is divided into three major blocks. The first (section II) will offer a critical analysis of this concept based on Keohane's classic article. This aims to provide an introduction to the conceptual bases—not apparent at some points—of pooled sovereignty with special regard to its relation to the traditional understanding of sovereignty and the reasons for justifying such an unconventional approach. The second (section III) will reflect the earlier conceptual points onto the *sui generis* governance model of the European Union and explains that it is pervaded by the idea of sovereignty pooling to a continuously broadening extent. Certain examples from the recent institutional setting will be also discussed to give a realistic view of the functioning of this strategy. And last, the third, concluding, block (section IV) will attempt to analyse the repercussions of the current European political crisis with regard to the probable failures of the idea of sovereignty pooling at certain dimensions of European Union constitutionalism.

[3] The general thrust of Keohane's classic article: RO Keohane, 'Ironies of Sovereignty: The European Union and the United States' (2002) 40 *Journal of Common Market Studies* 743.

[4] For example, one of the leading French manuals on constitutional law discusses power and state power in a very elaborate chapter in which the analysis of sovereignty also plays an important role. See F Hamond and M Troper, *Droit constitutionnel* 33rd edn (Paris, LGDJ, 2012) 85–206, esp 194–202.

II. KEOHANE'S IDEA OF POOLED SOVEREIGNTY

A. Sovereignty and the Emergence of a Modern State: An Inextricable Relationship

Since 1576, when Jean Bodin published his (in)famous *Six livres de la République*[5] the term 'sovereignty' has constantly been in the centre of various—mostly political, legal, constitutional, and international—controversies. These debates and the transformations in the perception of sovereignty—for its subjects and scope—during the centuries had already been well documented;[6] moreover the denial of sovereignty as such is also a part of the European political and academic thinking.[7] All in all, one may argue that sovereignty as a core concept has a more than four centuries long history in Europe, that is, considering it as an outstanding component of the European political tradition is definitely not an exaggeration.

However, largely because the term 'sovereignty' has never remained within the boundaries of the pure academic discourse but has widely been used to justify or oppose practical, often contradictory, political claims, on both national and international levels, its basic or elementary meaning seems almost to have passed into oblivion. Thus, the first step in making ourselves familiar with the European tradition of sovereignty is to detach this core meaning from the layers of interpretation accumulated in the course of subsequent scholarly and political discussions. Indeed, the later intellectual turbulences are secondary from our respect, as they have been propelled by ad hoc and age-dependent political interests.

It can hardly be questioned that Michael Oakeshott—as a historian of political ideas—is among those scholars who accurately identified the core of sovereignty in the context of modern European political history as he interpreted it in its proper historical context: the birth and formation of the modern state, the emerging unit of governance in post-medieval Europe. Thereby, he created a historical and descriptive—that is, not value

[5] J Bodin, *Les six livres de la République* (Paris, Gérard Mairet, 1583), Chapters VIII and X. In general, Bodin argues that 'La souveraineté est la puissance absolue et perpétuelle d'une République ...' and 'J'ai dit que cette puissance est perpétuelle, parce qu'il se peut faire qu'on donne puissance absolue à un ou plusieurs à certain temps, lequel expiré, ils ne sont plus rien que sujets'. On the absolute nature of sovereignty Bodin points out its totally unconditional nature: 'Aussi, la souveraineté donnée à un Prince sous charges et conditions, n'est pas proprement souveraineté, ni puissance absolue ...'. See ibid, 111, 112 and 119.

[6] For a detailed discussion of the concept of sovereignty and the changes in its interpretation see H Kelsen, *Das Problem der Souveränität und die Theorie des Völkerrechtes* (Tübingen, JCB Mohr (P Siebeck), 1920).

[7] See, eg, TJ Biersteker and C Weber (eds), *State Sovereignty as Social Construct* (Cambridge, Cambridge University Press, 1996).

or interest biased—understanding of sovereignty as an essentially historical phenomenon.

In Oakeshott's view sovereignty has to be associated with the emergence of the modern state, that is, its roots go back to the era of early Modernity. In fact, it is a necessary political precondition for the formation of the modern state characterised by a single governing authority in contrast to the multifaceted and fragmented exercise of political and coercive power in the Middle Ages.[8] In addition, the emergence of this single—sovereign—governing authority cannot be separated from the power potential of modern states based on the monopoly of coercion as well as the efficiency of bureaucracy.[9]

Oakeshott uses the Latin terms of *potestas* and *potentia* to shed light on the historical uniqueness of the modern state with respect to its unprecedentedly strong powers as compared to the earlier oscillating forms of European governance components.[10] That is, in a historical sense, sovereignty as a term refers the unitary and centralised nature of state powers through a single governing authority, and, therefore, the modern state has been the socio-political entity first enabled to use this substantively new set of powers for the achievement of its internal and external aims. The following, centuries-long and multilevel discussion about sovereignty has mainly been dedicated to the problem of approaching and interpreting this phenomenon of political and administrative power concentration from various angles including scholarly differences and ordinary political debates.

B. Keohane on Sovereignty Pooling: A Deconstruction of a Cultural Character

So, Oakeshott's view on sovereignty, identifying it as the power status of a single political authority, offers a perfect starting point to presenting the concept of pooled sovereignty as developed by Robert O Keohane. In sum, Keohane stresses that the European approach to sovereignty had made a substantive turn in parallel with the emergence of the European Economic Community as it was capable of transcending the traditional view centred on

[8] For the historical details see N Davies, *Europe. A History* (New York, HarperPerennial, 1998) 291–468.

[9] *cf* Max Weber's idea on the key role of bureaucracy in the emergence of modern state. M Weber, *Staatssoziologie* (Berlin, Duncker und Humblot, 1956).

[10] In the words of Oakeshott: 'Now, these characteristics of modern European governments may be summed up by saying that in a modern state: (i) Governing is recognized to be a sovereign activity. (ii) Governments are exceedingly powerful. These features refer, respectively to (a) potestas, the legal authority of governments; and potential, the actual, physical power of a modern government disposes.' M Oakeshott, *Lectures in the History of Political Thought* (Exeter, Imprint Academic, 2006) 368.

the necessary existence of a single governing authority in internal and international politics. In contrast, the North American approach is attached to the 'classical interpretation' coined by Bodin and his followers.[11] Although Keohane's thesis seems to be relatively simple, his line of argumentation is composed of insights that should be discussed in a more analytical way.

As an introductory step, Keohane argues—in line with the contemporary trends of political philosophy[12]—that political thinking is composed of concepts that have no single or permanent meanings, but their interpretations may diverge along with different cultural contexts. Thus, it is argued by Keohane that culture—understood in the broadest sense—has a decisive impact on the meaning of political concepts. And, therefore, the understandings of sovereignty may also diverge as they may be associated with various connotations emerging in dissimilar cultural contexts.[13] Keohane implies here that sovereignty as a concept is heavily culture dependent; consequently, its cultural embeddedness has always been taken into account when invoking it in a given discourse.

He further points out that at the end of the twentieth century Western Europe embraced an ideal of sovereignty that differed fundamentally from the way the concept remained understood in the United States, although both concepts are rooted in the same premise. The earliest appearance of this premise can be found in Bodin's vision, who argued that sovereignty, as the sum of the king's final powers, is undivided and it forms a basis for an ultimate political authority.[14] This kind of absolute sovereignty offered an excellent tool for legitimising the modern state as a political entity as well as limiting the external actors' practical room for 'international' or 'interstate' political actions when interacting with another sovereign unit. That is, the concept of sovereignty, as articulated by Bodin, helped to promote and establish order by imposing obvious limits on political behaviour in the turbulent era of pre-Westphalian Europe.[15]

However, in contrast to this common heritage, the understanding of sovereignty on the two sides of the Atlantic had begun to diverge substantially from the post-World War II decades. Basically, the commencement of the European integration process initiated this departure. In Keohane's

[11] For a detailed discussion of the formation of the 'American' approach of sovereignty see Keohane, 'Ironies of Sovereignty', 749–54. Interestingly, Keohane points out that the evolution of the concept of sovereignty in the United States had an opposite direction as compared to the European way since at the birth of the US the concept of unitary external sovereignty was an almost unimaginable term partly due to the federal political framework and the autonomy claims of the States; however, it began to take shape around the beginning of the 20th century.

[12] *cf* R Dworkin, 'Hart's Postscript and the Character of Political Philosophy' (2004) 24 *Oxford Journal of Legal Studies* 1. With special regard to the critique of the Archimedean approach of conceptualisation.

[13] Keohane, 'Ironies of Sovereignty' 743.

[14] ibid, 746.

[15] ibid, 747.

view the recent distinction between the two intellectual and political poles is due to four major factors: the difference in (i) societies, (ii) political institutions, (iii) national histories and (iv) geopolitical interest.[16] Therefore, a given account of sovereignty in international politics is a complex interplay of various factors, thus, it cannot be reduced to pure political interests. As it is, the main group of factors certainly has a historic-cultural character since differences in societies, institutions and perceptions of histories always go back to cultural premises.

The European idea of pooled sovereignty means a qualitative novelty with respect to international or interstate cooperation. While the traditional, so to speak Bodinian, approach fostered the establishment of a predictable and therefore more manageable framework for international cooperation by strictly delimiting political units, thereby structuring interstate relationships, it set forth robust inherent constraints on state cooperation. On the one hand, this approach prevented the final delegation of state powers—sovereign competences—to external authorities by its very nature; and, on the other, it also required unanimity in multi-player decision-making processes thereby protecting the sovereign units' final say in their political affairs.[17] Thus, the classical interpretation of sovereignty lies behind the idea of intergovernmentalism in international affairs.[18]

However, the European approach of pooled sovereignty drastically challenges this conventional view on international cooperation as it facilitates the transfer of some competences of final legal authority in some policy fields to the Community—or 'common'—institutions with specific individual, therefore supranational, political identity. That is, the formerly indivisible single governing authorities—the Member States—intentionally decided to give up—that is, pool—their sovereignty in certain policy areas as they recognise and acknowledge that this move is a necessary precondition for acting more efficiently in these fields.

Keohane sharply points out the main motives behind this unconventional, and even irrational according to the classic view, course of state actions resulting in the establishment of a new, supranational level of community institutions with a multitude of individual competences. This was mainly propelled by the recognition that the states participating in the European project had been in an externally and internally interdependent situation in the post-World War II world, therefore, due to rational expectations,

[16] ibid, 746.

[17] *cf* ibid, 748.

[18] For an excellent account of the features of intergovermentalism in the context of the European Union see SC Sieberson, 'Did Symbolism Sink the Constitution? Reflections on the European Union State-Like Attributes' (2007) 1 *UC Davis Journal of International Law and Policy* 5–16.

the pooling of sovereignty in certain areas may have made them together more efficient than acting alone in these fields.[19] So, in conclusion, socio-economic and political interdependence can create a historical setting where the strategy of pooling sovereignty under the supervision of community institutions may be a favourable political claim for each participant, even though this is clearly contrary to the conventional canon of sovereignty-centred state behaviour.

In addition, Keohane also argues that behind this Copernican turn in coordinated state behaviour a change in the attitude towards sovereignty may also be discovered. He points out that the European idea of pooling sovereignty implies that sovereignty is no longer a static account of final political powers but 'a resource to be used'[20] in achieving individual state aims and interests. Thus, sovereignty is no longer regarded as a *conditio sine qua non* for the very existence of a state in European eyes, but a toolkit for obtaining their aims through a system of 'co-operative mutual interference'.[21] Therefore, the claims based on sovereign competences can freely be used in the interstate bargaining processes when setting up the framework for particular community policies.

For instance, the so-called 'empty chair crisis' which started in 1965 exemplifies the extent to which sovereignty claims could be used to shape the institutional setting of the Community along with particular national interests, but to not endanger its very, embryonically supranational, nature.[22] Here, by vehemently referring to French sovereignty in the context of the Common Agricultural Policy and obliging the French representative to leave the Council of Ministers, de Gaulle essentially created the basis for such a political compromise in decision making that made it possible to defend 'vital national interests' and preserve the achievements of the qualified majority voting system in certain important policy areas at the same time.[23] Thus, in the political life of the Community sovereignty started to lose its meaning as a country's final political power *status*—remember at this point Oakeshott's definition[24]—and was gradually transformed into a strong argument for backing the Member States' individual policy preferences when cooperating with other Member States and Community institutions.

[19] Keohane, 'Ironies of Sovereignty', 748.

[20] ibid, 749.

[21] ibid, 749.

[22] For an in-depth analysis see J Ziller, 'Defiance for European Influence—The Empty Chair and France' in A Jakab and D Kochenov (eds), *The Enforcement of EU Law and Values* (Oxford, Oxford University Press, 2017) 422.

[23] On the Luxembourg compromise see K Lenaerts and P van Nuffel, *Constitutional Law of the European Union* (London, Thomson, 2006) 420.

[24] *cf* J Austin, *The Province of Jurisprudence Determined* (London, John Murray, 1932) 199–201.

In addition to providing an excellent description of the phenomenon of pooled sovereignty and mapping the major incentives behind it, Keohane also sets forth some normative insights—namely, he reflects on the ways to assess this transformation and how to learn from it in world politics. First of all, he argues that even though the European Union cannot be treated as a universal model for supranational integrations due to the uniqueness of political and cultural factors in the background of this development, its success has an obvious message for the world,[25] implying that successful interstate cooperation can be established without overemphasising state sovereignty claims as these may be tamed through supranational institutional innovation efficiently. That is, if a country is willing to pool certain pieces of its sovereignty it is certainly not a sign of political weakness but that of 'strength and self-confidence'.[26] Thus, sovereignty must not be regarded as a matter of 'all or nothing', a zero sum game as it were, but as a phenomenon with numerous layers and components that can freely be ceded when bargaining for common institutional frameworks that increase the potential of all participating actors.

Furthermore, Keohane also puts serious emphasis on the conclusion that if one considers sovereignty in such a way, this entails a serious decrease in the political value of an imagined, and strongly desired, full sovereignty *status*.[27] At that point, the attainment of full and perfect sovereign competences loses its urgent political relevance as the use of the pre-existing fragments becomes much more relevant in political terms. That is, the European success of pooled sovereignty suggests that attraction of the idea of full and absolute sovereignty may fade away in a mutually interdependent political and economic context.

Lastly, Keohane also identifies a major precondition for embracing the idea of pooled sovereignty. He argues that this way of cooperation strategy can only be successful and legitimate in the eyes of the participants if 'one's practices are in harmony with the partners' expectations'.[28] Thus, a higher level of political trust is a necessary prerequisite for the emergence of an approach of sovereignty which accepts that certain components thereof are, for any reason, to be pooled via a common institutional structure. Apparently, a common understanding among the participating states based on a shared historical and cultural memory may definitely facilitate the formation of such mutual interstate trust. Nobody can deny that the openness towards and understanding of other actors' expectations are also deeply rooted in cultural experience, and indeed may even be regarded as cultural questions.

[25] Keohane, 'Ironies of Sovereignty', 755.
[26] ibid, 755.
[27] ibid, 756.
[28] ibid, 760.

C. Assessing Keohane's Idea

In its entirety, Keohane's concept is logical and coherent. It originates from the recognition that the emergence of the European Community decisively—and partly invisibly—transformed the understanding of sovereignty in Europe from the 1950s, while the US political thinking is still strongly attached to the classic, Bodinian, interpretation. In the background of this renewal process one can identify two major impetuses. First, cultural differences reflected in the social, political and historical perceptions of the Continent resulted in such a renewed understanding and, second, this process was also facilitated by substantially diverging geopolitical interests (the re-unification of the Western World), too. In sum, the effect of cultural and geopolitical factors moved the Continent's view on sovereignty away from the classic pattern.

However, the scholarly novelty of Keohane's intellectual construction may be explained more lucidly through comparing it with the main trends of the intensive European sovereignty debates that are directly or indirectly attached to the birth of European Union constitutionalism. Contemporary assessments of European sovereignty debates[29] have already made laborious attempts at structuring this diverse and colourful discussion. In Byers and Sinclair's eyes both a purely theoretical and an 'integrationist' line of discussion about sovereignty have been taking place on the European scene in recent decades. The former is focused on either the specificities of sovereignty[30] or the taxonomy of its various appearances,[31] while the latter tries to assess its relevance from the aspect of the European integration process as well as the emerging European polity.[32] These pieces revealed interesting insights and points with respect to the possible roles of sovereignty in such a *sui generis* constellation of interstate integration. However, this discourse has been unable to recognise what has already been uncovered by Keohane in a convincing way.

Keohane points out that the general understanding of sovereignty has qualitatively been changing in Europe and, compared to this, the further, even insightful, nuances of taxonomy—as for instance: differentiating

[29] See S Besson, 'Sovereignty in Conflict' (2004) *European Integration Online Papers* vol 8 No. 15; eiop.or.at/eiop/texte/2004-015a.htm 6–12. M Byers and A Sinclair, *American and European Conceptions of Sovereignty: Two Sides of the Same Coin*, www.sussex.ac.uk/webteam/gateway/file.php?name=byers-sinclaironsovereigntyaug20072&site=12, 50–73.

[30] *cf* N MacCormick, *Questioning Sovereignty* (Oxford, Oxford University Press, 1998) 123–26.

[31] See, eg, A Hasenclever et al, 'The Future of Sovereignty: Rethinking a Key Concept of International Relations' (1996) *Tübinger Arbeitspapiere zur Internationalen Politik und Friedensforschung* 26, 1–13.

[32] See, eg, W Wallace, 'The Sharing of Sovereignty: The European Paradox' (1999) 48 *Political Studies* 503.

between sovereignty as a concept or phenomenon, then subdividing it as a phenomenon into legal and political categories[33]—may acquire only secondary importance. It seems that many European scholars are lost in the very details and, therefore, they appear unable to grasp the essence of the transformation. Naturally, this may be due to their internal, European, and often deeply involved, perspective. One of Keohane's main scholarly advantages is definitely his external position as compared to the European disputes.

Keohane's idea, and the concept of pooled sovereignty as such, was directly challenged by Samantha Besson by introducing her concept of cooperative sovereignty. The idea of cooperative sovereignty is more than a simple criticism of pooled sovereignty as it points to a real—but manageable—deficiency in Keohane's idea. Basically, as it is argued by Besson, the concept of pooled sovereignty only reflects a unidirectional relationship between the Member States and the Community's institutional architecture, that is, it acknowledges that Member States pool certain competences from their sovereignty to ensure the efficient functioning of Community institutions, but it is unable to handle the other side of the coin: by creating such kinds of sovereignty pool in certain policy areas the Community institutions also acquire some sovereign or sovereign-like competences. By doing so, it establishes a power relationship with two poles in which the Community actors also have a certain, obviously incomplete, but still extant, sovereign *status*.[34] The idea of a 'pluralistic constitutional order' developed by European constitutional law scholarship is underpinned by the recognition of this phenomenon: the complex interplay between the two levels of sovereigns.[35]

Besson suggests that, due to this deficiency of the idea of pooled sovereignty, the *status quo* of the European constitutional architecture can much more plausibly be described by relying on the concept of cooperative sovereignty. In fact, she argues that the *de facto* existence of sovereignty may only be preserved in this pluralistic order if cooperative duties underpin the running of the whole 'system'. That is, she is deeply convinced that the existing sovereign units in the Community—on the level of both those of the Member States and the Community institutions—have a strong obligation to cooperate as the pluralistic nature and the equilibrium of this order

[33] For details see Byers and Sinclair, *American and European Conceptions of Sovereignty*, 55–56.

[34] *cf* Besson, 'On this model, both national and European authorities retain their sovereignty but in having to be sovereign together, they cannot escape a certain degree of competition, emulation and cooperation which characterizes sovereignty in a pluralistic constitutional order.' Besson, 'Sovereignty in Conflict', 18.

[35] Clearly, the term sovereign is not used in the usual way here, but in the context of sovereignty pooling.

may only be safeguarded this way.[36] However, at this point, she suddenly changes the quality of her argument as she slides from the earlier descriptive perspective to a normative one.

First of all, she sets forth that 'it is important to understand that these duties of coherence and cooperation are duties of political morality rather than legal or institutionalised duties'.[37] Second, she also submits that cooperative sovereignty only works in a community that has a constant intent to continue integration towards a more advanced level.[38]

Needless to say that these normative premises cannot really be managed with a *realist* attitude[39] as the last years in the history of European integration revealed that Member States are always willing to set aside moral duties, including the duty of sincere cooperation, if their specific national interest is at stake.[40] And, if one detaches this moral and normative element from the concept of cooperative sovereignty, what remains is the idea of pooled sovereignty with the important addition that Community institutions, and the Community itself, may also behave as sovereign-like entities. This is a logical consequence of a strategy that was ignored by Keohane while focusing solely on the Member State dimension of sovereignty pooling.

III. SOVEREIGNTY POOLING IN EU CONSTITUTIONAL LAW

Apparently, sovereignty pooling as all the general political concepts embraces a wide range of connotations and implications: from pure political theory, through the justification of political claims and considerations, to a number of issues relating to international and constitutional law. Therefore, this chapter narrows the scope at this point as it will discuss one single component of this variety of issues: the rise of provisions in the law of the European Union that paved the way towards a constitutional framework for sovereignty pooling. By doing so, it will miss many valuable insights that may derive from the analysis of the political side of sovereignty pooling, but it is hoped that it provides such a sharp and precise analysis that may give rise to further interest.

[36] Besson, 'Sovereignty in Conflict', 19. *cf* this argument with Daniel Halberstam's point emphasising the need for both constitutional and extra-legal (structural, popular and political) constraints for the effective functioning of federations. See D Halberstam, *Federalism: A Critical Guide* 27–28. Available at SSRN: ssrn.com/abstract=1924939.

[37] Besson, 'Sovereignty in Conflict', 19.

[38] ibid.

[39] *cf* HJ Morgenthau, *Politics Among Nations. The Struggle for Power and Peace* (New York, Alfred A Knopf, 1985) 3–17.

[40] For a detailed analysis on the role in and effect of national interest on EU law in general, see M Varju, *Between compliance and particularism: Member State interests in European Union law*, Manuscript. Available at hpops.tk.mta.hu/uploads/files/MSInterestsYEL.pdf.

It is submitted by Paul Craig that the precise 'configuration of power sharing' within the European Union—that is the real power relationship between the Union itself and the Member States—may only be determined if treaty provisions on both competences and precise decision making—sometimes hidden in the TFEU—are read together.[41] Based on this insight, one may argue that the rules about division of competences are the 'static' side of Union decision making, in general, as they provide a conventional frame to channel the cooperative power exercise between the Member States and the Union, whereas the precise rules of decision making are to be regarded as the 'dynamic' dimension since they enable the actors to come to successful agreements on political or policy issues. Undoubtedly, qualified majority voting (QMV), regardless of the specific configuration of voting, has a crucial role from the aspect of pooled sovereignty in decision making. The option of QMV can make the whole idea of sovereignty pooling function in reality as it enables the decision makers—the Member States in general—to overstep peculiar individual political interests thereby empowering all the actors to make agreements in line with the interests of the entire community.[42]

In the following, this chapter examines how and to what extent the constitutional law implications of the idea of sovereignty pooling emerged and appeared in the course of the European integration process. The main point submitted here is as follows: sovereignty pooling has always been an underlying principle of the community toolkit of establishing its constitutional architecture even though it had been almost unnoticeable in the early period of integration. In addition, the actual—post-Lisbon—configuration of competence sharing and broad range of QMV decision making are logical consequences of the earliest intents of sovereignty pooling.

A. The Early Phase of Sovereignty Pooling in European Union Law: The Idea in Embryonic Form

Unsurprisingly, the question of how to avoid the political traps of unanimity decision making when community interests are at stake had already been an important issue when drafting the future provisions of the Treaty on the European Economic Community. For instance, Paul Henri Spaak passionately argued that 'unanimity formulae are the formulae of impotence',

[41] P Craig, 'The Lisbon Treaty, Process, Architecture and Substance' (2008) 33 *European Law Review* 147.

[42] *cf* A Moravcsik, *The Choice for Europe. Social Purpose and State Power from Messina to Maastricht* (Ithaca, NY, Cornell University Press, 1998) 67.

and he suggested that 'the ancient notions of sovereignty' had to be transcended by the introduction of the principle of majority voting in general.[43] However, contrary to all these considerations, unanimity voting was placed in the centre of community decision making at the moment of founding the Community in 1957, mostly for simple pragmatic political reasons.[44]

Nevertheless, the treaty makers also left the door open to QMV, that is, for the realisation of sovereignty pooling at certain, limited but important, policy fields. The Treaty of Rome itself scheduled the phasing-in of QMV in community decision making from 1965. In theory, almost 40 areas of Community activities had to be decided by way of QMV from 1965: mostly budgetary affairs, competition and commercial policy segments, and Common Agricultural Policy decisions were those areas where the Community decided to introduce QMV decision making to replace the previous unanimous decisions.[45]

Significantly, this extension of QMV procedure to sensitive policy areas, such as agriculture, was unacceptable at that time in the eyes of the French political establishment, and gave rise to the most serious crisis in the history of the Community: the so-called 'empty chair' crisis.[46] The six months during 1966 while France boycotted community decision making sharply brought into relief where the inherent 'cultural' limits of pooling sovereignty in Europe were at that time. But, and this is the most telling point from our point of view, even the fierce opposition by de Gaulle was insufficient to discredit the idea of QMV and sovereignty pooling in the name of a putative complete sovereign *status*. The Luxembourg compromise, providing a *de facto* veto in QMVs if a 'vital national interest' is concerned, besides all negative consequences resulting in the standstill and politically frozen but institutionally developing decades of the next period of 'Eurosclerosis',[47] made the survival of the idea of sovereignty pooling and its most important symbol, QMV, possible.

Moreover, besides all political stalemates in the 1960s and 70s, the European Court of Justice (ECJ) had started to develop the community architecture towards a more supranationalist framework in an almost invisible way.

[43] See SC Sieberson, 'Inching Toward EU Supranationalism: Qualified Majority Voting and Unanimity Under the Treaty of Lisbon' (2010) 50 *Virginia Journal of International Law* 933.

[44] For the background see R McAllister, *From the EC to the EU. A Historical and Political Survey* (London and New York, Routledge, 1997) 12–22.

[45] For the complete list see V Miller, 'The Extension of Qualified Majority Voting from the Treaty of Rome to the European Constitution' (2004) *House of Commons Research Papers*, 7 July, 10–11.

[46] *cf* Ziller, 'Defiance for European Influence'.

[47] For an insightful discussion of this period in the history of the European integration see A Awesti, 'The Myth of Eurosclerosis: European Integration in the 1970s' (2009) *L'Europe en formation*, 2009/3, 39–53.

The establishment of the principles of direct effect[48] and supremacy[49] as well as the birth of the doctrine of implied Community powers[50] all reinforced the idea of sovereignty pooling in practice. These developments intentionally limited the scope of Member States' sovereign competences by federal-type constitutional law solutions almost exclusively in relation to the completion of the common market.[51]

As for the clarification of Community competences—the 'static' dimension of sovereignty pooling—the ECJ also made a considerable contribution from the 1970s. Originally, the Treaty on the European Community did not contain any specific competence clause suggesting a federal solution,[52] but it dominantly applied the terms 'task',[53] 'purposes',[54] 'activities',[55] 'limits'[56] or 'powers conferred upon'[57] when delineating the areas of community action. This set of terms on the activities of the Community had a rather 'open-textured'[58] character—as it is argued by Joseph Weiler[59]—therefore the ECJ was given ample room to further interpret and determine the real scope of Community competences.

Unsurprisingly, in some cases, the ECJ argued for the exclusive nature of Community competences if these were vital for the smooth functioning of the economic community. Both the area of common commercial policy[60] and the conservation of sea biological resources were subjected to exclusive Community competence by the case law of the ECJ,[61] and the external competences of the Community were clarified through a rather community-friendly reading.[62]

In addition to these developments, as Joseph Weiler points out, the ECJ also started to extend Community competences via various sophisticated and less overt methods (namely: extension, absorption, incorporation

[48] Case 26/62 *NV Algemene Transport- en Expeditie Onderneming van Gend & Loos v Netherlands Inland Revenue Administration* [1963] ECR 1.

[49] Case 6/64 *Flamino Costa v ENEL* [1964] ECR 1339, 594.

[50] Case 22/70 *Commission of the European Communities v Council of the European Communities* [1971] ECR 263, para 28.

[51] *cf* Weiler, 'The Transformation of Europe' 2410–31.

[52] *cf* eg The Austrian Federal Constitution Arts 10–15; the Constitution of Belgium Arts 74 and 77; the Basic Law for the Federal Republic of Germany Arts 70–75; and the Constitution of the United States Art I 8–10.

[53] Art 2 TEC.

[54] Art 3 TEC.

[55] Art 3 TEC.

[56] Art 5 TEC.

[57] Art 5 TEC.

[58] See HLA Hart, *The Concept of Law* (Oxford, Oxford University Press, 2012) 124–35.

[59] Weiler, 'The Transformation of Europe', 2433.

[60] *cf* Opinion of the Court of 11 November 15 in *1/75, Draft OECD Understanding on a Local Cost Standard drawn up under the auspices of the OECD* [1975] ECR 1355.

[61] Joined Cases 3-4/76 and 6/76, *Cornelis Kramer and others* [1976] ECR 1279.

[62] For a detailed analysis see R Schütze, *From Dual to Cooperative Federalism. The Changing Structure of European Law* (Oxford, Oxford University Press, 2009) esp 312–20.

and expansion)[63] and this line of case law also forced the melting of sovereign competences in certain policy areas thereby paving the way towards the substantively new understanding of sovereignty that was analysed by Keohane from a political philosophy angle.

In sum, it may be argued that modest but definite steps were taken within the initial political and institutional framework of the Community in the direction of sovereignty pooling from the 1960s onwards. These were rather fragmentary, technical and sometimes even almost imperceptible, but they prove that the intent towards pooling sovereignty had never ceased in the Community even though political pragmatism raised hard constraints in its uncertain course of development. Further, due to the impasse in the political sphere of the 1960s and 70s, the ECJ must have played a pre-eminent role in this process of keeping the idea alive.

B. From 1986 to the Lisbon Treaty: Serious Institutional Steps Towards Sovereignty Pooling

By the enactment of the Single European Act in 1987 a new phase started in the European history of sovereignty pooling. Although this Act only extended the scope of QMV to a rather limited extent—namely seven community policy areas were changed from unanimity to QMV and five new ones were introduced into the corpus of the EC Treaty, from which the majority was directly linked to the functioning of the common market and the future evolution of the internal market[64]—one may convincingly argue that this was the overture to a completely new chapter in the proliferation of QMV in Community decision making. With the subsequent treaty modifications (Maastricht (1992), Amsterdam (1998) and Nice (2001)) QMV voting was considerably extended to pre-existing policy areas as well as to new Community competences which were introduced subject to QMV. In addition, the birth of the initially intergovernmental pillars in 1992—Common Foreign and Security Policy and Cooperation in Justice and Home Affairs—has also to be taken into account as these two new fields of action opened up new potential areas for future QMV decisions considered as core components of state sovereignty by the conventional Bodinian understanding, such as foreign and security policy or refugee and immigration policies.[65] By the modifications of the Nice Treaty only 66 provisions in the Treaties remained subject to unanimity decision making, a part of these related to the institutional structure of the Union, while another considerable

[63] For the details see Weiler, 'The Transformation of Europe', 2437–50.

[64] For a detailed list see Miller, 'The Extension of Qualified Majority Voting',11–13.

[65] For a detailed list see ibid, 13–17.

segment dealt with decisions of a high level of foreign and security policy relevance.[66]

The process of this extension of QMV decision making in the Union's constitutional architecture was further enhanced with the Lisbon Treaty modifications by the introduction of the so-called ordinary legislative procedure.[67] On the one hand, the Lisbon Treaty subscribed to the former dynamic of shifting from unanimity to QMV procedure and many segments of the institutional issues and policy areas were touched upon by these changes.[68] Further, the Lisbon Treaty also created a previously unknown mechanism to extend QMV decision making to some new areas; this is the inclusion of the rather unique *passerelle* provisions enabling either the European Council or the Council, with the consent of all Member State parliaments, to introduce QMV for future decisions by a unanimous vote.[69] This unconventional solution is certainly efficient from an institutional aspect, as it makes it possible to further extend QMV without being engaged in any treaty modification process. On the other hand, the Lisbon modifications also incorporated several new areas subject to QMV into the Treaties that were previously outside the scope of Community action or were subsumed under the options established by Article 308 EC, the Community's 'necessary and proper clause'.[70] However, to make this picture really complete, it should also be mentioned that even in some of the areas subjected to QMV under the new Lisbon provisions a certain 'veto power' or safeguards were retained by allowing the invocation of national policy preferences.[71]

In sum, from a static point of view, one may argue that the changes introduced by the Lisbon Treaty concerning QMV were predominantly extended to technical issues only and, therefore, do not affect the core components of Member States' sovereignty.[72] This assessment is certainly not untrue when evaluating the Lisbon Treaty modifications in themselves. However, if one regards the Lisbon Treaty modifications as a phase in a much longer and broader historical process that had begun with the consolidation of EC decision making as provided by the Single European Act and evolved with both the subsequent treaty amendments and the birth of the European Union starting to integrate two originally intergovernmental pillars into the

[66] For a detailed list see ibid, 20–22.

[67] See Art 294 TFEU.

[68] For details see Sieberson, 'Inching Toward EU Supranationalism' 940–66.

[69] The provisions relate to the fields of CFSP, budgetary planning, family law issues with cross-border effects, enhanced cooperation and EU programmes on environmental protection; ibid, 953.

[70] *cf* Schütze, *From Dual to Cooperative Federalism* 133–43.

[71] eg Art 31(2) TEU or Art 48 TFEU.

[72] This line of argument is summarised by Sieberson, 'Inching Toward EU Supranationalism', 954.

previously common-market centred framework, a different interpretation may also be arrived at.

In fact, the entire process that resulted in the Lisbon Treaty modifications may also be regarded as the triumph of sovereignty pooling in many Community, later Union, policy areas. Obviously, this does not mean that the European Union as a whole has become a completely supranational entity based on sovereignty pooling, but in many policy areas—from institutional matters through the various issues of the internal market to cooperation in justice and foreign policy—sovereignty pooling became a definite reality. If one compares today's situation with the situation of 1966, when the possible introduction of QMV into the common agricultural policy decision making gave rise to a political crisis with a threatening effect on the future of European integration, the success of sovereignty pooling becomes irrefutable.

The Lisbon Treaty also meant a great step forward in the settlement of the division of competences between the Union and the Member States from the perspective of sovereignty pooling. Until the Lisbon modifications the system of vertical division of competences had been clarified mainly by the case law of the ECJ, that is, apart from some basic treaty provisions on the Community/Union activities it had a strong judge-made law character.

However, for the very first time in the course of European integration, the Lisbon modifications introduced a complete 'competence clause' similar to federal solutions providing a detailed description on the division of Member State and federal competences. Articles 4 and 5 TEU set forth the main principles of competence sharing—the principle of conferral, delimitation of Member State competences etc—while Articles 2 to 6 TFEU define the various categories of union competences and declare the principle of pre-emption with regard to shared competences.

Hence, a seemingly federal approach to competence sharing between the central or national government, the Union, and the Member States was declared by the Lisbon Treaty, although it should also be admitted that in substantial terms this new constitutional framework does not modify the earlier *status quo* between these two levels of governance in the European Union. In addition, certain key federal competences—for instance military affairs, foreign policy and federal fiscal policy—are still in the Member States' hands almost completely, therefore the emergence of a United States of Europe cannot be inferred, let alone promulgated.[73]

Nevertheless, the appearance of this fully fledged federal attitude in the wording of these provisions may strengthen the impression that the creation

[73] For a detailed discussion see B Fekete, 'Does the Emperor Really Have New Clothes? A Critical Assessment of the Post-Lisbon Regime of Competences' in *Hungarian Yearbook of International Law and European Law, 2013* (The Hague, Eleven, 2014) 75–91.

of a smooth legal framework for sovereignty pooling at a general level is among the future aims of the integration process. And, as occurred in the 1970s and 80s, the ECJ may have a decisive role in the clarification of these provisions, with special regard to the fact that a political stalemate has begun in the last ten years that can be compared to the period of 'Eurosclerosis'.

C. The Place of Sovereignty Pooling in the Current Union Architecture

From the foregoing it seems undeniable that the intent for sovereignty pooling is one of the main motives behind the evolution of the European Union constitutional architecture. It is well reflected in the recent constitutional setting that provides a structure in which state—Member State—sovereignty can hardly be interpreted in the conventional Bodinian way as many sovereign competences are either eroded by the work of the Union institutions or conferred to the Union level. Further, the formation and evolution of the European Community, later the Union, constitutional architecture convincingly illustrates the validity of Keohane's broad concept of sovereignty pooling as a major impetus.

From a different angle, evidently, no one can convincingly argue that the European Union's existence is predicated on the complete realisation of sovereignty pooling. Still, there are many important policy areas—the three most important being fiscal, defence and foreign policy—that are under the dominant control of the Member States.

In sum, in harmony with Keohane's insights, the recent status of sovereignty pooling is certainly not an 'all or nothing' issue in the European Union constitutionalism, but a balance swinging between total sovereignty and complete sovereignty pooling with numerous nuanced intermediate positions. In the post-Lisbon situation, it can be argued that sovereignty pooling was a clear success in policy areas related to the internal market in the broadest sense while it had only modest or even little impact on other important policy areas mostly associated with the traditional core of sovereignty.

However, the European crisis which began in 2009 exposed political and legal phenomena that seem to suggest that the strategy of sovereignty pooling—in spite of its earlier manifest successes—has inherent limits in Europe. Basically, it seems that Member States in times of crisis[74] prefer to invoke the classical understanding of sovereignty as a panacea for all newly emerging problems. This happens not exclusively on the level of pure

[74] Here, the term 'crisis' is applied in the sense of Schmitt's 'exceptional situation'. See C Schmitt, *Politische Theologie: Vier Kapitel zur Lehre der Souverenität* (München and Leipzig, Duncker & Humblot, 1922).

everyday political rhetoric, but the general attitude towards EU law obligations has also been affected by this noticeable shift in the approach to sovereignty. The next section will make an attempt to formulate some lessons from the various experiences of this on-going process with respect to the idea of sovereignty pooling.

IV. THE NIGHTFALL OF SOVEREIGNTY POOLING IN EUROPE?

In the main, the events of this decade have been full of political or legal developments that implied yet another general and substantial shift in the European understanding of sovereignty. These developments indicate that the spreading and dominance of the idea of sovereignty pooling in the European Union's constitutionalism is not the final point in the European story of sovereignty. In essence, one may have the impression that sovereignty as it was conceptualised by the classic approach has gradually been reanimated in the European constitutional and political discourse. Numerous different patterns can be identified in this renewed discourse on sovereignty—from the intensifying of the references to 'constitutional identity' to the open political claims for full sovereignty as exposed during the debates on the Brexit referendum. Thus, a comprehensive overview and analysis would be worth even an independent monograph.

However, it is apparent that the main dividing line among these various new patterns of sovereignty discourse is whether they are associated with specific legal problems or they have a dominantly political character. Obviously, those which put the new sovereignty discourse into a(n often daily) political context are to be examined by the methods of political discourse analysis, therefore they stand far from the scope of this chapter focusing on a constitutionalism-oriented approach to European Union law. However, the other aspect, when the sovereignty issue is embedded in a specific legal dispute, seems to be a proper subject for analysis. Thus, the following parts will be dedicated to two segments within the general EU law discourse, both with high relevance regarding the transformation of the overall attitudes towards pooled sovereignty.

A. External Judicial Resentment of the Deepening of Sovereignty Pooling

A potential field for studying new tendencies in the understanding of sovereignty pooling may be the comparative analysis of some relevant decisions of Member State constitutional and supreme courts. It can be argued that the judicial system of the European Union, a structured network of the Member State and European Union courts, has a considerably interconnected nature, although the term 'dialogue' may seem to be too excessive to describe properly the relationship between the EU and national courts in some cases.[75] Therefore, the national constitutional court decisions may also have something to say on European Union constitutional issues such as sovereignty pooling by representing and articulating the Member State view. These national decisions may even shed light on the 'national' attitude (which is often not explicit enough) towards the main constitutional issues of integration. These can be valuable additions to the 'official perspective' promoted by the various EU institutions and high functionaries.

First, one may notice that the number of those national constitutional court decisions that have some relevance in this specific case have certainly increased in the last 15 years as compared to the 'golden age' of the European project. This is, of course, mostly due to the fact that the European Union had started to move in a more and more federal direction since the early 2000s and this evolution had certain repercussions for the core competences of sovereignty—they have been relevant from the national constitutional law perspective.[76] Thus, it can be argued that the birth of such national decisions has been a natural consequence of the substantial deepening of the integration.

Second, it should also be taken into account, however, that the latest wave of national decisions interpreting EU constitutional law issues have mostly, but not exclusively, been made by courts of the new, Central and Eastern European, Member States. That is, national judiciaries of the newly entrant Member States evince a high degree of sensitivity to the constitutional law aspect of integration and the consequences thereof to the national legal orders.

In order to demonstrate the attitude of this stream of case law, a number of decisions will be analysed hereafter with respect to their attitude towards sovereignty pooling, as this may uncover some national attitudes towards pooling sovereignty in a supranational framework.

It would be very tempting to argue that these national constitutional court decisions reveal both a high level of scepticism towards the current constitutional status of the European Union and a concomitant fondness for the concept of sovereignty as an absolute and irreducible political status. However, this line of argument would be a serious oversimplification. It is true that these decisions focus on and praise sovereignty to a great extent. As for instance, where the Supreme Court of Estonia points out that 'the sovereignty clause of the Estonian Constitution is strict in wording, providing that the independence and sovereignty of Estonia are timeless and

[75] For an insightful discussion of the problem of 'judicial dialogue' in the EU see M Claes and M de Visser, 'Are You Networked Yet? On Dialogues in the European Judicial Networks' (2012) 8 *Utrecht Law Review* 100–14.

[76] This controversy, the potential conflict between the national constitutional system and community law, first appeared in Germany. *cf Solange I* Beschluss (BVerfGE 37, 271) (1974).

inalienable'[77] or the Polish Constitutional Tribunal stresses when discussing the case of a potential collision between an EU law provision and a national constitutional one that 'such a collision may in no event be resolved by assuming the supremacy of a Community norm over a constitutional norm'.[78] Further examples of this attitude can be found in the cited or other decisions in great numbers.[79] That being said, the language of these decisions is certainly disposed towards sovereignty, which may suggest that these courts are definitely not against the concept of (national) sovereignty in general.

However, if one examines the arguments about the collision of sovereignty and European Union law obligations another relevant point becomes apparent. By citing the concept of absolute sovereignty, these courts do not claim to recoil from European Union law commitments, but try to point out the 'internal' legal limits of the Union's sphere of actions, thereby defending the core of their national constitutions, frequently labelled as 'constitutional identity'.[80] In the words of the Constitutional Court of Latvia: 'The Constitutional Court recognises that the State of Latvia is based on such fundamental values that, among the rest, include basic rights and fundamental freedoms, democracy, sovereignty of the State and people, separation of powers and rule of law', therefore the 'delegation of competences cannot exceed the rule of law and the basis of an independent, sovereign and democratic republic based on the basic rights'.[81] Or, the Hungarian Constitutional Court submits that the main components of the constitutional identity of Hungary can definitely be identified even though this is not a closed and final list; in the eyes of the Hungarian justices, civil liberties, separation of powers, republicanism, autonomies under public law, freedom of religion, rule of law, parliamentarianism, equality before the law, judicial power and the rights of the nationalities are all main components of this perceived constitutional identity, fundamentally characterising the Hungarian legal order.[82] Moreover, the Hungarian justices also stress that constitutional identity as a sum of these values and legal institutions cannot be given up in any circumstance, only the cessation of sovereignty may lead to their rejection.[83]

[77] Constitutional Judgment 3-4-1-6-12 (Judgment of the Supreme Court en banc), 128.

[78] Judgment of 11 May 2005, K 18/04. *Poland's Membership in the European Union (Accession Treaty)*, 13.

[79] eg Decision of the Hungarian Constitutional Court, 22/2016 (XII.5) para 60; Judgment on behalf of the Republic of Latvia, Riga, 7 April 2009, Case No 2008-35-01, 14.

[80] For a classic and comprehensive account of 'constitutional identity' see GJ Jacobsohn, 'Constitutional Identity' (2006) 68 *The Review of Politics* 361–97.

[81] Judgment on behalf of the Republic of Latvia, Riga, 7 April 2009, Case No 2008-35-01, 17.

[82] Decision of the Hungarian Constitutional Court, 22/2016 (XII.5) Section 65.

[83] Decision of the Hungarian Constitutional Court, 22/2016 (XII.5) Section 67.

In sum, the phrasing of these decisions envisages the relationship between the EU and national legal orders as a dynamic 'liaison' that may imply potential collisions between the EU and Member State legal provisions and general values. That is, the relationship between these two levels of legal orders—a supranational one and the national one—is not only about a harmonious cooperation, but also competition and collision.[84] Therefore, the boundaries of European Union legal actions must be defined in a precise way enabling the Member State courts to defend their own legal orders against any illegitimate encroachment by EU powers. Needless to say, these questionable interferences may mostly stem in the future from policy fields pervaded by sovereignty pooling.

Therefore, one may argue that there certainly exists a noticeable reluctance in the practice of national constitutional or supreme courts toward the extension of sovereignty pooling, led by Central European and Baltic judiciaries,[85] to such novel fields that are closely linked to the core of sovereignty, in other words, to the constitutional identity of a legal order. This reluctance, or scepticism to a certain degree, towards pooling sovereignty in relation to more political and value-oriented issues may be interpreted to mean that the relationship between the two levels of governance—the 'European' and the 'national'[86]—in the European Union are still not settled. Neither in a political, nor in a legal sense.

B. Internal Scepticism Towards the Deepening of Sovereignty Pooling

Parallel to the reluctance of some national supreme courts the continuous extension of sovereignty pooling to new policy areas has also been challenged within the decision-making framework of the European Union. A major example of this has been the serious controversy engendered by the so-called 'migrant quotas decision' enacted in September 2015.[87]

[84] *cf* with the position of Daniel Halberstam arguing that this kind of controversy may help in the identification of the values of constitutionalism in Europe, therefore this unsettled situation cannot be regarded as a simple source of conflict. D Halberstam, 'Constitutional Heterarchy: The Centrality of Conflict in the European Union and the United States' in JL Dunoff and JP Trachtman (eds), *Ruling the World? Constitutionalism, International Law and Global Governance* (Cambridge, Cambridge University Press, 2009) 326.

[85] For a similar argument from Western Europe see, eg, Décision n° 2006-540 DC du 27 juillet 2006, 19, and UK Supreme Court, *R v The Secretary of State for Transport*, 22 January 2014, 207.

[86] For some lessons from the US see M Tushnet, 'Enforcement of National Law against Subnational Units in the US' in A Jakab and D Kochenov (eds), *The Enforcement of EU Law and Values* (Oxford, Oxford University Press, 2017) 316.

[87] Council Decision (EU) 2015/1601 of 22 September 2015 establishing provisional measures in the area of international protection for the benefit of Italy and Greece.

The story of this Council decision and the follow-up events provide a vivid illustration for many relevant legal aspects of the on-going sovereignty discourse.

In sum, this Council decision was enacted as an emergency answer to the grave problems raised by the influx of 'nationals of third countries'—mostly refugees and migrants from Syria and the Sub-Saharan regions—starting in earnest from 2014. As is well known, this inflow affected the European Union in a very disproportionate manner. For simple geographical reasons, it was predominantly Greece and Italy that had to cope with this enormous challenge. Further, the so-called Dublin regulation, setting up the general frame of asylum policy in the European Union, left the competence to examine the claims of the applicants—who entered the territory of the European Union irregularly and who did not—for the purposes of international protection in national hands.[88] The authorities of Greece and Italy had to manage a serious and lasting humanitarian crisis situation on their own—largely because of the provisions of the Dublin regulation—which had serious repercussions for the entire European Union. The Council decision's main goal was to provide efficient help to both countries by making it possible to relocate around 120,000 third country asylum applicants to the other Member States on the basis of a proportionate quota set up by the experts of the Commission. Having been the subject of fierce political battles beforehand, the decision was made on the basis of Article 78(3) TFEU enabling the Council to adopt provisional measures in an emergency situation where a country experiences a 'sudden inflow of nationals of third countries'.[89]

The justification of the decision was twofold. First, the decision argued that an obvious emergency situation obtained in the Mediterranean due to 'exceptional migratory flows in the region' that called for a common and coordinated action by the entire European Union.[90] Second, the decision also set forth that such exceptional situations may only be effectively countered by subscribing to the principles of solidarity and the fair sharing of responsibility among the Member States.[91] Thus, the enactment of the decision was determined by the motives of pooling sovereignty, and it was mostly due to the circumstances of a situation that cannot effectively be managed by individual Member States alone, but needed coordinated action

[88] Regulation (EU) No 604/2013 of the European Parliaments and of the Council of 26 June 2013 establishing the criteria and mechanisms for determining the Member State responsible for examining an application for international protection lodged in one of the Member States by a third-country national or a stateless person, Art 13(1) and (2).

[89] Art 78(3) TFEU.

[90] *cf* Preamble of Council Decision (EU) 2015/1601 of 22 September 2015, paras (3), (9) and (21).

[91] *cf* Preamble of Council Decision (EU) 2015/1601 of 22 September 2015 paras (2), (5), (16), and (30).

under the supervision of autonomous supranational institutions designed to act in accordance with the Union's interest as a whole.

For practical reasons, the decision had to be made in a QMV vote although many members of the Council as well as the Commission openly favoured and promoted a unanimous and thus consensual decision in such a sensitive case. In the event, the representatives of the so-called Visegrad Group—except Poland—and Romania voted against the 'quota decision', while Finland abstained from voting. These countries rejected the setting up of a mandatory quota system that would deprive them of sovereign decisions in similar cases for the future.[92]

This outcome was not unexpected, as the opposing countries announced through various diplomatic channels their doubts about this way of problem solving and their disenchantment with QMV decision making.[93] As a further step, Slovakia and Hungary lodged parallel applications to the European Court of Justice in which they sought the annulment of this Council decision made in December 2015. The applicants enlisted manifold arguments to support their claim, but, in general, they specifically contested the application of QMV decision making in this matter.[94]

The history of the enactment of this Council decision is open to many different political and legal interpretations in addition to the special relevance it has for the currently evolving constitutional position on sovereignty pooling in the European Union.

First of all, it has to be emphasised that the issue of 'migrant quotas', or asylum policy in more general terms, is an area situated much closer to the 'core' of sovereign competences compared to fields where sovereignty pooling has traditionally been successful, such as the policy areas closely related to the internal market. This means that Member States have only had limited experiences—as for instance when cooperating in justice and police issues—in the pooling of sovereign competences and may therefore be averse to pooling when any other competence is at stake. Thus, the scepticism towards pooling competences in the second and third pillars is a logical reaction, further buttressed by the traditionalist understanding of sovereignty.

Second, it is tempting to simplify the political divide around the contested decision to a binary opposition between the rationalism and value orientation of Western politics and the emerging populism of some Central

[92] From a comprehensive and neutral summary of the story the Council Decision see J Barigazzi and M de la Baume, 'EU Forces Through Refugee Deal' *Politico* (23 September 2015) <www.politico.eu/article/eu-tries-to-unblock-refugee-migrants-relocation-deal-crisis/>.

[93] For the details see J Barigazzi and M Baume, 'Tusk's summit task: European Unity' *Politico* (21 September 2015) <www.politico.eu/article/the-eu-nuclear-option-on-migration/>.

[94] Action brought on 2 December 2015—*Slovak Republic v Council of the European Union* (Case C-643/15) OJ C/41–43. Action brought on 3 December 2015—*Hungary v Council of the European Union* (Case C-647/15) OJ C 38/43–44.

European countries. Naturally, the rejection of the mandatory quota system to relocate asylum applicants cannot be separated from political populism,[95] but there is also a hidden, but equally influential motive in the background of the unusual behaviour of Central European Member States in this case. This is the general public sentiment of fear from losing independence.

In general, the development of Central European constitutionalism has been to a much broader extent dominated by various public sentiments than acknowledged by the Western literature. It can be proved that fear of losing independence, inter alia, was a prominent factor in tailoring the new, post-Socialist, constitutions and this affective impetus gave rise to unusual provisions in Central European constitutionalism.[96] As sovereignty as a political status is a key point with respect to the independence of any country, it can be argued that the rejection of the quota system that entitles the Commission to determine how many asylum applicants must be settled in a given Member State was also propelled by the public sentiment of fear from losing important components of sovereignty, thus endangering national independence.

Third, one may recognise that two different concepts of sovereignty collided in the case of this 'quota decision'. The logic of pooled sovereignty offered a clear-cut answer to the crisis situation, but some of the Member States, lacking the same prehistory and thus emotionally of a different, more traditional, predisposition towards sovereignty, rejected this way of problem solving. This confrontation was solved by the option of QMV voting that led to the enactment of the decision; however, the opponents challenged this by citing legal objections almost immediately. Thus, the opposing Central European countries expressed their rejection of the results of the QMV procedure by contesting its legal validity, by bringing an action for annulment to the ECJ. This clearly implies that these countries cannot subscribe to the tradition of pooling sovereignty as they are unwilling to accept the very essence of QMV voting by which individual state interests are to be overridden in the interest of the whole community with the help of win-win compromises. This sequence of events shows a close similarity to the French attitude during the 'empty chair crisis'.

Last but not least, it should be mentioned that the law plays an important role in this—almost existential—conflict in allowing the translation of the political rejection of a decision to be expressed in quasi-neutral, professional terms. Thus the law assumes the role of taming the heated debate, providing it with a more rational frame than a mere political quarrel with

[95] For an analytical and scholarly discussion see G Mesežnikov, O Gyárfášová and D Smilov (eds), *Populist Politics and Liberal Democracy in Central and Eastern Europe* (Bratislava, Institute for Public Affairs, 2008).

[96] For details see B Fekete, 'On the Role of Public Sentiments in the Emergence of Post-Transitory Central European Constitutionalism' (2016) 57 *Jahrbuch für Ostrecht* 243, esp 249–52.

its concomitant stalemate. Now it is up to the ECJ to decide whether or not Article 78(3) TFEU provided a proper legal basis for this Council decision. Moreover, future judgments and their reception are likely to further expose the rifts and divergences among Member States with regard to the concept of sovereignty pooling.

C. Is Absolute Sovereignty now Back in Europe?

In conclusion, one may point out that the idea of Bodinian sovereignty never ceased to exist and never lost its appeal in European political culture. This is demonstrated—inter alia—by the outcome of the Brexit referendum and the judicial reluctance to any further extension of sovereignty pooling to 'sensitive', politically more central, policy areas. It might be more precise to observe that recent developments have provided a strong indication that the obvious success of the pre-Nice phase of integration—four decades of peace and prosperity in Europe—only froze the doubts and hostility towards the idea of pooled sovereignty among the European public and did not by any means eradicate them. At the very moment when this normal course of successful integration was interrupted by an unprecedented chain of consecutive crises—the European debt crisis, the crisis of Greece, and the growing inflow of asylum-seekers from 2014—the problematic and weak points of the European project came into sharp relief, immediately awakening the traditional concept of Bodinian sovereignty. This, in turn, provided a potential tool for some Member States' political leadership with a populist or nativist attitude to act upon their own, domestic, agenda. The inevitable conflict between the tendency to stake out or even reclaim sovereignty and the recent constitutional architecture of the Union can easily be predicted as it was duly demonstrated in the case of the 'migrant quota' decision.

All in all, the main conclusion of this analysis is that the cultural embeddedness of sovereignty pooling cannot only be regarded as an advantage facilitating and propelling the evolution of this interstate cooperation strategy; it can be a disadvantage, too. Basically, in a crisis period,[97] when the political stalemate between the Union institutions and the Member States reveals the incapacity of the Union's political and constitutional mechanisms to offer efficient solutions to individual national problems,[98] Member States may easily and swiftly incline to adopt a more conventional approach to sovereignty which offers the illusion of autonomous and competent political

[97] Yet another reference to Carl Schmitt's interpretation of crisis.

[98] *cf* with Herman von Rompuy's argument calling for common action based on the co-responsibility of Member States if a Union level crisis breaks out: H von Rompuy, 'The Discovery of Co-Responsibility: Europe in the Debt Crisis', Speech at the Humboldt University, 6 February 2012, 3.

behaviour. The logic of popular democracy also provides a favourable context for legitimising individual state behaviour that diverges substantially from the cooperative and community-oriented tradition of supranational institution-building and joint action.

In sum, the thesis of this chapter is that the more political the goals to be achieved via sovereignty pooling in times of crisis are, the less chance there is to realise them in a political culture that has not forgotten, has not overwritten, the original concept of sovereignty, only abandoned it temporarily during times of peace and prosperity.

7

EU Agencies in the Internal Market: A Constitutional Challenge for EU Law

MARTA SIMONCINI

I. INTRODUCTION

THE EUROPEAN INTEGRATION process presents specific challenges to constitutionalism beyond the state. The European Union (EU) as a legal order is caught between a phenomenon of supranational delegation from the Member States and autonomous constitutional developments. This peculiar nature has significant institutional implications, among others, on the development of EU administration. The comprehension of *agencification* as a phenomenon of the EU internal market integration cannot be fully understood if the roles of the supranational polity and of the Member States are not distinguished in their contribution to supranational administration.

The internal market has created cross-border interdependencies between markets and regulatory regimes. The need to prevent different regulatory philosophies from clashing has been addressed through coordination and harmonisation in the internal market. This regulatory process has boosted the growing importance of administration at the supranational level and it particularly involved the establishment of sector-specific EU agencies. From the original model of a Community allocating administration to the Member States, the EU has become a complex legal order where administrative tasks are increasingly allocated to institutions, agencies and bodies of the EU. In addition, the intensity of their regulatory cooperation has steadily increased. The tasks of a few EU agencies have evolved from being purely executive to including some regulatory content. In some cases, EU agencies have been allocated powers increasingly relevant to the rule-making process;[1] in other

[1] See M Busuioc, 'Rule-making by the European Financial Supervisory Authorities: Walking a Tight Rope' (2013) 19 *European Law Journal* 111; E Chiti, 'European Agencies' Rulemaking: Powers, Procedures and Assessment' (2013) 19 *European Law Journal* 93.

cases, they have developed the traditional recommendatory and advisory powers in models of administration through soft law standards that are increasingly able to constrain the decision-making process of both the EU institutions and the Member States.[2] In addition, in other specific cases, EU agencies have been allocated some powers to issue binding decisions.[3]

This chapter aims to investigate the legal legitimacy of EU agencies' powers in this complex context of European integration. Extensive studies have contributed to understanding the reasons for establishing EU agencies. After more than 20 years, the findings of the 1997 Special Issue of the Journal of European Public Policy on European agencies remain seminal. In the deadlock of intergovernmental politics, EU agencies responded to the integration demand by neutralising conflicts under the cover of technical expertise. By providing specialised skills, EU agencies support European integration through the development of harmonisation and coordination practices that shape Member States' enforcement policies in the light of EU objectives and rules, with no need to centralise further regulatory powers in the EU institutions.

According to Dehousse, 'agencies owe their existence to a paradox. On the one hand, increased uniformity is certainly needed; on the other hand, greater centralisation [in the European Commission] is politically inconceivable, and probably undesirable'.[4] According to Shapiro, agencies were conceived as a kind of neo-functionalist experiment, aimed at integrating Europe 'indirectly' by creating 'Europe-wide epistemic communities whose technical truths transcend intergovernmental politics'.[5] Also Kreher saw in agencies a phenomenon of administrative integration.[6] By fostering interdependencies, administrative integration can prosaically contribute to enhancing the connections between the different Member States beyond ambitious political projects.

[2] See S Vaughan, 'Differentiation and Dysfunction: An Exploration of Post-Legislative Guidance Practices in 14 EU Agencies' (2015) 17 *Cambridge Yearbook of European Legal Studies* 66. On the effects of soft law in EU law see F Terpan, 'Soft Law in the European Union—The Changing Nature of EU Law' (2015) 21 *European Law Journal* 68; O Stefan, 'European Union Soft Law: New Developments Concerning the Divide Between Legally Binding Force and Legal Effects' (2012) *The Modern Law Review* 879; O Ştefan, *Soft Law in Court: Competition Law, State Aid, and the Court of Justice of the European Union* (Alphen aan den Rijn, Kluwer, 2013); L Senden, *Soft Law in European Community Law* (Oxford, Hart Publishing, 2004).

[3] See S Griller and A Orator, 'Everything under control? The "way forward" for European agencies in the footsteps of the Meroni doctrine' (2010) 35 *European Law Review* 3; see also P Weismann, 'The European financial market supervisory authorities and their powers to issue binding decisions' (2012) 27 *Journal of International Banking Law and Regulation* 495.

[4] R Dehousse, 'Regulation by Networks in the European Community: The Role of European Agencies' (1997) 4 *Journal of European Public Policy* 246, 259.

[5] M Shapiro, 'The problems of independent agencies in the United States and the European Union' (1997) 4 *Journal of European Public Policy* 276, 281–82.

[6] A Kreher, 'Agencies in the European Community—A Step towards Administrative Integration in Europe' (1997) 4 *Journal of European Public Policy* 225.

By keeping out politics, enforcement of EU law is believed to be less susceptible to variations.[7] This enhances consistency in the implementation of EU law, whereas it allows EU institutions to outsource operational functions and concentrate on core tasks.[8] As Rittberger and Wonka have pointed out, this phenomenon can be analysed from two different perspectives: the politics of the creation of EU agencies and the functionalist approach to the problem of credible commitment.[9] On the one hand, political strategies determine the establishment of EU agencies and inter-institutional bargaining affects their powers and organisation. On the other hand, EU agencies' design can rationally respond to functional needs. These approaches are not mutually exclusive and contribute to explaining different aspects of European *agencification*: the political momentum for their establishment and the regulatory objectives that their establishment pursues.

When analysing the legal legitimacy of EU agencies, this chapter reconnects the development of EU agencies to the composite nature of the EU as a Union of Member States with the aim of showing that the development of EU agencies' tasks responds to constitutional challenges embedded in the governance of the internal market. The analysis explains that the legitimacy process is more complex than the bottom-up approach of the supranational delegation and it relies on the development of the specific EU constitutional framework.

As the Court of Justice (CJEU)'s case law points out, legally speaking the evolution of administrative powers at the EU level cannot be explained only through the pure lens of the supranational delegation from the Member States. The regulatory relationship that this administrative kind of delegation embodies presupposes the development of an autonomous supranational order that constitutionally frames EU agencies' powers. Only the existence of a constitutional principle at the EU level concerning the conditions for the delegation of powers conferred upon the EU institutions to EU agencies explains if and how EU agencies may legitimately retain regulatory powers. This principle, generally known as the Meroni doctrine, was developed and recently updated in the CJEU's case law. When dealing with the conditions for the allocation of powers to EU agencies, this doctrine shows

[7] See B Rittberger and A Wonka, 'Introduction: agency governance in the European Union' in B Rittberger and A Wonka (eds), *Agency governance in the EU* (London, Routledge, 2012), 2, 3.

[8] See R Dehousse, 'Regulation by Networks in the European Community: The Role of European Agencies', above n 4, 254–55; G Majone, 'The New European Agencies: Regulation by Information' (1997) 4 *Journal of European Public Policy* 262, 272. See also Communication from the Commission to the European Parliament and the Council COM (2002) 718 of 11 December 2002, The operating framework for the European Regulatory Agencies; Communication from the Commission to the European Parliament and the Council COM (2008) 135 of 11 March 2008 European Agencies—The way forward [2008] OJ C135.

[9] B Rittberger and A Wonka, 'Introduction: agency governance in the European Union', above n 7, 4.

the autonomous foundation, in the domain of EU law, of the responsibilities and tasks of EU agencies at the supranational level.

At the same time, the powers of EU agencies shall be framed within the composite nature of the EU polity as a Union of Member States. The guarantees for the exercise of their powers can only be explained within this original nature of the EU legal order. This means considering the accountability and legitimacy issues on broader grounds. Both the supranational framework of EU powers and the multilevel structure of the EU shall contribute to understanding the legitimacy of the exercise of administrative powers by EU agencies. This means that not only the Meroni doctrine, but also the regulatory approach to EU integration may contribute to re-connecting the EU administrative developments to the legitimate functioning of the EU legal order. On these grounds, only a more comprehensive public law approach can effectively contribute to understanding the constitutional challenges to the phenomenon of *agencification*.

The chapter is structured as follows. First, EU agencies' action is framed within the double-edged nature of the EU legal order as caught between its derived legitimacy from the Member States and the legal autonomy of its constitutional developments (section II). Subsequently, the chapter presents the constitutional foundations of EU agencies' powers in the EU legal framework as developed in the case law under the Meroni doctrine (section III). On these grounds, the chapter emphasises that the conferral of powers on EU agencies raises constitutional challenges that need to be framed in the double-edged nature of the EU legal order (section IV). This particularly affects the accountability structures, which operate with due regard to both the EU and the Member States. The final remarks consider the need for a comprehensive public law approach to EU law that takes into account this double nature of the EU and in this light, justifies the exercise of administrative powers to supranational administrative bodies.

II. EU AGENCIES IN THE COMPLEX NATURE OF THE EU INTEGRATION PROCESS

A clear distinction shall be marked between the supranational delegation of powers from the Member States to the EU and the subsequent allocation of powers which may autonomously take place at the EU level. Supranational delegation is a concept describing a political phenomenon of diffusion of specialised normative powers which does not question the political centrality of nation states. The conferral of administrative powers to EU agencies is, instead, a phenomenon of pluralisation and specialisation of EU powers that is legally autonomous from supranational delegation and that legally speaking, takes place only in the autonomous framework of EU public law. From different standpoints, both aspects contribute to explaining the EU integration process.

The reading of EU integration as supranational delegation conceives the idea that EU institutions retain regulatory powers conferred by the Member States with the aim of satisfying functional demands, but upon the condition of overseeing the exercise of the conferred powers. This approach was first developed by political science scholarship, which emphasised that the technocratic power of the EU was a means for Member States to insulate themselves from political pressures and commit to implementing EU policies.[10] Subsequently, legal scholarship has also further explored the regulatory approach to EU governance and considered the EU as a form of deliberative supranationalism, distinct from a constitutional experience.

Lindseth has particularly described EU integration as an administrative phenomenon, as it regards the conferral of specialised regulatory powers not on the basis of the expression of a general democratic will, but on the grounds of a delegation of powers from nation state institutions.[11] As legitimacy derives from the national constitutional systems, this approach shares the theories that base the legitimacy of the EU on the national democratic circuits.[12] Lindseth considers the political-cultural nature of such an administrative integration and he presupposes and implies the absence of autonomy of the EU as a constitutional legal order. According to Lindseth, the EU benefits from a 'mediated form of legitimacy' that stems from its Member States and their citizens. Member States are thus understood as the principals overseeing the EU agent.

This approach can explain EU governance historically and politically. Legally speaking, it is expressed by the principle of conferral set in Article 5 TEU. When transferring competences from sovereign Member States to the EU, this principle holds that:

> 1. The limits of Union competences are governed by the principle of conferral. The use of Union competences is governed by the principles of subsidiarity and proportionality.

[10] See G Majone (ed), *Deregulation or Re-Regulation? Regulatory Reform in Europe and the United States* (London, Pinter, 1990); G Majone, 'The European Community. An "Independent Fourth Branch of Government"?', in G Brüggemeier (ed), *Verfassungen für ein ziviles Europa* (Baden-Baden, Nomos, 1994) 23; G Majone, *The European Community as a Regulatory State* (Leiden, Brill Nijhoff, 1995); G Majone, *Regulating Europe* (London, Routledge, 1996).

[11] P Lindseth, *Power and Legitimacy: Reconciling Europe and the Nation State* (Oxford, Oxford University Press, 2010); P Lindseth, Equilibrium, 'Demoi-cracy and Delegation in the Crisis of European Integration' (2014) 10 *German Law Journal* 529; P Lindseth, 'The Perils of "As If" European Constitutionalism' (2016) 22 *European Law Journal* 696.

[12] See A Moravcsik, *The Choice for Europe: Social Purpose and State Power from Messina to Maastricht* (Ithaca, NY, Cornell University Press, 1998); JHH Weiler, 'The Community System: The Dual Character of Supranationalism' (1982) 1 *Yearbook of European Law* 267; JHH Weiler, 'The Transformation of Europe' (1991) 100 *Yale Law Journal* 2403; K Nicolaïdis, 'The New Constitution as European "Demoi-cracy"?' (2004) 7 *Critical Review of International Social and Political Philosophy* 76; K Nicolaïdis, 'Sustainable Integration: Towards EU 2.0?' (2010) 48 *Journal of Common Market Studies* 21.

2. The Union shall act only within the limits of the competences conferred upon it by the Member States in the Treaties to attain the objectives set out therein. Competences not conferred upon the Union in the Treaties remain with the Member States.

Within the domain of the devolved competences, however, the EU is only committed to the implementation of the Treaties and the exercise of its powers is only limited by the principles of subsidiarity and proportionality as set in EU law. The oversight of Member States is therefore constrained by the rule of the Treaties which thus founded the constitutional legitimacy of the EU legal order and its institutions.[13]

If the oversight of Member States is mediated by the Treaties and their institutions, the linearity of the supranational delegation paradigm is not able by itself to explain the autonomous developments of the EU public law framework. As Weiler has observed, the EU appears to be a 'specified interstate governmental structure defined by a constitutional charter and constitutional principles'.[14] Legally speaking, Court of Justice of the EU case law clearly affirms the constitutional nature of the EU as an autonomous community based on the rule of law and the protection of fundamental rights.[15] It also shows that when applying the principles of proportionality and subsidiarity, as well as when recognising the competences falling within the EU domain, the Court of Justice of the EU has adopted a standard of review which favours the autonomous evolution of EU action and responsibilities.[16] Without taking into account this legal autonomy of the EU from its Member States, based on this peculiar constitutional nature of the Treaties, the further development of EU powers beyond the supranational delegation from the Member States cannot be legally explained.

When understanding EU law, the idea of a supranational administrative governance shall be complemented by and adjusted to the existence of

[13] On the commitment to the rule of law as a condition for any theory of global constitutionalism see J-B Auby, 'Global Constitutionalism and Normative Hierarchies', this volume.

[14] See J Weiler, 'The Transformation of Europe', above n 12, 2407.

[15] See particularly 294/83, *Les Verts v Parliament* [1986] ECR 1339, para 23; Joined Cases C-402/05 P and C-415/05 P, *Yassin Abdullah Kadi and Al Barakaat International Foundation v Council of the European Union* [2008] ECR I-06351, paras 281–85.

[16] See P Craig, *EU Administrative Law* (Oxford, Oxford University Press, 2012), Chapters 14, 19–20; S Weatherill, 'The Limits of Legislative Harmonization Ten Years after *Tobacco Advertising*: How the Court's Case Law has become a "Drafting Guide"' (2011) 12 *German Law Journal* 827; T-I Harbo, 'The Function of the Proportionality Principle' (2010) 16 *European Law Journal* 158; R Schütze, *From Dual to Cooperative Federalism: the Changing Structure of European Law* (Oxford, Oxford University Press, 2009), 250; T Tridimas, *General Principles of EU Law* (Oxford, Oxford University Press, 2006), Chapters 3–4; M Kumm, 'Constitutionalising Subsidiarity in Integrated Markets: The Case of Tobacco Regulation in the European Union' (2006) 12 *European Law Journal* 503; A Estella, *The EU Principle of Subsidiarity and its Critique* (Oxford, Oxford University Press, 2002); G de Búrca, 'Reappraising Subsidiarity Significance After Amsterdam', Harvard Jean Monnet Working Paper, 7/1999.

an autonomous dimension of the EU legal order which cannot be explained only as a delegation of regulatory powers from the Member States, but needs to be understood within the specific categories of EU law. These are two faces of the same coin: if you look from the perspective of the Member States, you must admit that they politically accepted to confer part of their powers upon supranational institutions and you can accept that these powers are regulatory in nature. If you look from the perspective of EU institutions, however, you see an autonomous supranational legal order fully committed only to the goals set in the Treaties, which binds Member States and shapes their individual legal orders according to the framework of the Treaties. When doing this, unforeseen legal instruments and new regulatory solutions can be autonomously developed under the framework of EU law.

The allocation of competence to EU agencies is a clear example of this double nature of EU integration. If supranational delegation may be considered a preliminary condition for the allocation of powers to EU agencies, it cannot explain either if or how such allocation may be legally justified. The legal substance of supranational delegation is shaped by the autonomous evolution of the EU legal framework. Owing to this autonomous dimension of EU public law, the principle of conferral has embedded new regulatory instruments into the domain of EU law.

The growth of EU agencies' powers in the internal market is the consequence of the need for specialisation and technical expertise.[17] However, this functional development of EU law has been legally constrained by the principle of conferral, as set in the Treaties and interpreted in the Court of Justice's case law. The principle of conferral shaping the (political) delegation of competences to EU institutions has the supranational effect of designing a system of division of powers at the EU level that cannot be arbitrarily changed by EU institutions.

The limits to the growth of EU agencies' powers have been legally defined by the non-delegation doctrine, which generally goes under the label of the Meroni doctrine.[18] The issue in this doctrine is the protection of the balance of powers as set in the Treaties, meaning that responsibilities cannot shift from EU institutions which legitimately retain competences, to other bodies outside the relation of supranational delegation from the Member States as

[17] See HCH Hofmann and A Morini, 'Constitutional aspects of the pluralisation of the EU executive through "agencification"' (2012) 37 *European Law Review* 419, 421–23; but see also MLP Groenleer, *The Autonomy of European Union Agencies. A Comparative Study of Institutional Development* (Delft, Eburon, 2009) 100–08 (who considers the functional needs and the political motives); P Magnette, 'The Politics of Regulation in the European Union' in D Gerardin, R Muñoz and N Petit (eds), *Regulation through Agencies in the EU. A New Paradigm of European Governance* (Cheltenham, Elgar Publishing, 2005) 3, 7–10 (who reads the need for agencies in the light of the Principal–Agent approach).

[18] 9/56 and 10/56, *Meroni & Co, Industrie Metallurgiche s.p.a. v High Authority* [1957–1958] ECR 133.

set in the principle of conferral. If this is the substantive issue, however, the evolution of EU case law on EU agencies' powers demonstrates that the balance of EU powers depends on the autonomous legal developments of the EU legal order. The connection with the Member States through the principle of conferral does not prevent EU law from implementing autonomous instruments of governance in the internal market.

The real issue about the delegation of powers to EU agencies concerns their constitutional status, on the one hand, and the nature and the guarantees to the exercise of their powers, on the other hand. As soon as some constitutional changes intervened in these regards, the limits to the conferral of tasks on EU agencies also changed in the interpretation of the Court of Justice. The judicial interpretation of the Meroni doctrine evolved in almost 60 years of integration with the aim of pointing out that the development of administrative powers in the EU has its legal foundations in the legal setting of the Treaties and their interpretation, and not in the supranational delegation from the Member States. When designing the institutional profile and the functioning of EU agencies, however, the issue of the 'mediated legitimacy' from the Member States cannot be ignored, as it remains a foundational aspect of this supranational constitutionalism.

III. THE CONSTITUTIONAL VALUE OF THE MERONI DOCTRINE

Unlike EU institutions, only recently have EU agencies been recognised as institutional actors under the Treaties. Before the Lisbon Treaty, agencies were not included in the Treaties and therefore they fell outside the principle of conferral.[19] Legally speaking, the evolution of their powers is a story connected to the development of the EU case law.

To preserve the allocation of competences as set in the Treaties and not to alter such legal framework, the CJEU developed in the Meroni doctrine the rules for reconciling the need to keep the structure of the supranational legal order unchanged with the need to delegate technical tasks to expert supranational bodies. This case law is based on the principle of the balance of powers which is the other face of the principle of conferral.

The principle of conferral pinpointed the principle of the institutional balance of powers within the European legal order. The balance of EU powers as set in the Treaties on the grounds of the principle of conferral could not be altered by further delegation of tasks implying the exercise of political discretion to bodies not included in the Treaties. By making the institutions able to act only in accordance with the powers they have been conferred by the Treaties, this principle further specifies the more general

[19] See K Lenaerts, 'Regulating the regulatory process: "delegation of powers" in the European Community' (1993) 19 *European Law Review* 23.

principle of division of powers within the framework of the European legal order.[20] Under the ECSC Treaty, *Meroni* questioned the delegation of power from the High Authority to two bodies under Belgian private law—the so-called Brussels agencies—for dealing with financial arrangements of the ferrous scrap regime. In doing this, the *Meroni* case set the necessary principles and conditions under which any delegation of powers from institutions could be feasible.[21]

The case held that delegation should find its structural limit in the impossibility of delegating those powers whose exercise requires a discretionary evaluation, since this would have involved a shift of responsibility not expected by the Treaty. In the *Meroni* case, the concept of wide discretion referred to a quasi-legislative power 'which may, according to the use which is made of it, make possible the execution of actual economic policy'.[22] Moreover, the delegation of powers should be explicit and in line with the principle of conferred competences: if necessary for the accomplishment of its tasks,[23] the delegating authority can provide an agency with powers only explicitly[24] and within the limits of the powers it retains. Tridimas has identified in the necessity requirement the further condition of proportionality for lawful delegation.[25] These tasks should then be performed by the agencies under the same conditions as the delegating authority would have performed them. This means that the execution of the delegated tasks should be subject to the same procedural guarantees to be applied by the delegating authority as a necessary condition for its legitimacy.

Subsequently, the non-delegation doctrine has been further developed in the *Romano* case. Under the EEC Treaty, *Romano* questioned the delegation of regulatory powers from the Council to a body established under

[20] See J-P Jacqué, 'The principle of institutional balance' (2004) 41 *Common Market Law Review* 383, 383–84.

[21] In this regard see T Tridimas, 'Community Agencies, Competition Law, and ECSB Initiatives on Securities Clearing and Settlement', in P Eeckhout and T Tridimas (eds), *28 Yearbook of European Law 2009* (Oxford, Oxford University Press, 2010) 216, 241–43; T Tridimas, 'Financial Supervision and Agency Power: reflection on ESMA', in N Nic Shuibhne and LW Gormley (eds), *From Single Market to Economic Union: Essays in Memory of John A Usher* (Oxford, Oxford University Press, 2012) 55, 60–62.

[22] 9/56 and 10/56, Meroni & Co, 173.

[23] 9/56, *Meroni*, 151; 10/56, *Meroni*, 172.

[24] In this regard see also C-154-155/04, *Alliance for Natural Health* [2005] ECR I-6541, para 90; C-301/02 P, *Tralli v ECB* [2005] ECR I-4071, paras 42–52; T-311/06, *FMC Chemical SPRL v European Food Safety Agency (EFSA)* [2008] ECR II-88, para 66, where the General Court rejected the argument that the Commission had delegated to EFSA its powers to adopt decisions having binding effects on third parties on the grounds that 'powers cannot be presumed to have been delegated and that, even when empowered to delegate its powers, the delegating authority must take an express decision to that effect'. It is interesting that in this latter case, the Court does not deal with the legal feasibility of such delegation of powers, so that it does not manage to question the validity of the *Meroni* doctrine.

[25] T Tridimas, 'Financial Supervision and agency power: reflections on ESMA', above n 21, 55, 60.

EC secondary law, the Administrative Commission on Social Security of Migrant Workers. In a preliminary ruling, the CJEU held that agencies cannot impose methods, interpretative rules or obligations on national administrations, but they can only help such national administrations by providing non-binding decisions,[26] so as to specify that agencies cannot exercise any rule-making power, but they can only have recommendatory powers.

As a result, only executive powers could be delegated from Treaty-based institutions to agencies and their use must be entirely subject to the supervision of the delegating institution. This has been interpreted as holding that no regulatory power can be delegated to agencies without prejudicing the design of powers as set in the Treaties. Administrative rule-making power has therefore been frozen with the aim of keeping the institutional structure unchanged and compliant with the principle of conferral. In this line, the non-delegation doctrine has become a constitutional principle of the EU legal order concerning the possible allocation of public powers.

Nonetheless, in so far as internal market development and its proper functioning require those administrative functions to be performed by supranational administrations, an increasing number of agencies have been performing functions which almost substantially touch upon a regulatory content. Even if formally these agencies have limited decision-making powers and issue opinions or draft technical standards to EU institutions or recommendations to Member States, they often retain powers that stretch the Meroni doctrine. The European Aviation Safety Agency (EASA), for instance, issues standards which effectively commit Member States to the implementation of EU regulation in the aviation sector.[27] More recently, the European Supervisory Authorities in the financial markets (ESAs) have been bestowed with more intense powers of supervision and regulation which were reviewed by the Court of Justice according to the Meroni doctrine.[28] In addition, the powers of the Agency for the Cooperation of Energy Regulators (ACER) to determine the electricity capacity calculation regions have proved to be controversial in nature, as they involve 'a certain *margin of appreciation* of methodological nature to precise [sic] the concrete requirements to be met to assess that there is a situation of structural congestion'.[29]

[26] 98/80, *Giuseppe Romano v Institut national d'assurance maladie-invalidité* [1981] ECR 1259, para 20.

[27] See M Simoncini, 'The erosion of the Meroni doctrine. The case of the European Aviation Safety Agency (EASA)' (2015) 21 *European Public Law* 309.

[28] See M Simoncini, 'Legal boundaries of European Supervisory Authorities (ESAs) in the financial markets. Tensions in the development of true regulatory agencies' (2015) 34 *Yearbook of European Law* 319.

[29] Decision of the Board of Appeal of the Agency for the Cooperation of Energy Regulators (ACER BoA) of 17 March 2017, para 108. See also H Kühnert, P Böhler and S Polster, 'A Tale of Delegation and Power: ACER and the Dichotomy of the Non-Delegation Doctrine and the Creation of a Genuine Internal Market in Electricity' (2017) 1 *European Competition and Regulatory Law Review* 47.

The recent *ESMA short selling* case has somehow opened the door to further EU administrative integration through the development of EU agencies' regulatory powers.[30] The case concerned the power of the European Securities and Markets Agency (ESMA) to prohibit or impose conditions on the entry by natural or legal persons into transactions in the short selling market or require such persons to notify or publicise their positions, if and when there is a threat to the orderly functioning and the stability of financial markets with cross-border implications; and no competent authority has already taken measures to address such threat.[31]

When reviewing the compatibility of the powers of the ESMA with the Meroni doctrine, the CJEU updated the Meroni doctrine to the changed constitutional framework of the Lisbon Treaty. First of all, the Treaty on the Functioning of the European Union (TFEU) has recognised agencies as legal actors within the EU legal order.[32] According to the Italian administrative law scholarship, this shall be considered as the end of the precondition on which the Meroni doctrine was based; that is, the absence of any constitutional foundation for agencies' powers.[33] Furthermore, the TFEU holds that legal remedies apply also to EU agencies' acts when 'intended to produce' legal effects on third parties and this makes explicit the principle of judicial review already present to the EU judiciary.[34] Against this changed constitutional backdrop, the CJEU confirmed the validity of the logic of non-delegation of discretionary powers, but it 'mellowed' *Meroni*,[35] whereas it probably set aside *Romano*.

[30] C-270/12, *United Kingdom of Great Britain and Northern Ireland v Council of European Union and European Parliament* ECLI:EU:C:2014:18. On this case in the literature see D Adamski, 'The ESMA doctrine: A constitutional revolution and the economics of delegation' (2014) 39 *European Law Review* 812; M Chamon, 'The empowerment of agencies under the Meroni doctrine and article 114 TFEU: comment on United Kingdom v Parliament and Council (Short-selling) and the proposed Single Resolution Mechanism' (2014) 39 *European Law Review* 380; H Marjosola, 'Bridging the constitutional gap in EU executive rule-making: The Court of Justice approves legislative conferral of intervention powers to European Securities and Markets Authority' (2014) 10 *European Constitutional Law Review* 500; M Scholten and M van Rijsbergen, 'The ESMA-*Short Selling* Case. Erecting a New Delegation Doctrine in the EU upon the Meroni-Romano Remnants' (2014) 41 *Legal Issues of Economic Integration* 389; R Van Gestel, 'European Regulatory Agencies Adrift?' (2014) 21 *Maastricht Journal of European and Comparative Law* 188; CF Bergström, 'Shaping the new system for delegation of powers to EU agencies: United Kingdom v European Parliament and Council (Short selling)' (2015) 52 *Common Market Law Review* 219.

[31] See Art 28 Regulation 236/2012.

[32] Art 298 TFEU.

[33] D Sorace, 'Una nuova base costituzionale europea per la pubblica amministrazione' in M P Chiti and A Natalini (eds), *Lo spazio amministrativo europeo. Le pubbliche amministrazioni dopo il Trattato di Lisbona* (Bologna, Il Mulino, 2012) 45, 56.

[34] Art 263 TFEU. In the case law see T-411/06, *Solgema* [2008] ECR II-2771, paras 36–37. This represents a further development in the sector of EU agencies and bodies of the more general principle of judicial review as the other side of the rule of law as held in the *Les Verts* case.

[35] See J Pelkmans and M Simoncini, 'Mellowing Meroni: How ESMA can help build the single market', CEPS Commentary, 18 February 2014, available at <http://www.ceps.eu/system/files/Mellowing%20Meroni.pdf>.

The CJEU recognised that the EU legislative power may legitimately confer administrative powers to EU agencies under defined conditions. The CJEU upheld the rules about delegation of powers defined in the *Meroni* case, but noticed that the allocation of direct supervision powers potentially involving a regulatory impact was grounded on well-restricted conditions which make the discretionary power of intervention subject to strict exercise and effective judicial review. Against the changed backdrop of the Treaties, the Court delineates a form of administrative discretion which is situated between the mere executive powers (exercised in completely bound administrative activities) and the 'wide margin of discretion', political in nature, at stake in the *Meroni* case.[36]

The CJEU held that it is in the full power of the EU legislature—as composed by the EU Parliament and the Council through the ordinary legislative procedure ex Article 289 TFEU—to confer administrative powers on EU agencies. This is an expression of the constitutional autonomy of the EU legal order, as the EU legislature is able to confer powers of an administrative nature not specifically allocated to EU institutions by the Treaties, on third bodies legally included in the Treaties. Even if the Council is composed of its Member States, nonetheless this is a different framework from that of supranational delegation, because of both the nature of the EU legislature and the nature of the powers in question. In fact, the EU legislature is a different institutional actor, whose acts are the result of a deliberative procedure of two EU institutions, the European Parliament and the Council. Moreover, the powers conferred on EU agencies express administrative competences that are directly exercised at the supranational level and aimed at internal market integration. However, in order to keep the conferral of these powers in line with the principle of institutional balance, guarantees about their nature and their exercise shall apply. Only because of these guarantees has the Meroni case law been mellowed.

The exercise of administrative discretion shall be subject to a series of criteria and conditions set in legislative acts which limit and guide the exercise of administrative powers. This is clear from the *ESMA short selling* case: the powers conferred on ESMA are subject to the principle of legality. They should be exercised according to the relevant regulations conferring the direct supervision powers and more specifically 1) only if a concrete risk to financial stability is at stake and no competent national authority has intervened; 2) by taking into account a number of factors delineated in the short-selling regulation, so that ESMA's intervention does not create further risks in the financial markets (for example, the risk of regulatory arbitrage, or the risk of reduction of liquidity or the creation of further uncertainty on the market); 3) by limiting the power of intervention to temporary and

[36] C-270/12, *UK v Council and European Parliament*, paras 41–42.

precise measures as outlined in the founding regulation; and 4) by notifying the competent national authorities.

As long as the Court recognises that the TFEU 'expressly permits Union bodies, offices and agencies to adopt acts of general application', the generally valid *Romano* principle can no longer apply to the specific case of EU agencies.[37] When setting the guarantees of judicial review, the TFEU only indirectly recognises the capability of EU agencies to adopt acts of general application. First, when addressing the plea of illegality by guaranteeing the inapplicability of acts of general application to specific proceedings, Article 277 TFEU implicitly recognises that agencies can issue acts of general application. Article 267(b) TFEU on the preliminary ruling addresses the interpretation of the acts of agencies and bodies as well as those of the institutions; furthermore, according to Article 265 TFEU, the failure to act can be contested to agencies as well, under the same conditions that apply to EU institutions. Nonetheless, these provisions admit that acts of general application are now in the domain of EU agencies.

What the *ESMA short selling* case actually did was to recognise the different constitutional status that EU agencies achieved within EU law: as far as the Treaties laid down guarantees about the exercise of their powers, the CJEU could mellow the severity of the Meroni doctrine without dismissing its general structure.

This judicial development shows that the evolution of the constitutional framework of the EU Treaties can give rise to administrative organisations of powers which are supranational in character and cannot be reconnected to the will of the Member States to delegate competences to the EU. It is the EU legislature in its functional autonomy that may create and allocate administrative competences at the EU level (within the scope of the Treaties). Such a judicial development of EU administrative law shows the autopoiesis of the EU legal order as an autonomous (constitutional) system.[38] However, the double-edged nature of the EU requires that a coherent discourse on EU agencies cannot disregard the theory of the original delegation of powers from the Member States to the EU. This shall assist in structuring the accountability and strengthening the legitimacy of EU agencies' powers.

IV. THE CONSTITUTIONAL CHALLENGES TO EU AGENCIES

The judicial evolution of the Meroni doctrine shows that from a supranational perspective, the EU is a legal order autonomous from its constituent Member States. The tasks of EU agencies evolved because of the legitimate

[37] C-270/12, *UK v Council and European Parliament*, para 65.

[38] On the theory of law as a self-generating system see G Teubner, *Law as an Autopoietic System* (Hoboken, NJ, Wiley-Blackwell, 1993).

conferral by the EU legislature on the grounds of political choices made at the EU level.

This autonomous development of EU administrative law may have great potential for supranational integration in the internal market, as well as side effects for the democratic accountability of the EU. The EU administrative framework can have a strong impact on effective harmonisation in the internal market, but it is also clearly disconnected from the national democracies adhering to the EU. As political science scholarship has underlined, this mismatch may raise significant trade-off issues between efficiency and legitimacy in the implementation of EU agencies' tasks.[39] By focusing on the connections between the Member States and the supranational level, the theory of supranational delegation from the Member States can contribute to covering the democratic issues embedded in the autonomous development of the supranational legal framework.

Administrative law can help to fill the accountability gap that such disconnection generates. The implementation of administrative law guarantees beyond the state can help to circumscribe the growth of powers at the EU level and contain the distance of these bodies from national democracies. However, this process has not clearly developed at the EU level and the effectiveness of the mechanisms to control EU agencies' action can be questioned. EU administrative law has not yet recognised the relevance and the role of administrative discretion and, consequently, has not developed a coherent accountability system that consistently frames supranational administrative action.[40] As Chiti has observed, when dealing with administrative power, EU administrative law has focused on how to functionalise it to the implementation of EU law, but it has not been concerned with the establishment of a conceptual framework aimed at understanding the exercise of administrative powers in conformity with the rule of law and democracy. The reason for this failure lies in the disconnection of the development of EU administrative law from its political roots and in its reduction to a functional means of integration.[41]

The double-edged nature of the EU is a reminder of these political roots and can help to structure a coherent accountability framework for EU agencies' powers. When looking at EU agencies' powers from the EU level, the existence of legal remedies to their action and their political accountability to the EU legislature shall shape the exercise of their powers. When looking at the same issue from the perspective of the Member States, procedural

[39] See M Egan, 'Regulatory strategies, delegation and European market integration' (1998) 5 *Journal of European Public Policy* 485, 499–501.

[40] E Chiti, 'Is EU Administrative Law Failing in Some of Its Crucial Tasks?' (2016) 22 *European Law Journal* 576, 587–91.

[41] ibid.

rules can limit and guide the exercise of agencies' powers[42] as well as the existence of organisational arrangements which allow a representation of Member States' interests in the agency's boards. In the current framework of EU agencies, these variables are articulated in different ways and not all are fully developed and in place. In the following sub-sections, I will point out the criticalities of the current legal arrangements and the challenges that they pose for European supranational constitutionalism.

A. The Political Accountability Issues

The EU legislature supervises the delegation of regulatory tasks to EU agencies through the enforcement of accountability mechanisms that aim to check that the exercise of the conferred administrative powers is in line with the mandate. Both ex ante and ex post mechanisms shall operate and ensure that EU agencies exercise only administrative powers within the scope of their remit. According to the (even revised) Meroni doctrine, any *in blanc* delegation of powers that implies a full shift of responsibilities cannot be legitimate, as far as delegation shall not involve a loss of responsibility for EU institutions, but only a further refinement of their tasks.

Besides the definition of clear conditions for the exercise of powers, however, the ex ante control of the EU legislature is not remarkable in the current framework of EU agencies' powers. On the contrary, agencies intervene autonomously and the counterparts of their action are directly the Member States' agencies and private parties operating in the sector of reference. In this regard, the presence of representatives of the Member States on the management boards of EU agencies may be a further link to tailor EU agencies' measures and this could help to find more sustainable regulatory solutions which take into account the diversification of national contexts. Empirical research has not provided conclusive findings on the *de jure* or *de facto* effects of vertical accountability mechanisms connecting members of the management boards and the correspondent national institutions. Findings express some variance; but these mechanisms are not able to effectively re-connect EU agencies to the national political legitimacy.[43]

However, the presence of national representatives on the management boards can also hamper EU agencies' autonomy and delay the exercise of

[42] On the role of administrative procedure as a means available to the Principal to ensure the accountability of the Agent see MA Pollack, 'Delegation, agency, and agenda setting in the European Community' (1997) 51 *International Organization* 99, 108.

[43] See M Buess, 'European Union agencies and their management boards: an assessment of accountability and demoi-cratic legitimacy' (2015) 22 *Journal of European Public Policy* 94, 101–07. As regards de jure accountability, Buess notes that the more independent and powerful EU agencies are (like the EMA, EASA, and the OHIM), the less accountable to national institutions they are.

agencies' powers in favour of more concerted measures which may not have the same effectiveness. In the case of the ESAs, for instance, adjudication powers aimed at requiring the competent national authorities to take the necessary action in accordance with EU law and if necessary, at substituting the competent national authorities' decisions and making decisions directly applicable to financial institutions,[44] have never been exercised in the five years since their foundation. One reason for the failure to fully use supervisory powers shall be sought in the structure of the governance of the ESAs. As their board of supervisors is composed of representatives of the national competent authorities, before the adoption of restrictive measures addressed to the same national authorities, they preferred to pursue the supervisory convergence goal by using non-binding mediation, persuasion and reputational instruments which are less burdensome on the addressed national competent authorities.[45]

Ex post accountability mechanisms operate with the EU legislature and mainly consist of the submission of an annual report to the European Parliament and the Council which shall give an account of the activities carried out.[46] If the annual report is the common method ensuring the accountability of independent agencies in the Member States, the highly technical nature of reports does not allow a substantive control of the EU legislature on the performance. For instance, a concise version of the report in layman's terms could be usefully submitted, so as to enhance the understanding of EU agencies' activities and allow politicians to effectively know the methods and see the results of EU agencies' performances.

This accountability framework shows that the EU legislature substantially confers powers on EU agencies, but it is not equipped with effective control powers. In this light, it is not by chance that the 2012 Common Approach has introduced an 'alert/warning system' to be activated by the Commission if it has 'serious reasons for concern' that an EU agency may act beyond its mandate, may violate EU law or may be 'in manifest contradiction with EU policy objectives'.[47] If the EU agency does not accommodate the Commission's request, the latter informs the European Parliament and the Council with the aim of settling the institutional conflict. Vos has suggested that

[44] Arts 17, 18, 19 of the ESAs' Founding Regulations.

[45] See Report from the Commission to the European Parliament and the Council on the operation of the European Supervisory Authorities (ESAs) and the European System of Financial Supervision (ESFS), COM (2014) 509 fin, 7.

[46] See Art 57, Regulation 216/2008 of the European Parliament and of the Council, of 20 February 2008, on common rules in the field of civil aviation and establishing a European Aviation Safety Agency, and repealing Council Directive 91/670/EEC, Regulation (EC) No 1592/2002 and Directive2004/36/EC; see also Art 50, Art 16(4) and 17 (8), ESAs' Founding Regulations, which also require ESAs to clarify future plans and include any information requested by the European Parliament on an ad hoc basis.

[47] Common Approach Annex to the Joint Statement of the European Parliament, the Council of the EU and the European Commission of 19 July 2012 on decentralised agencies, para 59.

this provision might be susceptible to the introduction of a form of 'ministerial responsibility for agencies' acts' in relation to EU commissioners.[48] The search for complementary accountability instruments that beyond their specific goals can set up a wider political accountability framework is key to reconnect EU agencies to the composite nature of the EU and to consolidate their legitimacy.

B. The Legal Accountability Issues

Alongside the political accountability framework, legal accountability can also play a significant role and limit possible illegitimate use of administrative powers. As seen, the existence of effective judicial protection is a necessary precondition for the allocation of powers to EU agencies. The nature of the judicial scrutiny on administrative acts is the issue at stake.[49] The question is what level of deference the judiciary takes towards EU agencies' acts when complex technical assessments are submitted to the judicial review.[50]

The preliminary issue, however, is the fact that EU administrative law has not theorised the notion of administrative discretion and it has strongly reduced EU agencies' powers to technical tasks.[51] Only recently, in the *ESMA short selling* case, has the CJEU started to recognise the existence of an area of discretion that cannot be easily assimilated to the exercise of the political discretion prohibited under *Meroni*. The dichotomy between technical assessments by EU agencies and political discretion by EU institutions has blocked the development of effective procedural guarantees that can ensure the legitimate exercise of administrative powers by EU agencies.[52] To avoid blending discretionary choices of EU agencies, the recognition of the existence of a specific administrative decision-making space in the EU is needed.

[48] See E Vos, 'European Agencies and the Composite EU Executive' in M Everson, C Monda and E Vos (eds), *European Agencies in between Institutions and Member States* (Alphen aan den Rijn, Kluwer, 2014) 11, 32–33.

[49] See AH Türk, 'Oversight of Administrative Rulemaking: Judicial Review' (2013) 19 *European Law Journal* 126.

[50] From this point of view, the American experience is paradigmatic, since in a few years the Supreme Court passed from the deep review of administrative decisions—the so-called hard look doctrine developed in the 1970s (see *Citizen to Preserve Overton Park v Volpe* (1971) 401 US 402; *Vermont Yankee Nuclear Power Corp v National Resources Defense Council* (1978) 435 US 519; *Motor Vehicle Mfrs Assn v State Farm* (1983) 463 US 29)—to a much more deferential approach in the case *Chevron USA v Council* (1984) 467 US 837.

[51] See J Mendes, 'Law and administrative discretion in the EU: value of comparative perspective' paper presented at the Comparative Administrative Conference, Yale, April 2016, <https://www.law.yale.edu/system/files/area/conference/compadmin/compadmin16_mendes_law.pdf> accessed 23 May 2017, 3. See also J Mendes, 'Bounded Discretion in EU law: A Limited Judicial Paradigm in a Changing EU' (2017) 88 *The Modern Law Review* 443, 444–48.

[52] See J-P Schneider, 'A common framework for decentralized EU agencies and the *Meroni* doctrine' (2009) 61 *Administrative Law Review* 29, 38.

The increasing growth of EU agencies' competences makes the legal identification of this space unavoidable. EU agencies' action needs to be confronted with a firmer conception of legality that goes beyond the dichotomy between political and technical tasks. Only on these grounds can a coherent system of legal accountability be developed.

Clearly, the scrutiny of facts, the compliance with the criteria of delegation and the enforcement of procedural rights when taking administrative measures and acts are essential elements for making the judicial review effective. In the EU courts' case law, when complex technical assessment is at stake, courts cannot substitute their particular appraisal of the case with that of the competent institution and judicial review shall focus on how the discretionary powers have been applied.

Since the leading case *Technische Universität München*, the criteria for such a control have been consolidated and judicial review has consisted of how the competent authorities have performed 'the duty ... to examine carefully and impartially all the relevant aspects of the individual case'.[53] Judicial review therefore consists of the evaluation of the law and the facts which grounded the decision in question, as well as of procedural review. When applying this standard to EU institutions, the EU courts applied the manifest error standard: as long as EU institutions have not exceeded the bounds of their discretion, only manifest distortions in the exercise of the conferred powers are illegitimate.[54] Even if EU agencies have different status from EU institutions, it is reasonable that EU courts apply the same standard of review, but within the different boundaries of (technical) discretion. This means also checking the delegation criteria.

According to *Technische Universität München*, if the fundamental guarantees of fairness—particularly the careful and impartial examination which is closely linked to the right to be heard and the duty to give reasons[55]—are not correctly enforced, the legitimacy of the administrative measures shall be successfully challenged. If EU agencies were called to follow a common EU administrative procedure, judicial review could be favoured and the exercise of discretion could be more controlled.

[53] See C-269/90, *Technische Universität München* [1991] ECR I-5469, para 14; see also T-13/99, *Pfizer Animal Health SA v Council of the European Union* [2002] ECR II-03305, para 171.

[54] See CJEU, C-331/88, *The Queen v Minister of Agriculture, Fisheries and Food and Secretary of State for Health, ex parte Fedesa and others* [1990] ECR I-04023, para 9; T-13/99, para 166. See also P Craig, *EU Administrative Law* (Oxford, Oxford University Press, 2012) 408–09 and 441–45. In the literature, see also AH Türk, 'Oversight of Administrative Rulemaking: Judicial Review'. Above n 48, 141, who considers the introduction of general provisions about the public participation in EU administrative rule-making as a means 'to enhance the legitimacy of the process' and as a method 'to ensure that the Union courts have an adequate administrative record for substantive review'.

[55] C-269/90, *Technische Universität München*, above n 53, paras 25–26.

Even if EU agencies adopt their own rules of procedure on the basis of general principles set in the founding regulations and in the case law, this cannot have the same legal value of a general law about the EU administrative procedure in terms of protection of procedural rights and controls over the exercise of administrative powers. In fact, the choice of procedural rules is not neutral to the final decision. The way the procedure is articulated allows the taking into account of some interests rather than others and this affects both fact-findings and decision making.[56] When leaving the definition of the procedure to EU agencies, the prioritisation of interests itself is left to agencies.

The autonomy with which EU agencies can organise their own administrative procedure seems to be at odds with the allocation of administrative powers of supervision and regulation to actors who are not legitimated through the democratic circuit and are also far from the national *demoi*. The implementation of procedural guarantees through primary law would positively affect the compliance with the constraints of the (even mellowed) Meroni doctrine. The democratic principles embedded in the Meroni doctrine would benefit from the existence of an administrative procedure law which ensures procedural legitimacy in the exercise of EU agencies' powers. The introduction of an EU administrative procedure law would make the exercise of (regulatory) powers more visible to the Member States, as well as to European citizens and sector operators.

V. FINAL REMARKS

By analysing the evolution of EU agencies' powers, this chapter aimed to point out the complexity of the EU identity as a legal order beyond the state. The autonomy of the EU and its derived legitimacy from the constituent Member States emerged as faces of the same legal reality. The powers and the limits of the EU legal order exceed the classification as an experiment of administrative governance, but at the same time, the legal autonomy of the EU cannot disregard its national roots when framing its constitutional status.

The case of EU agencies is a good example of how autonomy and interdependency are strictly connected in the development of administrative powers to be exercised at the EU level. The evolution of the Meroni doctrine in the EU case law has shown such complexity. When setting the constitutional principle of the limits to delegation of EU institutions' powers to other entities, the Meroni doctrine demonstrated its sensitivity towards the mutation

[56] See G della Cananea, 'The European Union's mixed administrative proceedings' (2004) 68 *Law and Contemporary Problems* 197, 207, who emphasises that the shape of administrative proceedings depends on the interests at stake.

of the constitutional framework of the Treaties. Only when EU agencies acquired a constitutional status in the Treaties and their powers have been clearly subject to defined conditions of exercise and explicitly recognised as amenable to judicial review, have they become legitimate actors able to exercise administrative powers with a regulatory impact.

When considering the 'mediated legitimacy' of the EU as a phenomenon of supranational delegation, the development of EU agencies' powers can be interpreted as further fragmentation of national normative powers which involves a relaxation of Member States' oversight aimed at the development of the (supranational) internal market. The autonomy of EU law legally justifies this development on the grounds of the constitutional status of the EU. To understand these two faces of the same phenomenon, a broader paradigm that compromises these competing approaches is needed. The constitutional autonomy of EU law needs to be grounded on the supranational delegation from the Member States and EU agencies' powers should be assessed within this composite framework.

Under a public law paradigm, EU law can accommodate its independent developments without disregarding its derived legitimacy from the Member States' constituencies. The legitimate powers of EU agencies shall be compatible with the principle of conferral as set in the Treaties and thus with the balance of powers within the EU. Benchmarks of the compatibility of EU agencies' powers can be identified through administrative law instruments which can re-connect the supranational administration to EU institutions, as well as to the Member States.

The balance of powers in the EU can be implemented by strengthening the political accountability framework and by settling possible illegitimate alterations through judicial review. From the perspective of the Member States, organisational arrangements and procedural restrictions to the exercise of EU agencies' powers can help to administratively protect against any unwanted extension of EU regulatory tasks. Procedural arrangements also protect individuals against arbitrary decisions of EU administrative bodies. Administrative law can thus provide the instruments for containing an unnecessary proliferation of administrative agencies.

As seen, not all these arrangements are in place and their effectiveness may be strengthened so as to implement the benchmarks of the Meroni doctrine. If more regulatory powers are conferred upon EU agencies, the implementation of these arrangements is a preliminary condition that allows the maintenance in equilibrium of the different powers composing the EU legal order.

EU law as a specific experience of public law beyond the state presents an original character where the derived legitimacy from the Member States is embedded in the constitutional structure of the Treaties and both these aspects contribute to explaining and nourishing the EU integration process. The supranational delegation approach particularly shows the gap between the legal dimension of the EU and its political nature and it recalls the need to safeguard democratic instance in the expansion of EU powers. The constitutional status of the EU is not structured as in the Member States according to the traditional state doctrine, but nonetheless it is legally enforceable and it also frames the supranational administrative governance.

A public law paradigm for EU integration contains and respects these different components in a broader framework. Cassese has shown the openness of public law and its capability to create new frameworks for law by combining different levels of regulation and meaningful interactions that generate institutional changes.[57] If we reflect in the more general terms of public law, we can better understand the goals and the limits of the EU. If we accept that a single category of law cannot explain the complexity of the EU, then we can engage different legal disciplines in a dialogue aimed at understanding the nature of the EU in the polymorphous domain of public law. The key is to go beyond the boundaries between the single areas and to approach the EU as a specific public law experience, which can be analysed but cannot be captured through the specific categories of the single legal disciplines.

[57] S Cassese, 'An International Society of Public Law' (2015) ICON S Working Paper Series—Conference Proceedings Series 1 No 1/2015.

Index